Planning • Environment • Cities

Series Editors: Yvonne Rydin and Andrew Thornley

The context in which planning operates has changed dramatically in recent years. Economic processes have become increasingly globalized and new spatial patterns of economic activity have emerged. There have been major political changes across the globe, not just changing administrations in various countries, but also the sweeping away of old ideologies and the tentative emergence of new ones. A new environmental agenda emerged from the Brundtland Report and the Rio Earth Summit, prioritizing the goal of sustainable development. The momentum for this has been maintained by continued action at international, national and local levels.

Cities are today faced with new pressures for economic competitiveness, greater accountability and participation, improved quality of life for citizens and global environmental responsibilities. These pressures are often contradictory and create difficult dilemmas for policy-makers, especially in the context of fiscal austerity. New relationships are developing between the levels of state activity and between public and private sectors as different interests respond to the new conditions.

In these changing circumstances, planners, from many backgrounds, in many different organizations, have come to re-evaluate their work. They have had to engage with actors in government, the private sector and non-governmental organizations in discussions over the role of planning in relation to the environment and cities. The intention of the *Planning, Environment, Cities* series is to explore the changing nature of planning and contribute to the debate about its future.

The series is primarily aimed at students and practitioners of planning and such related professions as estate management, housing and architecture as well as in politics, public and social administration, geography and urban studies. It comprises both general texts and books designed to make a more particular contribution, in both cases characterized by: an international approach; extensive use of case studies; and emphasis on contemporary relevance and the application of theory to advance planning practice.

Planning · Environment · Cities

Series Editors: Yvonne Rydin and Andrew Thornley

Published

Philip Allmendinger
Planning Theory

Patsy Healey
Collaborative Planning

Michael Oxley
Economics, Planning and Housing

Yvonne Rydin
Urban and Environmental Planning in the UK (2nd edn)

Geoff Vigar, Patsy Healey and Angela Hull (with Simin Davoudi)
Planning, Governance and Spatial Strategy in Britain

Forthcoming

Anna Davies, Bob Evans and Sue Percy
Environmental Policy and Planning in Britain

Ted Kitchen
Skills for Planning Practice

Peter Newman and Andrew Thornley
Planning World Cities

Other titles planned include

Introduction to Planning
Planning for Diversity
Urban Design

Planning, Environment, Cities
Series Standing Order
ISBN 0–333–71703–1 hardback
ISBN 0–333–69346–9 paperback
(*outside North America only*)

You can receive future titles in this series as they are published by placing a standing order. Please contact your bookseller or, in the case of difficulty, write to us at the address below with your name and address, the title of the series and an ISBN quoted above.

Customer Services Department, Macmillan Distribution Ltd
Houndmills, Basingstoke, Hampshire RG21 6XS, England

Economics, Planning and Housing

Michael Oxley

First published 2004 by
PALGRAVE MACMILLAN
Houndmills, Basingstoke, Hampshire RG21 6XS and
175 Fifth Avenue, New York, N.Y. 10010
Companies and representatives throughout the world

PALGRAVE MACMILLAN is the global academic imprint of
the Palgrave Macmillan division of St. Martin's Press, LLC and of
Palgrave Macmillan Ltd. Macmillan® is a registered trademark in
the United States, United Kingdom and other countries. Palgrave is a
registered trademark in the European Union and other countries.

ISBN 0–333–79245–9 hardback
ISBN 0–333–79246–7 paperback

This book is printed on paper suitable for recycling and made from fully
managed and sustained forest sources.

A catalogue record for this book is available from the British Library.

A catalog record for this book is available from the Library of Congress.

10   9   8   7   6   5   4   3   2   1
13   12   11   10   09   08   07   06   05   04

Printed in China

*To Dianna, Russell
and Natasha*

Contents

List of Tables and Figures

Tables

Figures

Acknowledgements

I am indebted to many people for their direct and indirect help in preparing this book. I am particularly grateful to Peter King as I have built on some of the material in our book, *Housing Who Decides* (Macmillan – now Palgrave Macmillan; 2000). Chapters 3, 4 and 10, in particular, have benefited from this input. My colleague Andrew Golland has made many helpful suggestions for changes to several chapters and diagrams. I gratefully acknowledge the advice and encouragement I received from Yvonne Rydin in her role as series editor and from my publisher at Palgrave Macmillan, Steven Kennedy. Their comments on earlier drafts have improved the structure and content. I am also grateful for the careful copy-editing provided by Paul Dennison and Keith Povey on behalf of Palgrave Macmillan. The material on the USA in Chapter 10 has benefited considerably from the generous provision of information and constructive comments from Daniel Anderson and J. Michael Pitchford of Bank of America.

Research projects for several organizations have informed some of the policy and practice context. In particular, work for the Greater London Authority (GLA) and Office of the Deputy Prime Minister (ODPM) undertaken with Three Dragons has enhanced my understanding of planning and affordable housing. Projects for central, regional and local government with Entec UK Ltd have contributed to my understanding of the theory and practice of urban capacity studies. Economic and Social Research Council (ESRC) funded research (award number R000223799) on the viability of urban housing development has informed the content of Chapters 5 and 8. This research was conducted jointly with Andrew Golland and Richard Weston. I thank them both.

The diligent word processing of the manuscript was begun by Justine Atkin and completed by Gabriela Afonso, to whom thanks are also due for her efficient production of the diagrams. My daughter Natasha Oxley read and commented on drafts of all the chapters. Her corrections and many constructive suggestions for improving the clarity of the text have been invaluable. I do, of course, take full responsibility for any errors that might remain.

MICHAEL OXLEY

Chapter 1

Introduction

London, Paris and New York all have severe housing shortages and an increase in the stock of housing would be valuable in each of these three cities. Why then do the authorities not promote building in Hyde Park, the Jardin du Luxembourg or Central Park? Quite obviously such construction would promote public outrage nationally and internationally because all three locations are cherished for the beauty, joy and amenity they provide. However, if houses were built in these parks there would be no shortage of people wanting to live in these pleasant and convenient places. No doubt substantial profits to the municipalities and to private developers could be generated by such prime residential developments. Alternatively, what about easing housing shortages by promoting housebuilding on land that is currently occupied by run-down industrial premises or using agricultural land just outside the boundaries of each urban area? The protests would be less severe than those that would meet proposals to develop globally renowned green recreational space, but there would still be opposition. In these cases, at least, there would also be powerful supporters. Whilst there would be some concern about the loss of potential employment land and the environmental losses associated with depleted agricultural land, there would be some support for the provision of extra dwellings. Diverse interest groups would lobby for and against the proposed new development.

The decision about whether or not housebuilding is allowed in each case in each city will not be made on the basis of how much money can be made from residential development. It will, instead, be made by considering the social and political costs and benefits of permitting or promoting the provision of new dwellings in particular locations. In other words, the decision on the use of land will not be determined by commercial market forces, it will be a public policy decision. The public policy will involve land-use planning, and the way that land-use planning mechanisms work in each country will vary. They will be a product of the history, culture, politics and chance that determine the shape and operation of the institutional

1

arrangements in each place. However, the aim of planning will in each case be broadly similar. It will be to achieve land-use outcomes that are socially desirable rather than only financially beneficial. The land-use decision will be made not simply by firms and households, but also by governments, the agents of governments and all those groups that influence governments.

The British government has stated that 'a key role for the planning system is to enable the provision of new homes in the right place and at the right time. This is important not only to ensure that everyone has the opportunity of a decent home, but also to maintain the momentum of economic growth . . . Planning is concerned with the provision of homes and buildings, investment and jobs . . . [It] reconciles a number of different demands for new development' (ODPM, 2003a, p. 3). It is also clear that planning is expected to 'secure more affordable housing' (ODPM, 2003b, p. 3). Similar views about the expectations of the planning system in relation to housing can be found in many developed countries. There is also a worldwide recognition that land-use planning addresses a multitude of objectives in addition to those associated with housing. A thorough analysis of the aims and the instruments of planning in a UK context can be found in Rydin (2003).

This chapter provides a descriptive overview of the policy issues that are to be considered and it introduces the economic theory that is to be applied to these issues. The chapter also sets out some signposts to the rest of the book, providing the reader with advance notice of what follows.

Planning and housing

The analysis in this book is relevant to all countries in which there is a land-use planning system that operates within a broadly market economy. That is, it is relevant to most of the countries in the world where there is some form of mixed economy in which governments work with and moderate market forces. Many of the examples come from Britain, but they are also drawn from the rest of Europe and from the USA. The benefits of a comparative approach are demonstrated in Chapter 10 where similar issues are considered in different contexts and, with regard to different policy instruments, in several countries.

In detail, planning systems are expected to do different things in different countries and objectives are pursued within different institutional structures. However, there are some broad similarities of purpose and method. Planning systems are used by governments to promote policy objectives. These objectives include securing sufficient quantities of new housing and ensuring that the location of this housing is appropriate. This means that housing is built where it satisfies consumer demand but does not conflict with other objectives such as containing road congestion and protecting the natural environment. Planning may also be expected to have some effect in making housing more 'affordable' for certain sections of the population. Affordability concerns typically relate to ensuring that low-income households have sufficient housing of an acceptable quality and that excessive housing costs are not a barrier to the supply of lower-income workers.

Planning objectives can thus relate to improving the well-being of certain groups, particularly low-income groups, but the objectives also encompass concerns for the local and national economies. Planning is expected to contribute to promoting local urban economic growth and national economic growth. Growth may be promoted by sufficient supplies of workers available in the right places and for the right wages or salaries. By promoting sufficient and appropriately priced housing, planning may be expected to promote the required supplies of labour. Using land for housing will frequently conflict with using land for the production of other goods and services, and planning will thus sometimes seek to influence the distribution of land between residential, industrial and retail uses, for example, with a view to the consequences for the value of the output of local and national economies. The origins of urban town planning are often viewed in the context of reducing slum housing to improve the health of the residents. It could also, of course, be expected that a healthier workforce might be an economically more productive workforce.

In promoting national economic growth, planning might be expected not only to ensure sufficient supplies of employment land, but also to contribute to an entrepreneurial environment. Thus it will be desirable for industry and commerce to be in locations that enhance the mutual dependency of firms and reduce production and transportation costs.

Governments in mixed economies have from time to time and in varying degrees been concerned about the effects of land ownership and development on the distribution of wealth, and a range of methods have been tried to limit the gains that property owners may achieve from increases in demand that are outside of their control. For example, planning in the form of restrictions on development rights, or requirements for developers to provide facilities for the community, such as roads or schools, has in many cases been expected to achieve redistributions of wealth. Planning is often associated with protecting the countryside but it is also expected to enhance the quality of urban life. Bringing people back into cities and making them better places in which to live is an increasingly significant planning objective.

This very broad agenda for planning is further evidenced by the environmental objectives that are now of great importance. Environmental concerns range from the very local to the global. In preventing proximate incompatible land uses, planning is expected to minimize the nuisance that new developments can cause to a neighbourhood. This ranges from stopping smokey factory chimneys being built in residential neighbourhoods, to stopping the extension to the house next door blocking out the light.

The environmental agenda embraces concerns about the balance between development on greenfield sites and brownfield sites. The former includes agricultural land and previously undeveloped land. The latter includes land that has been previously developed, and has thus been used, for example, for industrial or commercial uses. A reduction in the use of greenfield sites for residential and industrial development is promoted to preserve natural habitats as well as the beauty and recreational benefits of open spaces. Traffic congestion is partly a function of the location of economic activities, and the disbenefits of congestion in terms of time wasted, costs incurred and energy consumed might be eased by improved local planning. Reductions in energy consumption might in turn be expected to have an effect on global warming and the well-being of future generations.

Although much of the economic analysis in this book is applicable to all forms of development, the emphasis is on residential development. The role of land-use planning in influencing the volume, type, location, allocation and affordability of new housing should be examined in the context of other policy measures designed to influence both new and existing housing. It is thus appropriate to examine the aims and the instruments of housing policy as well as planning policy. The aims of housing policy stretch wider than those addressed by planning, to include securing housing of at least minimum quality standards for all households. This will include households who have a 'need' for decent housing but lack the financial resources necessary to afford such housing. Policies will sometimes include a desire to promote particular housing tenures, especially owner-occupation, and increasing home ownership has been and is a policy objective in many countries.

Ensuring a sufficient supply of, and fair access to, rental housing is also a widespread objective.

Most governments also have concerns about the relationships between housings markets and the wider, or macro, economy. The interrelationships between house price inflation and general inflation in the economy, between mortgage rates and interest rates generally, and between housing expenditure and national expenditure will all be legitimate areas of concern for governments anxious to ensure compatibility between housing objectives and macroeconomic objectives. A refreshing overview of the application of economics to a wide range of housing issues can be found in O'Sullivan and Gibb (eds, 2003).

The instruments of planning policy can include the designation of land for specific purposes in land-use plans; the granting of planning permission for acceptable development and controls on the density of development; the layout of estates; the design of buildings and the type of materials used. We can extend our view of planning to encompass controls on the structure, safety and energy consumption of buildings. The instruments of housing policy extend further to include the use of subsidies to the consumers and producers of certain types of housing, and influences over the cost and availability of credit to buy and develop housing. The exact mix of instruments varies from country to country, and the type and degree of government control does in detail depend on the history, politics and values of each society.

In addition to the traditional planning instruments listed above, several countries are expanding the complementary use of fiscal policy instruments, including tax concessions and financial penalties, to achieve both planning and housing objectives. At several points in this book the pros and cons of this expanded range of policy instruments will be debated.

Much of this text is about the role of planning policy instruments in solving problems. There will also, however, be recognition of arguments that suggest that planning and government activity more generally are the cause of problems. There are often suggestions that planning causes shortages of development land, contributes to low levels of housebuilding and pushes up house prices. There are also views that some of the problems tackled by planning, such as the provision of affordable housing, are better addressed through other means. These views of planning will be set out and examined. The aim is to provide a critical analysis of planning and housing policies. This analysis should aid an understanding of what is happening and encourage better approaches to policy in the future.

Economic analysis

Economics is about choices. These choices are made by individuals, households, firms, governments, international organizations and a whole range of local, national and international committees, clubs and groups with a multiplicity of configurations. Usually economists assume that choices are made with some objective in mind. The objective usually relates to making things better. Some intended improvement is thus behind the choice. Various schools of economic thought have focused attention on differing decision-makers and differing objectives.

Neoclassical economists, whose thinking dominated Western economics in the late nineteenth century and much of the twentieth century, focused their attention on consumers and firms as decision-making units whose aims were to use resources to maximize individual well-being and to maximize profits. The decisions were made logically and rationally with purposeful actions following a weighing of the available information on the possible choices and their outcomes. Key contributions in neoclassical thought came from the works of Jevons (1871) and Menger (1871) and later Robinson (1933) and Chamberlin (1933).

According to neoclassicists, individual well-being or utility came from the consumption of goods and services and firms made profits from the production of goods and services. Decisions were essentially made through choices expressed in markets where goods and services, and the factors of production necessary to make those goods and services, were traded. An examination of how markets work, and in particular the formation of market prices, was a central component of neoclassical analysis. Prices would change so as to balance the demands from purchasers and the supplies from sellers; balance or equilibrium in markets was a situation in which there were no shortages and no over-supply. Competitive markets, through adjustments towards equilibrium, allocated factors of production and goods and services to those who gained most benefit from their use. Neoclassical economics, however, is not a simple and cohesive body of thought. There are many 'sub-schools' and divisions which emphasize certain concepts such as utility or equilibrium, or concentrate on particular issues such as the reasons for different market forms including monopoly and oligopoly although there is much emphasis on the workings of competitive markets in which there are many buyers and sellers.

The neoclassical domination of economics has been challenged by economists who have criticized the simple assumptions on which it is founded. The reductionist approach of the neoclassicists has been set aside by economists who have emphasized the complications of the real world. Institutional economists, such as Coase (1937), Buchanan (1968) and Demsetz (1969), in particular, have emphasized the role of rules, organizations and administrative arrangements in understanding how economies function. The role of information and transaction costs in influencing the operation of markets has been emphasized by modern institutional economists who have viewed the virtual dismissal of these issues by neoclassical economists as a fundamental weakness of their approach. However, as one of the most authorative sources on the history of economic thought has stated:

> For better or for worse, and despite all the arguments and counter-arguments, the vast majority of economists the world over subscribe to the received corpus of neoclassical economics centred around the concepts of utility-maximising households and profit-maximizing enterprises. (Blaug, 1990, p. 234)

Despite the shortcomings of neoclassical economics and the advances in modern economics, it continues to have a considerable influence on what we might call 'mainstream economics'. This is the dominant form of economics taught as introductory economics on undergraduate courses in the Western world. The emphasis in mainstream economics is on microeconomics (which examines the operation of specific markets) and macroeconomics (which considers the functioning of national economies and their international interactions). Rather like neoclassical economics, mainstream economics is not a neatly bounded and easily defined body of knowledge. However, the content of standard introductory economics texts such as Lipsey and Chrystal (1995) and Samuelson and Nordhaus (2001) is principally mainstream economics. The emphasis in the microeconomics of such works is on markets in which individuals and firms trade competitively to achieve well-defined objectives.

This sort of microeconomics colours some of the economics in this text. There is, however, no attempt here to explain all the intricacies of mainstream microeconomics. Readers seeking a systematic introduction to this may find it useful to consult basic texts such as those by Begg *et al.* (2003), Harvey (1998) and Mulhearn and Vane (1999). Readers without prior knowledge of economic theory will, however, find sufficient explanation in this text for the value, application and implications of the economic concepts to be clear. When basic economic ideas such as 'demand', 'supply' and 'market price' are applied they should not be used in a crude and uncritical fashion. They should be used with an appreciation of their meaning, with caution around their implementation and sensitivity about their relevance to specific circumstances. This is true of all applications but there are particular problems that arise in relation to housing and land.

Housing is a complex commodity that is purchased for a variety of reasons including to provide a shelter, a home and an investment. It might be a one-roomed apartment or a 20-bedroomed mansion. It might be in the centre of town or on a remote island. Housing may be supplied by many sorts of providers including housebuilders, homeowners selling their property, private landlords seeking profits and social landlords trying to satisfy local wants. Both the location of the housing and the details of the rights and privileges that the purchaser acquires have a major impact on what the housing is worth.

The same complexities concerning location, rights and privileges apply to land. Land is also purchased for a variety of reasons including its potential to grow food, accommodate housing and provide recreation. The use to which land is put will, importantly, have implications not just for those who own or occupy the land, but also for those who live or pass nearby. Whether it is used for housing or some other purpose may even have implications through the environmental impacts for people in other countries.

Despite these complications, a basic contention of this book is that it is useful to think of markets in housing and land. These markets do not, however, exist in the absence of customs, laws and conventions that are determined by social and political processes. Markets do not exist independently of the state and governments. A recurring theme of this text it is that is wrong to think of 'government intervention' in housing markets and land markets, for this suggests that it is possible to have complex markets without governments. In making links between economic activity and the actions of governments, this book is in the tradition of political economy. This connects economic and political processes. The text examines government activity which seeks to compensate for the failure of markets to promote efficiency. It does this from the contrasting perspectives of (a) a liberal interventionist approach which maintains that governments can usefully take actions to compensate for the inevitable inefficiencies of markets and (b) a public choice perspective which suggests that governments may fail to improve on market outcomes if they have insufficient regard for the strengths of markets and the weaknesses of governments. Governments work with markets in many intricate ways, and the methods by which governments can moderate and steer market outcomes is a key concern of this book. To be successful in achieving policy objectives, governments should understand what might happen to markets with and without further governmental actions. Economic theory can assist in this process.

Economic analysis involves abstract thinking. It involves modelling of the real world. Useful economic theories do not necessarily provide good descriptions of the real world; that is not their purpose. By processes of abstraction and simplification they aid understanding of what has happened and what might happen. The test of a good theory is whether it is helpful in providing an answer to a question. The questions in this book are policy questions; they are about how to improve well-being by the use of policies that are framed and executed by the various arms of government. Economic theory can help in formulating both policy problems and policy solutions, and can thus help structure the questions as well as offer answers. Economic analysis is an aid to decision-making. The policy decisions will, however, have to be made by politicians, not economists. The economists can provide analysis and they will often provide analyses of alternative options, but the choice of which option to take can best be seen as informed by, but not determined by, economic analysis.

Economics should be an aid to evidence-based policy formation. Evidence from economists is ideally a combination of useful theories and useful empirical information, since theories are of little value if they do not connect with information about reality. Information outside the framework of a theory is also of limited value. We might have masses of data on house prices and land prices but on their own such data will give no indication of whether house prices influence land prices or land prices influence house prices, or both. Some sort of theory is necessary in order to permit an analysis of the data.

Introductory economics texts typically make a distinction between positive economics, which offers objective explanations of how an economy works, and normative economics, which offers recommendations based on personal value judgements (see, for example, Begg *et al.*, 2003 pp. 10–11). The emphasis in mainstream economics is on a positive approach. The textbook argument is usually along the lines that positive economics questions can be answered by an appeal to appropriate evidence, whereas normative issues are a matter of opinion on which differing views are inevitable. Whilst in principle this distinction has some value, in practice it is often hard to maintain. Take for example the following hypothetical statements (which are similar to those frequently made about planning in South-East England): 'Planning forces up land prices and house prices. It would therefore be a good idea if planning was made less restrictive so that house prices would not rise so much'. Whether or not planning forces up land and house prices involves questions that can be addressed by positive economics. There are theories about the connections between planning and land prices and house prices, and there are data that can be used in testing these theories. However, there are alternative and competing theories and there are different ways of using the data. There are differing opinions amongst economists on which theories are 'best' and how the data should be interpreted. Thus despite positive analyses of the problem, there will be different views on the best objective process. Even if there was total agreement based on agreed positive analysis that planning did force up land and house prices, and there was agreement on the amount by which prices rose as a result of planning, it does not follow that it would be a good idea for planning to be relaxed. There might be agreed evidence that planning achieved benefits; the value of these benefits compared with dis-benefits of higher prices could be investigated using positive analysis; but even faced with the evidence of this analysis, the balance of the relative costs and benefits might well remain a matter of opinion. If the problem is formulated not as a planning problem but as a question of why land prices and house prices are rising, positive analysis can provide evidence about the causes of such inflation. It may be that factors other than planning are deemed, through such evidence, to be the most significant in pushing up prices. What to do in the face of such evidence will again be a normative issue.

The positive and the normative are not easily disentangled in housing and land-use issues. One function of economic analysis is to separate as much of the positive as is possible from an issue and apply reasoned analysis to those elements of a problem. In applying a positive approach economists make a claim to be social scientists (see, for example, Samuelson and Nordhaus, 2001). In their scientific approach economists test hypotheses and examine evidence. Social scientific methodology involves careful appraisal of alternative explanations for events and systematic consideration of alternative courses of action. The methodology frequently, but not always, involves quantification. However, precise measurement of economic phenomena is not always possible. This does not devalue the merits of applying the relevant concepts. For example, in this text it will be argued that one of the arguments for planning is that it can in principle bring the external costs and benefits that can arise from development into decision-making calculations. These costs and benefits are frequently intangible and either very difficult or impossible to quantify precisely. This does not mean that they do not exist or they are not important. A scientific approach reveals their significance and argues for their consideration, irrespective of whether exact numbers can be attached to them. Social scientific investigation does not lead to universally applicable laws; it does rather rest on propositions that can be accepted or rejected by an appeal to evidence.

This text applies aspects of economics which can be found elsewhere under a variety of headings including welfare economics, environmental economics, land economics, urban economics, housing economics and regional economics. Welfare economics, with its concerns for collective rather than just individual well-being and its recognition of the failure of markets to achieve social objectives, is central to the arguments of much of this book. Environmental economics, which examines both the remedies and the reactions to the failure of markets to promote environmental objectives, provides important insights into the environmental role of planning. Land economics, with its critical insights into the pricing of land and the role of location in determining land use and land value, is at the centre of arguments about the distributional role of planning. Urban economics includes analyses of the connections between urban housing markets, labour markets and transportation as well as the determinants of local income levels and the sources and functions of local public finance. Housing economics embraces analysis of the functions of, and failures of, housing markets and the problems and tools of housing policy. Regional economics includes spatial analyses of production, consumption and land use within and between geographical regions. There are no clear boundaries to these different branches of economics and no two texts containing the pertinent terms in their titles cover exactly the same ground. Between them they provide ideas and information that inform much of our understanding of the connections between economics, housing and planning; eclectic borrowing from each of these areas will be encountered as a variety of issues are discussed.

Structure of the book

Chapter 2 introduces the basic concepts of demand and supply of housing and land. It explains how housing and land prices are expected to be determined according to basic mainstream economics. The important distinction between housing demand and housing need, which is essential to analysis of housing policies, is set out. The importance of distinguishing housing supply and housing production, and understanding the relationship between the output of new housing and trading in the existing stock are examined. The basic tenets of simple location theories and their contributions to explaining market-oriented land-use patterns are sketched out. The role of institutional analysis in challenging and, it is argued, complementing basic market analysis is examined. There is also an introduction to the concept of efficiency. This is important to analysis of the role of planning in promoting improvements in the efficiency with which land is allocated.

Chapter 3 shows how welfare economics provides the theoretical foundations for governments to modify market outcomes in order to achieve social objectives. Planning offers some options but these ultimately have to be assessed in relation to the merits of alternative policy instruments. The role of governments in promoting equity or fairness as well as efficiency is seen to be central to the case for policy instruments that seek to improve the well-being of society as apposed to the well-being of individuals.

The failure of competitive markets to achieve efficiency in the use of resources is explored in Chapter 4. The concepts of external costs and external benefits, or externalities, are central to this analysis; these are the costs and benefits that individual decision-makers do not necessary consider. They do, however, when added to the private costs and benefits that are directly considered in competitive markets, give the social costs and benefits which are compared in assessing social welfare. It is argued that externalities are a pervasive and inevitable feature of housing and land markets. Further difficulties for competitive markets arise through their failure to provide optimal quantities of public goods and through their tendency to disequilibrium. It is thus argued that 'market failure' provides the foundations of the case for governments to promote an efficient use of resources through implementing a range of policy instruments including some form of land-use planning.

Chapter 5 links environmental economics and sustainable development. The role of environmental economics in both formulating environmental problems and suggesting policy responses is explored. The wide view of environmental issues which is taken embraces local concerns such as the amenity value of views over open countryside, as well as the global impact of energy consumption patterns. It is shown that economics provides valuable insights into the role of planning in pursuing sustainable development objectives. These objectives include resource conservation, the quality of the physical environment and social equality and they address the well-being of future as well as present generations.

Public choice theory raises significant questions about the ability of planning to respond efficiently to market failure and sustainable development agendas, and a public choice critique of planning is presented in Chapter 6. The challenge that public choice theorists have posed to the welfare economics that underpins the liberal interventionists' perspective of market failure and planning is examined. It is argued that a public choice view of the world highlights the possible costs and negative outcomes from planning and shows that, without proper regard for property rights and pricing issues, planning is likely to fail.

The distributional role of planning, particularly in relation to the rewards from the ownership and use of land, is examined in Chapter 7. Theories of land value determination and economic rent are used to explore arguments about the effect of planning on land values. Whilst many forms of taxation have tried to capture the returns to land that in some sense 'belong' to the community rather than an individual, they have usually been unsuccessful in both their conception and implementation. The prospects for site-specific planning conditions capturing some of this 'surplus value' are argued to be potentially greater than blanket taxes.

Chapter 8 considers how in principle and practice land values may be effectively appropriated through the planning system to help provide 'affordable housing'. The provision of such housing for households on low incomes has been pursued through the planning system in several countries in different institutional contexts, and both the efficiency and the equity of promoting 'affordable housing through planning' are examined.

The urban renaissance agenda which has gained favour on both sides of the Atlantic is examined in Chapter 9. This agenda expects planning to contribute to more compact patterns of development in order to achieve energy-saving and countryside-preserving objectives. The environmental concerns driving the agenda are matched by a desire to promote cities as pleasant places in which to live and work even though residential development is expected to be at higher densities. The role of economic analysis in appraising this agenda is set out. The policy instruments, including financial incentives as well as conventional planning controls, that might address urban renaissance objectives, are considered.

Chapter 10 examines planning and housing policy instruments in a comparative context. It is shown that examining issues in different countries, in varying institutional contexts, can generate critical analyses of policies in use in individual countries and promote debate about the feasibility and desirability of transferring policies between countries. Several contrasts are drawn between both the objectives and the instruments of housing and planning policies in Europe and the USA. The role of inclusionary zoning in promoting affordable housing through planning instruments in the USA provides a contrast with the 'affordable housing through planning' practices adopted in Britain.

Ideas on the economic consequences of planning are explored in Chapter 11. Microeconomic, macroeconomic, welfare and market-specific impacts are considered, and the problems of isolating the effect of planning are acknowledged. There is a review of theory and evidence about the connections between planning controls and land and house prices. It is argued that the impact of planning controls on housing production needs to be examined in the context of the many determinants of residential development. The effect of changes in the rate of housebuilding on house prices will furthermore depend on the relative significance of production changes compared with all the factors that influence house prices, including the power that house-builders have within the housing market. This market power varies with institutional arrangements, and is influenced by the degree of competition that housebuilders face from dwellings traded within the existing housing stock.

An overview of the relationships between economics and planning, economics and housing, and planning and housing is provided in Chapter 12. The recurring theme of the book – the relationships between markets and governments – is emphasized and the conclusions on the range of issues covered are summarized.

The text is accompanied by 16 diagrams, placed within boxes that contain explanatory notes. The diagrams provide stylized and succinct ways of explaining concepts and problems, although the main text can be read without any reference to the diagrams if the reader desires. Alternatively, the diagrams can provide additional formulations, reinforcements and extensions of the ideas that are set out in words. Whilst the text can be read without the diagrams, the diagrams should not be used without reference to the text; they present simple abstractions of complex real-world phenomena. It is in the text that the complexities of the concepts and the complications of applying the ideas implicit in the diagrams are revealed.

Throughout the book the role of economics in providing ideas, in formulating problems and encouraging a theoretically-informed and evidence-based approach to policy formation and implementation is to the fore.

Chapter 2

Markets, Development, Institutions and Efficiency

Throughout the world the development of housing depends on the combined operation of markets and public policy. In detail, markets work in different ways in different social, political and institutional contexts, but they have key elements that pervade a variety of settings. The process of development involves changes in the use of land and buildings that create new built-environment assets. Governments are not content to allow markets to wholly determine this process and the results or outcomes, and they therefore influence these processes through public policy. An important element of such public policy is land-use planning.

In this chapter we provide a backcloth against which the policy and planning rationale, actions and outcomes of subsequent chapters can be displayed. An essential feature of this backcloth is an examination of how housing and land markets might be expected to operate in the absence of planning. This will be done by applying the concepts of mainstream economics to the demand for housing and land and the production of new housing. As explained in Chapter 1, in mainstream economics individuals and firms trade competitively in markets to maximize utility or individual well-being and to maximize profits. We will examine the role of prices, the nature of explicit and implicit markets, and the problem of determining the boundary of a housing market area.

An important theoretical strand to the economics of land use and development has been provided by location theories, and some key elements of such theories, their propositions and limitations will be set out. Conceptualizing and modelling location are issues that have challenged economists and planners, and the issues will be explored and the options examined.

Mainstream economists' market-orientated analyses of development processes have in recent years been both challenged and supplemented by institutional analysis. Several institutional perspectives will be explored, the nature and role of property market institutions will

15

be examined, and the contribution of an institutional approach eval-uated. It will be shown that institutional analysis provides a useful complement to, rather than a substitute for, mainstream economics.

An important aspect of the case for public policy to modify the processes and outcomes of markets is that markets can be inefficient, and it is therefore necessary to consider the concepts of efficiency and inefficiency. The application of these concepts from mainstream economics and institutional perspectives will expose the various interpretations that are available. Whilst basic mainstream econom-ics provides a very simple explanation of how markets work, it can provide useful insights into how planning may modify market outcomes.

Housing and land markets

Housing markets bring together buyers and sellers of housing. Land markets bring together buyers and sellers of land. Buyers offer demand and sellers offer supply. The exchanges between buyers and sellers occur at prices which reflect the willingness of buyers to purchase and the willingness of sellers to sell. If prices are not fixed by governments or an administrative body, mainstream economics suggests that prices only reflect the decisions of buyers and sellers. If a degree of fixing or control occurs, the decisions of buyers and sell-ers are moderated in a fashion that reflects the degree of fixing or control. We can assume at this stage that the degree of fixing or control is minimal and thus that the prices of housing and land are a consequence of the demands and supplies of those who express their preferences through market transactions. As explained in Chapter 1, housing and land are in reality complex items demanded for a variety of reasons and supplied via a variety of processes. An application of basic demand and supply analysis involves consider-able simplification and abstraction.

Housing demand

Demand involves a willingness and an ability to purchase, and thus depends on preferences and financial resources. We can think of indi-vidual demand which is expressed by a single person or a household, and aggregate demand which is the sum of a set of individual demands. The individuals may be aggregated in several ways, espe-cially by location and the type of housing under consideration. Thus we may, for example, conceptualize the aggregate demand for housing in England, or London or the borough of Kensington and Chelsea. Or we may consider the aggregate demand for owner-occupied housing or for terraced housing, and consider this demand for any of these locations. Defining with precision the item traded in a housing market is difficult. Dwellings have a variety of physical, locational and legal attributes and the 'units of housing' exchanged in a housing market can have several configurations.

With all other influences on demand held constant, there is an expectation that households will demand more rather than less housing if the price of housing falls. If the price of housing rises it is expected that less housing will be demanded. These basic propositions involve the elementary *ceteris paribus* assumption which allows the relationship between two items (in this case price and quantity demanded) to be considered whilst nothing else changes (see Figure 2.1).

The expression of individual demand implies a choice between options. The options might be, for example, a bigger or smaller house, a house near work or a house near schools, a house in London or a house in Cambridge, a house to buy or a house to rent. The complexity of the choice and options reflects the complexity of the item under demand. In demanding a house an individual is expressing a preference for a physical commodity and a location, both of which will have many attributes. The attributes of the house include, for example, its size, number of bedrooms, presence or absence of a garden and garage. The attributes of a location include its proximity to work, schools, shops, open space and transport facilities. Giving examples of these attributes does of course involve considerable simplification; many subtle differences in the configuration and style of a house and attitudes to and images of competing locations will influence the demands that individuals make for alternative dwellings.

If a dwelling is demanded as an asset to be purchased, another set of characteristics which define the attractiveness of the property as an investment will influence the choice that is made. A dwelling that is demanded for owner-occupation may, for example, be particularly attractive because its value is expected to rise rapidly. A potential landlord may place a high demand on a dwelling that will yield a high rental income and have low maintenance costs.

It is useful to consider any dwelling as having a set of property rights (Jaffe, 1996; Becker, 1997) associated with it which define the privileges and obligations that the purchaser is endowed with on acquiring the property. One may thus think of individuals demanding

Figure 2.1   *Demand for housing*

(a) A demand curve for housing

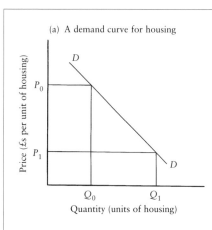

(b) Shifts in a demand curve for housing

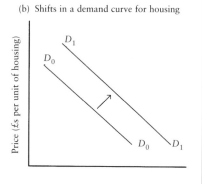

We may consider DD to be either (i) a demand curve for an individual household, or (ii) a demand curve for a group of households – in this case it is an aggregate demand curve. The demand curve in both cases shows the relationship between the price of housing and the quantity of housing demand. The price might be the purchase price of owner-occupied housing or rental payments for rented housing. The demand curve shows a desire to 'buy' (this might mean purchasing a house or renting a house) backed up by the financial resources to buy. If prices fall from P_0 to P_1 quantity demanded increases from Q_0 to Q_1. The change from Q_0 to Q_1 is caused only by a change in price with all the other factors influencing demand remaining constant.

A shift in a demand curve for housing is caused by a change in something other than the price of housing. For example an increase in income (of an individual household or incomes of a group of households) may cause the demand curve $D_0 D_0$ to shift to $D_1 D_1$. An increase in the total number of households in an area may also cause the aggregate demand curve for the area of shift from $D_0 D_0$ to $D_1 D_1$. Or again, lower interest rates may shift the demand for owner-occupied housing in a country from $D_0 D_0$ to $D_1 D_1$. At any given price, demand is greater with $D_1 D_1$ than with $D_0 D_0$.

sets of property rights associated with a physical property rather than just demanding the physical object. The particular bundle of property rights on offer will influence the attractiveness of the dwelling. A house in a street where the occupants have to bear the responsibilities and costs for maintaining the road and pavement may be less in demand that an otherwise equivalent house where local government takes on these obligations. A dwelling where planning permission exists for constructing a new house in the garden has a different set of property rights to a dwelling where this opportunity does not exist.

The concept of housing demand can be applied to the various forms of private and social renting that exist throughout the world. In acquiring the right to occupy a dwelling in return for rental payments, a tenant is buying a very different bundle of property rights from an owner-occupier who buys the right to occupy and resell the dwelling. Legal contracts between buyer and seller and between tenant and landlord will help define the property rights that are being traded. Differences in property rights are likely to be reflected in differences in demand and ultimately the prices and rents which the dwellings attract.

For social-rented dwellings the process by which demand is expressed and rents are determined will be different than those prevailing for private renting. The degree of choice that the prospective tenant is afforded varies between the many types of social-renting systems. Increasingly systems are being adapted throughout Britain and Western Europe which allow social-sector tenants more choice in the property they occupy. For example, a choice-based letting system which originated in the Netherlands is, with encouragement from central government, being applied in England with the objective of reducing bureaucracy and increasing tenant satisfaction. (For an example of the application of this 'Delft system' of allocation see Brown *et al.*, 2003.) There are also shifts in favour of social rents reflecting the relative demands for properties rather than bureaucratic decisions based on such factors as the size of dwellings or the historic costs of production.

Despite more choice than in the past, social-housing systems typically allocate dwellings according to need rather than demand, two very different constructs. A need for housing is a socially determined requirement for accommodation. A household may have a need for housing but not have the money to demand that housing. Housing need is also complemented by housing standards that define a socially determined minimum level of quality. Just as we can think of adding together individual housing demands to create aggregate housing demands, we can think of aggregate housing need. This has been defined as

> The quantity of housing that is required to provide accommodation of an agreed minimum standard and above for a population given its size, household composition, age distribution etc., without taking into account the individual household's ability to pay for the housing assigned to it. (Robinson, 1979, pp. 56–7)

As we shall see in later chapters, planning systems typically attempt to respond to housing need as well as housing demand. In Chapter

10 there is a review, in an international context, of measures to stimulate demand and supply to tackle problems of housing need.

Returning to housing demand, economists expect individual and aggregate demand to be influenced by household incomes, the price and availability of substitutes and the price and availability of complementary goods. Individuals will tend to demand more housing and better quality housing at higher than at lower incomes. As household incomes generally increase, one would expect the demand for housing to increase. This relationship is, in formal terms, called 'the income elasticity of demand for housing'. Numerically, this is the percentage change in quantity demanded divided by the percentage change in income. Thus, for example, if a 10 per cent increase in income was associated with a 5 per cent increase in housing demand the elasticity value would be 0.5. If a 10 per cent increase in income was associated with a 10 per cent increase in demand the value would be 1, and there would be 'unitary' income elasticity of housing demand with respect to incomes. Only if increases in income led to reductions in housing demand would the income elasticity value be negative. Empirical estimates of the income elasticity of demand for housing vary widely, which is not surprising given that the exact specification of the income and demand changes measured vary from study to study. Monk (1999) provides a useful summary of estimates for markets in the UK and the USA and shows several sets of results clustered around values between 0.5 and 2.0.

Economists expect, on most specifications, income elasticity of demand for housing to be positive (although there may be exceptions: for example the demand for poor-quality housing may fall with an increase in incomes). However, 'price elasticity of demand' would be expected to be negative. Thus with price elasticity measured by the percentage change in quantity demanded divided by percentage change in price, if a 10 per cent increase in price was associated with a 5 per cent reduction in quantity demanded the elasticity value would be –0.5. Again, empirical estimates vary with exactly what is being measured (Rosenthal, 1984). Monk (1999) quotes UK and US estimates that cluster around –0.2 to –1. In principle, in such elasticity estimates only the two variables, price and quantity demanded, are considered, with all other items assumed to be constant. In reality, many things change at the same time and isolating the effects of individual variables can involve complex modelling. The assumption of the constancy of other items (the *ceteris paribus* assumption) is important in understanding and interpreting elasticity information. For example, one would normally expect the price elasticity of demand for housing to be negative, but if house prices increased this might lead to a change in expectations in that households might expect house prices to rise further. The changed expectations may raise demand and, thus in turn, house prices. A simple set of observations that ignored the effect of expectations might erroneously conclude in such circumstances that the price elasticity of demand for housing was positive (Figure 2.2 gives a diagrammatic presentation of the price and income elasticities of demand for housing).

Changes in the price of complementary goods may be expected to influence housing demand. For example, large increases in transport costs may reduce the demand for rural houses that had previously been very attractive to households commuting to cities. If local property taxes are viewed as complementary goods, one can again postulate an elasticity of demand for housing with respect to such

Figure 2.2 *Price and income elasticity of demand for housing*

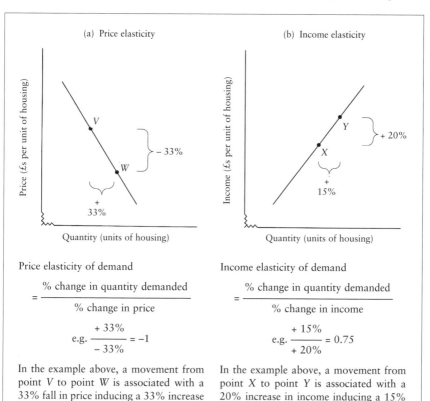

(a) Price elasticity

(b) Income elasticity

Price elasticity of demand

$$= \frac{\% \text{ change in quantity demanded}}{\% \text{ change in price}}$$

e.g. $\dfrac{+33\%}{-33\%} = -1$

In the example above, a movement from point V to point W is associated with a 33% fall in price inducing a 33% increase in quantity demanded.

Income elasticity of demand

$$= \frac{\% \text{ change in quantity demanded}}{\% \text{ change in income}}$$

e.g. $\dfrac{+15\%}{+20\%} = 0.75$

In the example above, a movement from point X to point Y is associated with a 20% increase in income inducing a 15% increase in quantity demanded.

taxation. With other items held constant, higher property taxes might reduce housing demand.

Housing of different types or houses in different locations will to some degree be substitutes for each other. The degree of substitutability depends on households' circumstances and their preferences for the options. General increases in rents might, for example, be expected to increase the demand for home ownership. A large increase in urban house prices may increase demand in suburban and rural locations. In principle, the responsiveness of housing demand to changes in the price of complementary and substitute goods can be measured by applying the concept of 'cross elasticity of demand' (see Begg *et al.*, 2003, pp. 47–8), which can be estimated by dividing the percentage change in demand by the percentage change in the price of the complementary or substitute good. One would expect the cross elasticity of demand for complementary goods to be negative (higher transport costs reduce rural housing demand) and for substitute goods to be positive (higher urban house prices increase rural housing demand). Because of the complexity of the modelling involved in isolating the effects of changes in the prices of complementary and substitute goods on housing demand, there are very few empirical estimates of the relevant cross elasticities (see Figure 2.3).

Simple models of markets assume that demand is determined independently of supply: that is, supply is not a direct determinant of demand. However, housing demand many be influenced by perceptions of what is available. Perceptions of the number of dwellings available, as well as their price, size, location and other attributes may influence the desire to purchase dwellings. The number of households in particular is an important determinant of aggregate demand. The very existence of households and the rate of household formation, as well as being a function of demographic factors, is likely to be influenced by the availability of dwellings. The complex interactions between supply and demand make the housing market resistant to the superficial application of simple models.

Housing supply

It is useful to distinguish between two sources of housing supply. These are: supply from the existing stock and supply from housebuilding, both of which combine to create the supply coming onto the market. Supply from the stock depends on all those factors that influence house-owners' decisions to put their properties on the market. Dwellings may be offered to the market largely because of

Figure 2.3 *Cross elasticity of demand*

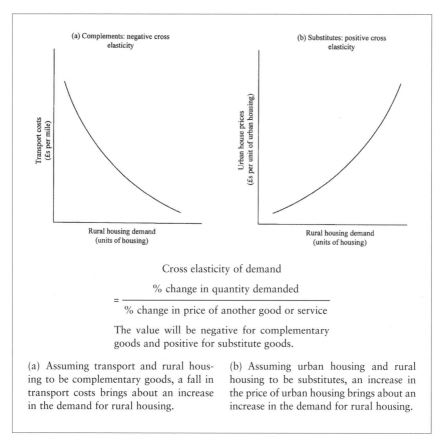

(a) Complements: negative cross elasticity

Transport costs (£s per mile)

Rural housing demand (units of housing)

(b) Substitutes: positive cross elasticity

Urban house prices (£s per unit of urban housing)

Rural housing demand (units of housing)

Cross elasticity of demand

$$= \frac{\text{\% change in quantity demanded}}{\text{\% change in price of another good or service}}$$

The value will be negative for complementary goods and positive for substitute goods.

(a) Assuming transport and rural housing to be complementary goods, a fall in transport costs brings about an increase in the demand for rural housing.

(b) Assuming urban housing and rural housing to be substitutes, an increase in the price of urban housing brings about an increase in the demand for rural housing.

changes in household circumstances. Job changes may prompt a desire to move to a new location; changes in family size may lead to a wish for a larger or smaller property; and changes in incomes may lead to a hankering to trade up or down. Increases in house prices are unlikely, *per se*, to bring more dwellings from the stock onto the market unless they prompt a desire to capitalize on the wealth accumulated in dwellings. There could thus be a desire to trade down to lower-priced properties or move to rented dwellings and use the surplus accumulated wealth for a non-housing purpose. Without such an effect it is unlikely that supply from the stock will be very sensitive to changes in price – that is: the price elasticity of supply from the stock is likely to be low.

Supply from housebuilding includes new construction and extra dwellings created from the conversion of existing properties. The price elasticity of this source of supply depends on the ability of the housebuilding industry to respond to higher prices. These higher prices with costs unchanged will mean increased profitability from housebuilding and firms might be expected to respond to the prospect of higher profits by increasing production. Constraints on the supply of factors of production such as labour and land will, however, limit the strength of this response. Further constraints may come from the ability of the existing stock to absorb more demand and provide more effective supply as prices rise. If there is a high vacancy rate in the existing stock, some reduction in this rate might also precede increased production. We might expect housebuilding firms to respond to expectations about future profit levels. Thus if firms do not expect higher house price levels to be maintained relative to future costs, they may conclude that extra output sold in the future is unlikely to achieve the profit levels that current prices would suggest.

As with demand elasticities, empirical estimates of the price elasticity of supply of housing vary widely depending on the specification of the model and the data used. Monk (1999) reviews a range of estimates which suggest low elasticity of supply figures for the UK compared with the USA. Malpezzi (1996) suggests that in the long run the elasticity of supply in the UK is between 0.9 and 2.1 (using post-1945 data), whereas the comparable range for the USA is between 9 and 16. Bramley (1993a) estimated housing supply elasticities by county for England with results that range from 0.15 to 1.8. The elasticity of the supply of new housing will depend on the actions, motivation and constraints on firms in the housebuilding industry.

The ways that housebuilders respond to higher house prices and to increased demand for housing depend firstly on how the housebuilding industry is structured and secondly on the willingness and ability of housebuilders to change the volume and composition of their output. The structure of the housebuilding industry and the composition of the output varies from country to country. In Britain, most new housing is built by private housebuilders who operate either as speculative developers or contractors for social-housing landlords. Supply is dominated by speculative developers building for owner-occupation. Most of this output, which constitutes around 80 per cent of total housebuilding, is supplied by a small number of large housebuilders who are taking a growing share of the market (Barlow, 2000). It is argued that

> The main risks associated with speculative housebuilding concern the price paid for the land and the timing of the scheme

in relation to the land and housing market cycles. Acquiring and managing a portfolio of land holdings is the critical feature of the speculative housebuilding process. Firms need to secure a steady flow of sites to feed their immediate business plans, as well as a flow of options or conditional contracts for longer term strategic plans. Stocks of land, whether owned outright or under contract (land banks), can help to increase development profit by keeping down land costs relative to house prices. (Barlow, 2000, p. 3)

Land shortages caused by the planning system are often seen as the main cause of supply inelasticity in Britain (see, for example, Evans, 1991, 1996). However, Ball (1999) suggests that slowly changing labour-intensive construction techniques weaken supply responsiveness and 'a higher rate of innovation, therefore, should improve supply elasticities and help to smooth out the housing market cycle'. It is also suggested that housebuilding techniques in North America enable an easier flow of labour into and out of the industry and contribute to greater supply elasticities than in Britain (ibid., pp. 15–17). A focus on land development profits rather than profits from houses is furthermore seen as a contributory factor to the low rate of construction innovation in Britain (ibid., pp. 19–21). Explaining differences in supply elasticities between countries requires an understanding of the complexity of differences in institutional arrangements, the organization of the housebuilding industry and the relationships between housebuilding and the land market. It has been argued that 'Not too much can be said on a comparative basis about relative supply responses internationally, apart from the fact that they are likely to be highly variable and depend on the competitiveness of the land market' (Ball, 2003, p. 914).

Government policies can have important influences on housebuilders. Adams and Watkins (2002) argue that the housebuilding industry in Britain will have to make big changes in response to the government's desire to see 60 per cent of future development on previously used brownfield land:

If speculative developers are to make a significant contribution to brownfield development, it is apparent that new skills and strategies will be required. The problematic nature of many brownfield locations means that developers will need to deliver value added from housing products rather than rely on gaining profits from inflation in land prices. (Ibid., p. 144)

Brownfield development issues are discussed in the context of the 'urban renaissance' agenda in Chapter 9.

In mainstream economics, demand and supply are together expected to determine the price of housing in the absence of controls on housing markets. They are also expected to determine the quantity available in the market, but this quantity may not be sufficient to satisfy the total need for housing. If governments wish to see housing

Figure 2.4   *Changes in the demand, supply and price of housing*

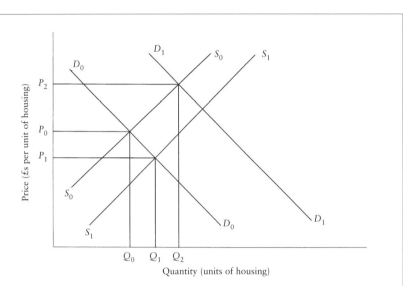

Assuming that $D_0 D_0$ and $S_0 S_0$ show initial aggregate demand and supply curves for owner-occupied housing in an area, the price at which demand and supply come together (the equilibrium price) is P_0. The equilibrium price 'clears the market', meaning that there is no excess demand or excess supply. The quantity demanded equals the quantity supplied and this equilibrium quantity is Q_0. The actual price and quantity of housing in the area may be quite different from P_0 and Q_0 if the market is not in balance (that is, the market may be in disequilibrium).

If the supply curve shifts from $S_0 S_0$ to $S_1 S_1$, the equilibrium price falls to P_1 and the equilibrium quantity increases to Q_1. The supply curve may shift because of an increase in supply due, for example, to more households wishing to sell their houses and/or housebuilders being willing and able to build and sell more houses.

If the demand curve shifts from $D_0 D_0$ to $D_1 D_1$, the equilibrium price increases to P_2 and the equilibrium quantity increases to Q_2. The demand curve may shift because of an increase in demand due, for example, to an increase in household incomes and/or more households wishing to live in the area.

One could also assume that Figure 2.4 depicts demand and supply curves for rented housing. In this case the price is the rental payment for housing.

need satisfied they may use a variety of policy instruments that influence both the demand for and supply of housing. These instruments
include planning measures (see Figures 2.4 and 2.5), and the variety
of options available in principle and those used in practice in several
countries are discussed in Chapter 10.

Figure 2.5 *Housing need*

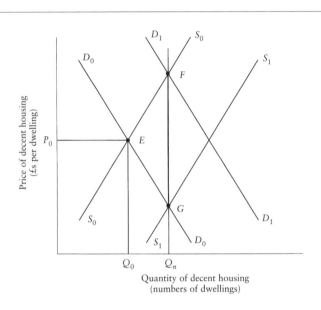

Quantity of decent housing
(numbers of dwellings)

Within a given area (or one could assume, within a given country) the demand and
supply curves for decent housing ($D_0 D_0$ and $S_0 S_0$) intersect at E to give an equilibrium
quantity Q_0. Decent housing is housing of a socially and politically determined minimum standard. If the total numbers of households in the area is Q_n and each household
needs decent housing, and total housing need in the area is Q_n.

With market equilibrium at E, there is unmet housing need equal to the difference
between Q_n and Q_0.

If government wants all households to have decent housing, they require policies
that eliminate the gap between Q_n and Q_0. Policies might try to (1) increase the demand
for decent housing (through housing allowances or housing vouchers for example) so
that with a new demand curve at $D_1 D_1$, equilibrium at F results in a new equilibrium
Q_n. Policies, alternatively, might try to (2) increase the supply of decent housing (by,
for example, making more land available for housebuilding, or providing subsidies or
tax concessions to suppliers of decent housing) so that with a new supply curve, $S_1 S_1$,
equilibrium at G results in a new equilibrium quantity at Q_n. Another policy approach
(3) would be for government to directly supply, or supply through government agencies, supply equal to Q_n minus Q_0. In practice, governments usually use some combination of approaches (1), (2) and (3).

More information on the options available in principle and those used in practice in
different countries is given in Chapter 10.

Demand and supply of land

The demand for land for residential development is a demand for a factor of production. In mainstream economics the demand for factors of production is viewed as a 'derived demand', that is it depends on the demand for the final good or service that is to be produced. Thus the demand for housebuilding land is derived from the demand for housing. The maximum amount that housebuilders are willing to pay for land may be ascertained from a residual valuation approach, where the residual value is equal to expected revenues from house sales minus the expected costs of all inputs other than land. A 'normal' or minimum acceptable level of profit, together with the expected levels of expenditure on labour, materials and finance are included in non-land costs. If more revenue from house sales is expected, other things being equal, the residual value will increase. Thus more expensive dwellings built on a plot, or a plot developed to a higher density, will raise residual values. If expected non-land costs increase without any expected increase in revenues from house sales, the level of demand for residential development land and the size of the residual values will fall.

In practice, whether or not houses may be built on a given plot and the density at which houses can be built are likely to be regulated by planning policies. Such policies control the bundle of property rights associated with the plot, and variations in this bundle will be reflected in variations in demand. The demand for a one hectare plot on which no houses or one house can be built will be very different from the demand for a one hectare plot on which 40 houses can be built.

It is important to distinguish between the stock of land and the supply of land. Within any geographically defined territory there will be a fixed stock of land. Unless major physical changes occur that result, for example, in land falling into the sea or being reclaimed from the sea, this stock has a constant size. Land supply is not a stock but a flow. It is the flow of land offered to the market over a given time period. This flow is not fixed but varies according to such factors as the price offered for the land and the nature and degree of planning controls (see Figure 2.6). To understand residential land supply it is important to examine the exact specifications of the land being offered to the market, and again the concept of property rights is useful. One may conceptualize bundles of property rights in land being offered to the market; one may think of rights to develop land offered to the market rather than market trading in physically defined factors of production.

Figure 2.6 *The stock of land and the supply of land*

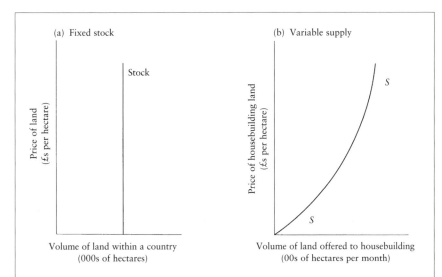

(a) Fixed stock

(b) Variable supply

Volume of land within a country
(000s of hectares)

Volume of land offered to housebuilding
(00s of hectares per month)

The stock of land is different from the supply of land.

(a) The stock of land within any geographically defined area (e.g. a country) is fixed. Changes in the price of land have no effect on this amount.

(b) The supply of land is a measure of the flow of land available to the market. The volume of land offered to the market for any purpose varies. For example, the volume of land offered to housebuilders for housebuilding will vary with price. At higher rather than lower prices more land will, in the absence of any controls, by offered for housebuilding. *SS* is a supply curve for housebuilding land.

The physical attributes will also be important, however, and will help to characterize the bundle of rights on offer. Land with planning permission that requires extensive drainage and the construction of access roads before residential construction can begin is quite different from land with a similar permission that comes complete with all basic infrastructure in place.

In the absence of planning controls one would expect the supply of land for residential development to vary with the price offered for such land, that is there will be some 'price elasticity of supply'. The prices offered for land in alternative, competing uses will have an important impact on this elasticity. If, for example, in rural areas agriculture and housing development are competing land uses and the demand for housing increases significantly relative to the demand for agricultural produce, it is likely that the price offered for land to transfer from agricultural to residential use will rise and there will be a significant land-supply response. There may therefore, in such a situation, be significant elasticity of residential land supply. If, in an urban area, office development and housing development are competing uses, an increase in the prices offered for land for housing development relative to land for office development will bring forth an increase in the supply of housing land and there may be some conversion of office land into housing land.

Planning regimes will have important impacts on the elasticity of supply of land for specific uses. If planning constrains the supply of residential land relative to, say, agricultural and office land, the effective elasticity of supply of residential land will be limited, and supply will become more inelastic. If the demand for housing land rises significantly one would, in these circumstances, expect the proportionate increase in the price of housing land to be greater than the proportionate increase in the volume of housing land offered to the market. This elasticity concept is particularly important to the further discussions of land supply and land value and the linkage to distributional justice and land taxation in Chapter 7 and the economic consequences of planning in Chapter 11.

Private-sector housing development

In a competitive environment one would expect the volume of housing production to depend on the profitability of building houses. This in turn would be a function of the demand and price of new dwellings and the costs of housebuilding. If housing supply is dominated by sales from existing stock, and 'new' and 'old' dwellings are good substitutes for each other, changes in demand for old dwellings will tend to have a strong influence on the price at which new dwellings can be sold. Housebuilders, in these circumstances, will in large measure be 'price-takers' rather than 'price-makers'.

Housebuilders' expectations about the price at which they can sell houses and the costs of building those houses (not including the costs of land) will influence the amount they bid for land. Expectations of higher house prices will, other things being equal, increase housebuilders' bids for land. Higher bids for land will, in the absence of planning controls, increase the volume of land supplied for housebuilding. Figure 2.7 gives a more complete exposition of the relationships between the housing market, land market and the production of new houses in a market framework without planning.

Explicit and implicit markets

There are explicit markets in houses and in land but there are no explicit markets in each of the characteristics that define a house or a plot of land. There are only implicit markets in the characteristics. In explicit markets, prices can be observed and recorded because monetary exchanges actually occur. Data on house prices and land prices obtained from explicit market transactions do, however, inevitably conceal wide variations in the bundles of characteristics of the properties that have been exchanged. A basic theory of implicit markets is set out by Evans (1995 pp. 6–10), which assumes that in principle each buyer is paying a price for a property which reflects their valuation of the characteristics of the property. If in the case of a house it was possible to break this value down into a price, for example, for each bedroom, the garage and the garden and for the proximity of the location to work and school, each attribute would have a price. The list of attributes in practice is much longer and one can easily see that examining the implicit markets in the wide range of attributes is a complex task.

Sophisticated statistical methods have been applied to implicit markets in order to reveal the prices of individual characteristics. These methods involve 'hedonic pricing' which attaches implicit prices to defined characteristics (Rosen, 1994) such as access to local amenities, environmental features and transport facilities (see for example Hughes and Sirmans, 1992; Smith and Huang, 1993; O'Byrne *et al.*, 1985). Hedonic pricing has also been used to create standardized house price indices which measure the changes in price over time of a hypothetical house with a uniform bundle of characteristics (Fleming and Nellis, 1984). Such indices thus show movements in house prices which are independent of changes in the mix of houses coming onto the market. In short, they do for house prices what the retail price index attempts to do for prices generally – that is, measure inflation in the price of a constant 'basket of goods'.

Housing market areas

To understand how housing markets operate and to link land-use planning mechanisms to market boundaries, it will be useful to consider a national housing market as a series of local markets. This immediately raises the question 'where does one housing market end and another begin?' Market areas will not necessarily coincide with administrative boundaries. This is recognized in Scotland, for

Figure 2.7 *The housing market, new house production and the land market*

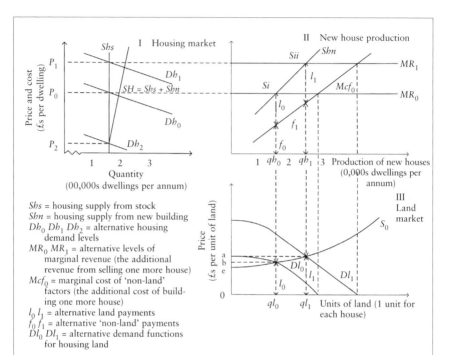

Figure 2.7 shows a model which examines the relationships between the market for existing houses, new house production and the land market. The model examines the flows of housing demand and supply. It is assumed that supply comes from the existing stock and new production. The supply from the stock is perfectly inelastic with respect to price, and thus dwellings come into the market because of decisions to change dwellings related to such factors as job moves or changes in family size, but increases in price, per se, do not induce sales. The model can be viewed as relating simply to the owner-occupied market or in a wider context to all private housing if the 'price' variable is interpreted as an imputed or explicit rent. In the explanation that follows, it is assumed that owner-occupied houses are under consideration. Consumers are assumed to be indifferent between old and new houses.

Section I
An initial demand function Db_0, gives a price of P_0

Section II
It is assumed that there is a competitive house-building market such that all builders are price-takers, and attempt to maximize profits. The house-building industry is a price-taker because its contribution to annual supply is small compared with that coming from sales of existing houses. Expected marginal revenue (MR) is initially at level MR_0. Mcf_0 shows an expected marginal cost of factors other than land (Mcf), and includes a normal profit element. Normal profit is the minimum profit necessary to ensure production. Mcf_0 slopes upwards because of the additional factor prices associated with committing an increasing volume of resources to housing construction. The industry is assumed to bid for land in a residual fashion such that the maximum land bid is equal to the expected revenue from

$\rightarrow$

$\rightarrow$

house sales minus the expected value of all other costs. Let the maximum land bid = l; this is the bid price per unit of land necessary for each new housing unit.

Generally, $l = MR - Mcf$,
Specifically at price P_0, $l = MR_0 - Mcf_0$.

At output level qh_0, l has a value of l_0.
From this relationship the demand curve for land, shown in Section III, can be derived.

Section III
With house price P_0, marginal revenue at MR_0, and 'other factor cost' Mcf_0, the demand for land is shown as Dl_0. S_0 is the supply curve of land for housing development; it shows the flow of land available for housing development at different prices. The base level Oe can be taken to be the price of agricultural land. One unit of land is necessary for one house. At an equilibrium land price of Ob (or l_0) ql_0 units if land are traded.

Section II, again (ii)
The initial level of house production is qh_0 dwellings per annum with a payment to 'non-land factors' of f_0 and a payment to land of l_0 per dwelling.

Section I, again (ii)
Let demand increase to Dh_1 and price to P_1. The additional supply from new building is assumed to be too small to have a significant effect on price. (In the very long run successive 'rounds' of extra supply from new building could add to the stock and shift the 'supply from the stock' curve, Sh_s, to the right and, without significant demand changes, this would affect price. The concern here is, however, with less than the very long run.)

Section II (iii)
Expected marginal revenue increases to MR_1.

Now, $l = MR_1 - Mcf_0$.

Section III, again (ii)
With house price level P_1 and 'other factor cost' Mcf_0, the demand for land is Dl_1. The equilibrium price of land is now Oa (or l_1).

Section II (iv)
The level of house production is now qh_1 dwellings per annum. The 'non-land' payment is f_1 and the land payment is l_1.

Differing levels of MR will give different land demand curves in section III and different levels of production in section II.

House price level P_0 gives output qh_0
House price level P_1 gives output qh_1

Points such as Si and Sii may be joined to give the supply cure of new housing Shn.

Section I (iii)
The supply curve information from section II can be transferred to section I (note the quantity scales are different in sections I and II). Shn is added to Shs to give SH. SH is the supply curve of 'old' and 'new' housing. The quantity of new housing produced is not large enough to have any significant effect on house prices (at Dh_2 house prices are too low to encourage any dwelling production). If a government expects output to be at qh_0 but wishes output to be at qh_1 it can attempt to achieve this goal by a variety of means. For example, demand may be encouraged, non-land factor prices may be subsidized, and land supply and prices might be influenced.

example, where housing market areas have been seen as superior to local authority areas as the most appropriate functional entities. Official guidance suggests rather imprecisely that housing market areas 'are ideally areas in which a self contained housing market operates. A pragmatic test is that a substantial majority of people moving house and settling in an area will have sought a house only in that area' (Scottish Office, 1996 p. 9).

The deficiencies of this definition are addressed by Jones (2002) who identifies a set of housing market areas in west-central Scotland by applying criteria which define migration self-containment. Using this approach a housing market area is defined as 'a continuous area comprizing a settlement or group of settlements with a high degree of housing market self-containment, and where in-migration . . . is of only minor significance' (ibid., p. 557).

The underlying economic principle in this approach to housing market areas is that buyers consider transactions at any point within the area to be appropriate substitutes for each other. This tends to lead to market prices for similar houses within the area being similar. If houses are reasonable substitutes for one another, one would also expect increases in prices at any point within a market area to lead to increases in prices of other houses within the area. Within a market area buyers are in direct competition with one another, as are sellers.

The degree of competition and the degree of substitutability between houses could be measured simply by observing the relationships between the levels of house prices and the rates of change in house prices within a location. It should be possible using price data to establish degrees of substitutability between dwellings and thus define housing market areas simply in terms of high degrees of substitutability.

The degree of substitutability between houses in London and houses in Chicago is almost certainly zero. Prospective buyers do not consider houses in either location as substitutes for each other nor do prospective sellers in either location consider themselves to be in competition with each other. The degree of substitutability between houses in the London borough of Barnet and the adjacent London borough of Brent will, in contrast, be very high. Buyers and sellers in the two boroughs will be in competition with each other and this will be reflected in house price movements in both boroughs. There will be a degree of substitutability between houses in Barnet and those 20 miles away, outside of London, in Stevenage. Some prospective buyers will be willing to consider living further from the centre of London in Stevenage as an alternative to living nearer the centre of

London in Barnet. There will also be some, lower, degree of substitutability between houses in Barnet and houses 55 miles away in Cambridge; there will be some connection between house prices in the two locations. If house prices were to increase significantly more in Barnet than in Cambridge, some demand would switch from Barnet to Cambridge. Thus the degree of substitutability considered will determine where we draw the housing market area boundary. With only a very high degree of substitutability considered, Barnet and Brent are part of the same market area; with lower and lower degrees considered, Stevenage and even Cambridge might be defined as being within the same market area.

Price, value and cost

The price, value and cost of a dwelling or a plot of land are very different things even though the terms are often used interchangeably. The market price of a house may be viewed as the sum of money for which the dwelling is exchanged between the buyer and seller. In a more complex formulation one could think of the price of occupying the house or consuming the services of the house over a given time period. Thus there may be, for example, a monthly price. For the owner-occupier this might include the costs of paying loans, property taxes, maintenance and depreciation. For the tenant this is rental payments and service charges.

Whilst price is a measure of what is paid for housing or land, value is a measure of what the property is worth. This might be the worth to the owner or to the tenant or in a wider sense to society or some segment of society, and it can be difficult to assess such value in precise monetary terms. If an individual buying a house is willing to pay, for example, £50,000 more than they actually have to pay, their personal valuation can be said to be £50,000 more than the price. The exchange price might nevertheless be termed by a property professional the 'market price' or 'market value' if it is assumed this is the sort of sum for which the property might reasonably be expected to change hands. The extra £50,000 of worth over and above the price paid might be termed 'consumer surplus'.

A farmer selling a plot of land might be willing to accept £500,000 and this can be equated with the personal valuation of the land or what it is currently worth the farmer accepting. If a housing developer buys the land from the farmer for £1m, the farmer receives a surplus, which may be called 'economic rent' (for an elaboration of this argument and further discussion of economic rent see Chapter

7). The value of land to housing developers will depend on the revenue expected from house sales and the costs of development. If development costs are very high relative to expected revenue because there are, for example, exceptionally high costs of treating polluted land before housebuilding can begin, or house prices in the locality are very low because of low demand, land can have a negative development value. The 'asking price' that the current land owner is trying to obtain for the land may be greater in this case than the developer's estimate of the value of the land.

The price at which a plot of land can currently be sold in the marketplace may be different from the value or worth of land to society. A rural hillside or an urban park can have an amenity value which is not reflected in any price because the respective parcels of land are either not available to be traded in a market or because any market trading is incapable of determining prices which reflect society's valuation (these arguments are elaborated in relation to environmental issues in Chapter 5).

Cost has a variety of meanings in relation to housing and land. The acquisition costs of a house will include the sum of money paid to the vendor and the transaction costs including surveyor's and conveyor's fees, and any taxes on the transaction such as stamp duty in the UK. It is possible to envisage a real user cost of housing services. Muellbauer and Murphy (1997a) show that this is a function of the real price of houses, the tax-adjusted interest rate, the depreciation rate or rate of maintenance costs including property 'taxation', and the expected rate of appreciation of house prices.

The production cost of a house is the sum of money required to construct the dwelling, and includes the costs of labour, materials and finance. It might also be defined to include 'normal profit', which is the minimum reward the housebuilder requires in order to build houses and which may be thought of as a necessary cost of production. If the housebuilder is to make an 'excess profit', or a 'super-normal' profit, the selling price for the dwelling must be greater than the broadly defined production costs.

Opportunity cost is a measure of the cost of consumption or production measured in terms of alternative options that are forgone. Thus the opportunity cost of living in a two-bedroom rather than a one-bedroom flat for one year might be measured by the value of the holiday that has been forfeited to afford the larger dwelling. The opportunity cost of developing housing on a piece of farmland may be measured in relation to the value of the agricultural produce that can no longer be produced.

Location theories

Housing and land markets, and real property markets more generally, are characterized by the fixed location of the items whose property rights are exchanged in the marketplace. The location of the dwelling or plot of land is a key determinant of its demand and market price. It is not the absolute location, in the sense of the latitude and longitude of the item, but rather the relative location, in the sense of the proximity to other activities that is important. Modelling the impact of relative location on property prices and demand has been the concern of location theorists who have attempted to add a spatial dimension to the analysis of markets. Theories of residential location, as set out for example by Alonso (1964) and Evans (1973, 1985), examine the effect of distance (from places that households wish to reach) on residential land values and house prices.

The simplest theories assume that urban households wish to travel to work to firms that are located in the centre of towns. Different households will have different preferences for location relative to the centre, trading off proximity to work, measured in more complex models by the cost as well as the time and distance travelled, against the amount of space they wish to consume. Competition between households will then determine relative residential prices. Some households will keep transport costs low by living near the centre of town, and others will have higher transport costs but lower prices or rents per square metre on the edge of town. In a circular urban area the relatively small supply of land near the centre compared to the periphery will, with competitive bidding, lead to higher prices near the centre and lower prices per square metre further out. Basic location theory, based on an assumption of a central point of attraction in a radial urban area, predicts that a rent gradient will develop with the highest rents per square metre in the centre of town and the lowest on the edge of town. High prices and high rents per square metre near the centre of town will in turn encourage development and the density of living will thus be high relative to the low-density development on the edge of town (see Figure 2.8).

Higher incomes and more competition for property within an urban area will be expected to increase property values generally throughout the area. Improvements in transport which make it cheaper and easier to get to the centre of town from the edge of town and beyond may be expected to raise peripheral property values and extend the boundary of the built-up area. Conversely, increases in transport costs and difficulties in getting to the centre are expected

Figure 2.8   *Location theory: bid rent curves and a rent gradient*

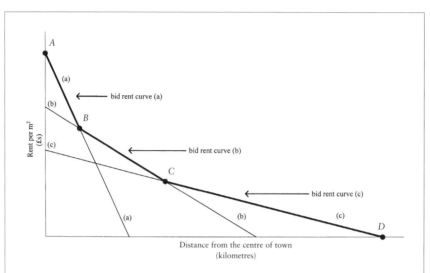

Bid rent curves show a willingness to pay rent at varying distances from the centre of town. Three bid rent curves of three sorts of households, a, b, and c are shown. Households with bid rent curve (a) wish to keep transport costs low and offer high rents per m^2 in the centre of town. Those with bid rent curve (b) offer lower rents than households with bid rent curve (a) near the centre of town, but bid more for property away from the centre. Those with bid rent curve (c) offer low rents near the centre of town but are willing to pay higher rents than other households near the periphery of the town.

With competitive bidding the actual rents paid give a rent gradient of *A B C D*. Households may pay higher rents per m^2 at the centre of town than those near the periphery but consume less space than those near the periphery, resulting in higher density living near the centre and lower density living near the periphery.

The bid rent curves shown above are for households. Firms will also have bid rent curves and compete for urban space. On the diagram 'distance from the centre of town' might be replaced by 'time to travel to the centre of town' or 'cost of travel to the centre of town' for both households and firms in more complex analyses.

to raise central property prices and further increase the pressure for high-density inner urban development (see Figure 2.9).

Elementary location theory is complicated by the inclusion of additional considerations including (1) households' locational preferences being influenced by factors other than work (for example shops, schools and recreational facilities), (2) work and other points of attraction being in non-central locations and there being several dispersed points of attraction, (3) households competing for locations with other market-orientated users such as industrial and commercial firms, and (4) market-orientated

Figure 2.9 *Location theory: changes in incomes and transport costs*

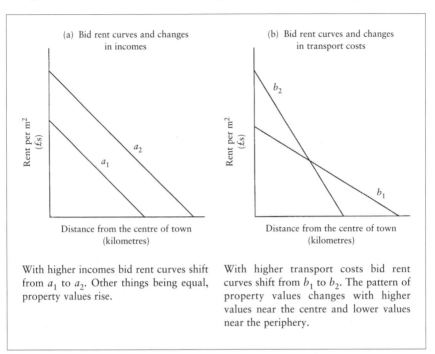

(a) Bid rent curves and changes in incomes

(b) Bid rent curves and changes in transport costs

With higher incomes bid rent curves shift from a_1 to a_2. Other things being equal, property values rise.

With higher transport costs bid rent curves shift from b_1 to b_2. The pattern of property values changes with higher values near the centre and lower values near the periphery.

residential, industrial and commercial land users competing with public sector land uses such as town halls, parks, schools and hospitals.

In a competitive framework, location theorists predict that land use will be determined by the highest monetary bid for a given location. Despite the inevitable simplifying assumptions of location theorists, they do provide useful predictions of what land-use patterns might be in a totally market-orientated setting free from any planning. The resulting configurations of land use are based on the decisions of households and firms expressing preferences based on a desire to find optimal locations that, subject to prevailing constraints, maximize utilities and profits. These decisions do not take account of the wider external costs and benefits of alternative locations and the resulting land-use patterns. As the arguments developed in Chapter 4 demonstrate, a major objective of rational land-use planning is to take account of these external costs and benefits. If planning is successful in achieving its objectives, the actual pattern of land use will differ from that predicted by simple market-orientated location theories.

Institutional perspectives

Basic mainstream economics assumes that market transactions occur between consumers and firms who wish to achieve fairly straight-forward objectives like maximizing satisfaction, utility, profits or market share. Individual decisions backed by such motivations and based on individual preferences are important. It is implicitly assumed that there are transactions in private property rights that give entitlements to use, exclusion and transferability. The contracts between buyers and sellers are, furthermore, implicitly simple, based on easily available and complete information and there are zero or insignificant transaction costs. It can, of course, be easily argued that the 'real world' does not accord with these assumptions, but it is not the intention of any worthwhile theory to provide a description of 'reality'. Theories abstract and simplify; they provide explanations (not descriptions) of how things are and predictions about how things might be in the future. Good explanations and good predictions can arise from theories whose assumptions are a long way from 'reality'. The complexity of the real world is such that any theory will need to abstract and simplify in useful ways.

Institutional approaches to property analysis have challenged the simplifying assumptions of basic mainstream economics and attempted to model housing and land transactions and, more generally, the processes by which residential development occurs, by taking account of the impact of 'institutions'. There are, however, several contrasting approaches to the analysis of institutions. There are institutional approaches within economics, but other disciplines including sociology, public policy and law have contributed to an array of ideas that shelter under the umbrella of 'institutional perspectives'.

In a review of institutions in British property research, Ball (1998) states that

> what constitutes an institution varies from theory to theory. Many studies take the meaning as obvious – the firms, public bodies and other agencies associated with property development constitute 'Institutions'. Another tack is a more formal one of highlighting property rights as the guiding framework for institutional defini-tion. Much of the institutionalist literature formally distinguishes between organizations (the players) and institutions (the rules). (1998, p. 1502)

And Keogh and D'Arcy (1999) state that:

In the most general sense, institutions are the rules, norms and regulations by which a society functions. They impart certainty and stability to social interaction, but they also change and develop over time as circumstances and experience dictate. Since institutions are created by human society, they are a reflection of the power and interests within that society. (1999, p. 2407)

Economic analysis has attempted to incorporate institutional dimensions through a variety of approaches including developing theories of transaction-cost minimizing and information (Ball, 1998, pp. 1503–6). The transaction-cost minimizing approach argues that institutions evolve to minimize the transaction costs associated with production and exchange. The characteristics of the activity and state of technology influence the pattern of institutions that emerges. Large integrated firms emerge, for example, where there are benefits from organizing production through a single entity with non-market linkages between the various parts of the enterprise. Smaller firms prevail where lots of small market transactions between producers and consumers are beneficial. Thus the complexity of organizing the linkages between land buying, housing construction and marketing together with some limited opportunities for economies of scale might explain the preponderance of large firms in the speculative housebuilding industry. In contrast, the less complex arrangements for repair and maintenance with few economies of scale might explain the large number of small firms engaging in this activity. Ball (1998) argues that since transaction costs are difficult to measure, transaction-cost minimizing explanations of institutional arrangements are difficult to verify and alternative theoretical explanations often seem equally plausible.

Rather than assuming information to be easily available and complete, information theory explores the implications of information deficiencies. Imperfect information about the future and an associated variety of attitudes to the risks of future changes in costs, demands and technology can be seen as an explanation for the existence of different sorts of property organizations. Speculative developers aim to make profits out of taking risks on future outcomes; property leases can reduce the uncertainty about future rents and security of tenure by having appropriate clauses to satisfy both landlord and tenant. Alternatively they can be seen as exploiting the power of one party or another in the face of uncertainty. The desire for improved information about the quality of properties and the legality of interests in property can be viewed as explanations for the widespread involvement of surveyors and lawyers in the property transaction process.

Jaffe (1996) has argued for an institutional perspective which focuses on the role of transaction costs and property rights in understanding the operation of housing markets: 'In terms of both public decision-making and private contracting, housing is deemed to be a special type of good traded in unusual markets, often resulting in relatively high transaction costs. This presumption has enormous implications for both public policy and for evaluating private behaviour'. (ibid., p. 427). Jaffe explores the connections between transaction costs and property-rights arrangements in housing markets. This is linked to an evaluation of contractual instruments used in housing markets, and it is claimed that 'not only can this process help to understand participant motivations and the relative values placed upon resources, this type of analysis can also serve to provide insights into why certain policies are likely to succeed or fail, and why some instruments are used in actual practice and others are not', (ibid., p. 432).

An institutional perspective that may be termed 'behavioural institutionalism' is characterized by an approach that seeks to 'identify particular types of agency – landowner, developer or financier – and suggest that they have behavioural characteristics, usually preferences, that are distinct from those implied by national profit-maximizing calculation' (Ball, 1998, p. 1509). Different types of landowners including the church, crown, manufacturing firms, financial institutions and local authorities have, in particular, received attention from this approach. Difficulties with behavioural institutionalism include generalizing from often small samples of landowners or financiers, erroneously assuming that observed behavioural differences are permanent, and incorrectly assuming that group behaviour rather than structural context is the cause of a given outcome (ibid., p. 1510).

'Structure–Agency Institutionalism' applied to property development has been particularly associated with the work of Healey (1992 and 1998), but Ball (1998) argues that the key concepts in this approach are poorly defined:

No precise definition is given of what constitutes a 'structure', an 'agency' or an 'institution'. Structure seems to be aspects of the broad context in which agents operate. Agents seem to be key people working in institutions, in which case institutions become wrongly personified as people, although it may be the case that institutions refer to broader social rules and regulations. The reason for all the confusion may be that the approach is concerned with practical research questions rather than theoretical niceties, and it argues that structures and agencies are important on pragmatic grounds. (1998, p. 1512)

Ball has developed an approach in which there is no dichotomy between agency and structure, and where the key concept is a 'structure of provision' (SoP). This SoP is, in relation to building,

> the contemporary network of relationships associated with the provision of particular types of building at specific points in time . . . Provision encompasses the whole gamut of development, construction, ownership and use. . . . The network of organizations (e.g. specific firms) and markets involved in a particular form of building provision is the 'structure' of that provision . . . Organizations and markets are both part of structures of provision, because of the two-way influence of each on the other . . . SoP is a conceptual device for incorporating institutions into analyses of the development process. It does not constitute a complete theory in itself rather it is a methodological theory – a series of statements about how to examine institutions and their rules rather than an explanation in itself. Other theories are needed to understand particular research questions formulated within its framework. (Ball, 1998, pp. 1513–14)

More generally, it is useful to see institutional perspectives as not providing complete theories in themselves. In contrast to the simplifications of basic mainstream economics, institutional perspectives alert us to the complications of the 'real world'. They do not provide explanations and predictions that are necessarily opposed to those provided by the concept of markets, and it is indeed very useful to view markets as a form of institution. Markets are social constructs which work within socially determined patterns and details of property rights. Institutional analysis can complement, rather than compete with, market analysis by aiding an understanding of the detailed operation and outcomes of complex markets in housing and land.

Efficiency and inefficiency

The concept of efficiency is central to economic analysis. As the discussion in Chapter 3 shows, according to Pareto (Winch, 1971, pp. 27–71) an efficient allocation of resources is one from which it is not possible to make a change that makes someone better off without making someone else worse off. So with Pareto efficiency, all factors of production are used in such a way that it is impossible to get extra output of one item without losing output of another, and all goods and services are allocated so that all reallocations that benefit some without disadvantaging others have been made.

A standard theorem of neoclassical welfare economics is that under clearly specified conditions, markets operating with perfect competition will promote Pareto efficiency (Cullis and Jones, 1998). For perfect competition to exist, a number of conditions must exist including: the existence of many buyers and sellers; freedom of entry to the market; homogeneous products; and full information. Evans (1995) argues that such conditions inevitably do not hold in property markets, and that these markets, including housing markets, are thus imperfect and consequently inefficient markets. In markets that are efficient it is difficult to make excess profits because the market efficiently discounts available information. However, Evans argues that

> The 'inefficiency' of the property market means . . . that with good information, which for the appropriate fee the property market professional will gladly provide, excess profits can more easily be made . . . It is no accident that so many millionaires made their money in the property market – it is a result of its inefficiency. (1995, p. 28)

In efficient markets, prices will reflect preferences and the values that participants in the market put on alternative resource-allocation options. Changes in prices perform a crucial role in shifting resources between alternative options in order to improve efficiency. When prices do not reflect the values that society places on resource allocations, welfare economics suggests that markets fail to promote Pareto efficiency. Thus, in the interests of society there is an *a priori* case for some form of government activity; this argument is developed in Chapters 3 and 4.

Keogh and D'Arcy (1999) consider efficiency from an alternative institutional economics perspective and argue that

> the institutional dimension alters the concept of efficiency and leads to a partial and contingent judgement on achieved efficiency. Instead of seeking a judgement on whether the 'property market' as an entity is efficient, the institutional approach allows the possibility that the property market process may be efficient for some market participants but not for others'. (Ibid, p. 2401)

Applying this approach, it is concluded that 'Institutional analysis suggests that there is little merit in trying to evaluate the collective social efficiency of a market structure when the market in question emerges out of dominant economic and social interests' (ibid., p. 2412).

The arguments developed in Chapters 3 and 4 are, in contrast, founded on the belief that it is worth taking a social view of efficiency, in that the resource-allocation arrangements that prevail will ideally promote outcomes that maximize social well-being. If markets in housing and land do not work in ways that promote social efficiency, then there are grounds for changing the structure, operation or outcomes of markets so that the result is more efficient. One role for planning is to promote a more efficient use of resources than that which currently prevails. Planning can do this in a variety of ways including promoting new institutional arrangements, new patterns of property rights and using fiscal instruments to promote a different set of prices. All these options are considered in subsequent chapters.

Conclusions

In this chapter the application of elementary demand and supply analysis to markets in housing and land has been demonstrated, and the housing demand of individuals has been shown to depend on a variety of factors including price and income. Aggregate demand is furthermore a consequence of demographic factors. The contrast between demand which depends on ability to pay, and need which depends on the norms and standards of society has been set out. The value of the concept of elasticity in examining the responsiveness of demand and supply to changes in prices, incomes and the price and availability of substitutes has been demonstrated.

It has been argued that in a market context it is useful to view the demand for land as a derived demand, dependent in the case of residential land on the demand for houses. The value of residential development land can be viewed as residually determined and an outcome of derived demands and the relative market strengths of developers and landowners. A very important distinction has been made between the stock of land and the supply of land. The stock of land within any geographically defined area is fixed; the supply of land is not fixed. Supply, in the sense of land available to the market, varies with price and the associated demands for different land uses. There is thus some price elasticity of supply of residential building land.

It has been shown that it is useful to view housing and land markets as means for trading property rights, which are a function of social, political and legal processes. The distinction has been made between explicit markets and implicit markets. In the former, prices for bundles of housing or land-specific property rights can be observed. In the latter, prices for items that are implicitly traded have to be imputed using techniques such as hedonic pricing. The benefit of viewing housing market areas in terms of the degree of substitutability of dwellings within the area has also been expounded, and the distinctions between price, cost and value have been set out.

Elementary residential location theory, whilst built on oversimplifying assumptions about household decisions, does provide some insights into land-use and land-value patterns in a market framework. With appropriate considerations of its restrictive assumptions, location theory can provide insights into the impact of planning on housing and land markets. It has been argued that institutional perspectives should be seen as complementing rather than competing with mainstream market analysis, providing useful insights into the real-world complexities of housing and land transactions.

The concept of efficiency has been introduced, which, together with the concept of equity or 'fairness', will be elaborated in subsequent chapters where the role of planning in promoting both efficiency and equity by moderating market outcomes will be examined.

Chapter 3

The Relevance of Welfare Economics

This chapter examines the theoretical basis of the links between land-use planning and housing development on the one hand, and welfare economics on the other. It starts from the proposition that without a planning system, land-use and housing development decisions would be determined by the operation of market forces. For market forces to operate, a framework of control and law is required and this framework is typically provided through the state and governments. Thus, even without a land-use planning system, the state will influence land and housing markets. It will protect and underwrite property rights that are fundamental to the functioning of markets. However, the existence of a planning system gives the state the opportunity to modify the operation of markets in the interests of society. It is a concern with the interests of society, as opposed to the narrower interests of the individuals which comprise society, that links planning with welfare economics.

This link is explored in this chapter in the context of arguments about the propensity of markets to produce efficient and equitable outcomes. The inability of markets to consistently achieve efficient and equitable land uses and efficient and equitable levels and patterns of housing development provides a strong case for planning. Welfare economics provides a framework for understanding this failure of markets, and provide a rationale for a planning system with social objectives. This rationale is examined in this chapter.

Planning and welfare

It has been suggested that 'Land use planning is a process concerned with the determination of land uses' (Cullingworth and Nadin, 2002, p. 2). However, markets in land are also concerned with the determination of land uses, and in the absence of planning, land use would in many societies still be determined by markets. They would

47

determine land use on the basis of decisions made by landowners and developers, and those decisions might be driven by a variety of motives including most probably the overriding motive of a desire to profit from the land use and to make as much profit as possible. Maximizing profit means examining the differences between actual or expected revenue from a given land use and the cost of that land use. It is likely that, in a market situation, there will be competition for land from different sorts of potential land users. Farmers wanting to grow crops on a field will be in competition with developers wanting to build houses on the field. One housing developer will be in competition with another housing developer. In the absence of planning, the land use will be determined by which potential land use offers the best return and which developer offers the most to the existing land user. The interests of individual landowners and individual developers will determine land uses. Houses will be built on the land if a housing developer offers high enough payments to develop the land, and if developer A offers more than developer B it is likely that A will do the developing rather than B. Private interests will thus determine land use in the absence of planning.

However, 'The broad objective of the UK system is to "regulate the development of land in the public interest" ' (ibid., p. 2). A concern with the public interest suggests a concern with the well-being of the public or of society, and it is this concern with society that makes welfare economics relevant to an examination of the purpose and methods of planning.

Economics is about choice. It is also about well-being and satisfaction. At its broadest level, welfare economics is about the use of resources to maximize the well-being of society. A succinct definition states that 'Welfare economics is the study of the well-being of the members of a society as a group, in so far as it is affected by the decisions and actions of its members and agencies concerning economic variables' (Winch, 1971, p. 13). The economic variables include: the factors of production, the goods and services produced from these factors, and the distribution of these goods and services along with the associated benefits. Welfare economics recognizes the significance of the objectives of society as a whole rather than the private objectives of its members. It also recognizes that private and public interests can conflict and that some actions make some people better off and others worse off (Begg *et al.*, 2003, pp. 211–28). Whether, on balance, such actions are desirable can only be answered by referring to the interest of society rather than the interests of individuals. Welfare economics acknowledges a social well-being which is different from the sum of the well-being of those who compose the society.

Planning is based on the proposition that land use can usefully be determined within a policy framework. A policy may be seen as a deliberate course of action designed to improve the welfare of society. For such action there must be objectives. Welfare economists have traditionally sought to make important divisions between what welfare economics can and cannot say about policy objectives. It has been argued that 'It is not possible for economic analysis to determine what the objectives of society ought to be, nor whether a particular social state is better than another. Such questions are the subject matter of moral and political philosophy' (Winch, 1971, pp. 13–14). Welfare economics attempts, according to this perspective, only to advise on the appropriateness of actions to achieve these objectives, not the appropriateness of the objectives themselves. The implied separation between policy objectives and policy instruments can, however, be highly misleading. Suppose that the welfare economist is told that an objective of society is to limit the increases in rents that tenants pay. The recommended course of action might be to control or fix rents. Rent control, as a policy instrument, might however be predicted to lead to unwanted consequences such as shortages of accommodation. By questioning the given objective and asking why rents should be limited, the welfare economist may discover that rent limitations are preconceived to be the means to some other end such as 'preventing exploitation' or 'making housing more affordable'. The economist has a role in questioning the objectives as well as prescribing possible instruments, and the questioning should lead to a clarification of the objectives as well as a better specification of the instruments. The clarification of objectives and a statement on what the *aims* of policy are is essential to any useful policy debate. If policy aims are agreed, the debate is about the most appropriate methods or instruments for achieving these aims. A political-economy approach to planning and housing policy is concerned with debate about both what the aims of planning and housing policy are, and what the most appropriate instruments are to achieve those aims. This approach is exemplified in the analysis that follows.

Barr (1998) makes much of the distinction between aims and methods, suggesting that 'There is general agreement that the major aims of policy in Western societies include *efficiency* in the use of resources; their distribution in accordance with *equity* or justice, and the preservation of *individual freedom*' (1998, p. 4; emphasis in original). These aims, it is acknowledged, can be defined in different ways and accorded different weights. The answer to the question, 'What are the *aims* of policy?' is argued to be 'explicitly normative and largely ideological' and is in marked contrast to the question, 'By what *methods* are those aims best achieved?' which 'should be treated not as ideological but as technical – that is it raises a *positive* issue' (ibid., p. 4). The very example that Barr gives to illustrate his point does however expose the difficulties and the limitations of the aims/methods and normative/positive distinctions. He suggests that: 'How much redistribution of income, wealth, power, and so on should there be?' is 'clearly ideological and normative; it is an aims question and so properly the subject of political debate'. But 'How should the economy best be run (for example the market system, central planning, or a mixed economy)?' is largely a question of method and a positive issue 'more properly the subject of technical than political discussion' (ibid., p. 4). However, it will be worth exploring whether redistribution is not an aim in itself but the supposed means to some other end. If, for example, redistribution is predicted to improve housing conditions, an improvement in housing conditions might be the true aim and the connection between redistribution and housing conditions is properly the subject of positive and empirical investigation and not a normative issue to be discussed only in terms of ideology. Likewise, the choice of central planning or a mixed economy will be correctly influenced by ideological stances about degrees of individual decision-making which are seen to be compatible with aims of individual freedom, equity and justice as well as positive issues about the efficiency of alternative regimes.

It will thus be necessary not just to separate aims from instruments but to clarify exactly what the aims are, why they are policy aims, and to examine the normative and the positive issues involved in the choice of policy instruments. We will return to these issues and examine the problems involved in closely specifying the aims and instruments of planning and housing policy in subsequent chapters, but it is instructive first to examine the prescriptions of welfare economics in relation to the all-embracing aim of maximizing the welfare of society.

Maximizing social welfare

The maximization of social welfare is conventionally analysed using the framework established by the Italian social scientist Vilfredo Pareto (see, for example, Winch, 1971, pp. 27–71; Begg *et al.*, 2003, pp. 213–17). The analysis is founded on explicit value judgements which state that, firstly, the individual is the best judge of his or her well-being or utility; secondly, society can be examined as the sum of the individuals who comprise society; and thirdly, the welfare of society is increased if the utility of one individual can be increased without reducing that of another. When no such increases are possible there is a 'Pareto optimum'.

When, with given tastes, technology and resources, an economy is organized so that it is not possible to make anyone better off without making someone else worse off there is an efficient allocation of resources. The notion of such an efficient economy or a 'Pareto efficient' economy has had much appeal. Efficiency in the sense used by Pareto requires that resources are used so as to ensure efficiency in production, and goods and services are distributed so that there is efficiency in the allocation of goods and services (see Figures 3.1 and 3.2). The relevance of Pareto efficiency is dominated by the link to a competitive economy. A central theorem in welfare economics is

Figure 3.1 *Efficiency in the production of housing*

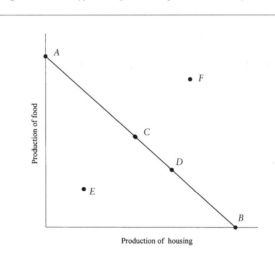

The maximum quantities of housing and food that can be produced within an economy are defined by *A B*: this is the efficiency frontier. If we are concerned only with the production of housing and food we see that with all productive resources devoted to food, amount *A* of food can be produced. With all resources devoted to housing, amount *B* of housing can be produced. Efficient outputs of housing and food occur at points such as *C* and *D*. These points and all points on *A B* involve Pareto efficiency in production: it is impossible to produce more housing or more food without a loss of production of the other good. At points such as *E* there is inefficiency because a movement to say *C* or *D* involves an increase in production of both goods. Productive capacity is not fully utilized at *E*. The economy has insufficient productive resources for an output such as *F* to be possible.

Figure 3.2   *Allocation of housing*

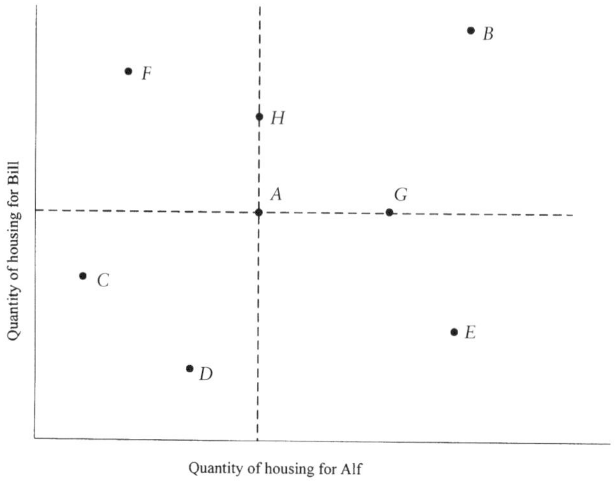

At point *A*, Alf and Bill have equal quantities of housing. A move from *A* to *B* makes both Alf and Bill better off in as much as they each have more housing. *C* and *D* are clearly worse positions than *A* in that both Alf and Bill have less housing than at *A*. Movement from *A* to *E* or *A* to *F* gives one person more housing and the other less housing. A conclusion on whether *E* and *F* are better or worse than *A* in a two-person 'society' comprising Alf and Bill requires a value judgement about the relative importance of housing to each person. It is not possible to make such a judgement on grounds of Pareto efficiency. Such judgements might, however, be made on grounds of equity. Movements from *C* and *D* to *A* are 'Pareto' improvements as are movements from *A* to *B* and *A* to *G* and *A* to *H* (at least one person is better off without anyone being worse off).

that, subject to a number of qualifications, universal perfect competition will result in a Pareto optimum (Cullis and Jones, 1998, pp. 1–8). The extent to which this theorem is accepted is of much significance to the type of economic system, and the associated political system, which is supported within a society. It does, in turn, provide the paradigm within which the aims and instruments of housing policy might be formulated.

A perfectly competitive economy is one in which there are markets that are not dominated by the power of specific buyers or sellers; there is perfect information and there is freedom to enter and exit markets. If the conditions necessary for perfect competition hold and there is a competitive and enterprise-driven economy, the argument suggests there is no need for governments to become involved in the provision of specific goods and services. Production and consumption decisions can be left to individual firms and individual consumers acting in a competitive and self-interested fashion. There is indeed an accordance between the optimality of Pareto and the 'invisible hand' that Adam Smith suggested would ensure an optimal allocation of resources (Barr, 1998). Each individual will by pursuing self-interest promote economic efficiency and the well-being of society if the Pareto and Smith propositions are accepted. The idea that 'market success' results in economic efficiency is a powerful and persuasive notion in promoting the concept and the practice of free-market economies with lots of atomistic choices and minimal collective decision-making. Challenging the notion of market success by the development of the concept of 'market failure' is thus central to the case against unfettered individual decision-making and the case for some collective decision-making and for some planning.

Efficiency

The concept of economic efficiency is not a narrow technical matter; it is rather a broad concept that relates to the desirability of arrangements that make the best use of limited resources. The Pareto concept of economic efficiency is about the production of goods and services and the consumption of goods and services. Efficiency is maximized where production and consumption activities are such that no one can be made better off without making someone else worse off, and in determining well-being the individual is assumed to be the best judge of his or her own welfare. An analysis based on the principles of Pareto does not challenge the initial distribution of resources, and in this sense it is an essentially conservative approach. However, there are explicit value judgements involved, and there is a normative underpinning to Pareto efficiency. In using the concept, economists are not trying to be value free; such a position for an activity that seeks to prescribe action to improve welfare would, of course, be untenable. Gains that make some people better off and make no one else worse off are efficiency gains, and it is such efficiency gains that can be argued to be compatible with several theories of society.

To argue for an efficient allocation of resources is, for example, to argue that the maximum output of housing and other goods and services should be produced from given resources. If more housing can be produced without reducing the outputs of other commodities then this should be done. The combination of housing production and other production should also take account of consumer preferences; it is not efficient to produce more housing if consumers do not value the housing, and this valuation will be a function of preferences. It is a combination of resource constraints and preferences that determine an efficient level of production. There is nothing mechanistic in this concept of efficiency, nor is there anything that is contrary to a concern with what people desire. The principal reason for Pareto optimality gathering normative significance is that it is based on value judgements that endorse consumer sovereignty. The coincidence of Pareto efficiency and perfectly competitive markets would not be of importance if individual preferences were not to be of paramount significance. Market processes tend to be supported on the grounds that they promote efficient allocations of resources that are responsive to consumer preferences. The arguments for state activity to counteract market failure are not arguments for ignoring individual choice or rejecting the preferences of individuals, they are, rather, arguments which rest on propositions that in given circumstances market processes are not able to produce outcomes which do fully respect individual preferences.

This does, of course, beg many questions about how preferences are to be known in the absence of market transactions, and how resources and commodities are to be valued in the absence of appropriate market prices. Because these are difficult questions to answer, it does not mean that one has to pretend that the market failure does not exist and revert to a reliance on markets despite their inadequacies. Thankfully, there are many able economists who have sought to address these questions and provide answers. For a summary of the key contributions see Cullis and Jones (1998), particularly chapter 4 entitled 'Collective decision-making: searching for the public interest' (pp. 71–91). The answers are, unsurprisingly, varied and often controversial, their acceptability varying with ideological positions as well as what is viewed as practical. For these reasons, the vast literature on valuations in the absence of suitable prices, the derivation of social choice from individual preferences and the reconciliation of conflicting preferences will continue to grow as long as there is a desire to address, rather than assume away, market failure and that effort is destined to promote efficiency.

Efficiency is not a simple value-free concept, nor does the application of the concept lead to a plan for achieving a unique position. Differences between alternative efficient combinations of resources will have to be judged by equity rather than by efficiency criteria. To argue for an efficient allocation of resources is to argue for avoiding producing items that are not wanted and for producing items that are wanted using methods that avoid waste. It is to argue for using productive resources rather than have them lying idle. An efficient housing system would produce dwellings that people wanted and it would not contribute to the production of items that were not desired, such as ill-health. If changes to the housing system do not produce more housing which people want, and less of what they do not want, the change is not an efficient change. Whilst acknowledging the many difficulties in determining whether a given change is efficient, those changes which depend only on individual, as opposed to collective, action are unlikely to bring about all the possible efficiency gains in any society.

Equity

Whilst economists sometimes try to keep the normative essence of efficiency subliminal, they are usually completely open about the normative nature of equity and economists firmly ensconced in the positivist school use this as a justification for drawing the boundary of their enquiry at this point. They believe that it is up to other disciplines to decide on the criteria for an equitable distribution of resources.

Equity, in the sense that is used here, is about fairness and justice. What is fair and just is a matter of opinion. This normative nature of equity is sufficient for positivist orientated economists to set it aside. However, even if one wishes to reserve one's opinion on the rights and wrongs of any change that is proposed on grounds of equity, the consequences of a change instituted in the name of equity will have resource implications. The broad view taken here is that both the rationale for planning and development changes, and the consequences of those changes are legitimate areas of enquiry for welfare economics.

Many land-use changes and housing developments redistribute income and wealth; some people are made better off and others are made worse off. There are some winners and some losers. Judgements about the desirability of such changes thus, in part, involve judgements about fairness and equity. A new housing development on the edge of a village may block the view over countryside enjoyed by existing residents, enhance the value of the land that is to be developed, bring profits to the developer, and house people currently in need of better accommodation. How are the benefits to landowner, developer and future residents to be weighed against the losses to current residents? This is a judgement to be made on grounds of equity. If the development goes ahead, some people will be better off and others will be worse off. In this situation, will society be better off or worse off if the housing development goes ahead?

If the decision is left to the marketplace alone, without any planning considerations, the development will go ahead if the developer can buy the land from the landowner and the developer judges that a profit on the development is likely. The distributional consequences connected with the losses to existing residents do not influence the decision. However, the operation of a planning system allows, in principle, the distributional consequences to be taken into account.

As has been stated, Pareto was concerned mainly with efficiency. The equity problem was a difficulty because it involved comparing levels of satisfaction or utility between people, yet such interpersonal comparisons of utility were deemed futile because satisfaction was an introspective concept. It lay within people and could not be measured in a cardinal fashion. Without units of measurement attached to utility, how do we know if loss in satisfaction experienced by one group of people is greater than the gain in satisfaction experienced by another? In our example, how do we know whether the losses experienced by existing residents, if the development proceeds, are greater or less than the gains to the landowner, developer and new residents?

Subsequent to Pareto's analysis, welfare economists have struggled with the equity problem from several perspectives. Some economists have devised compensation tests that pose questions about the ability of those who are made better off to compensate those made worse off and therefore make everyone better off after the change plus compensation. Others have devised indicators of well-being to make the problem of the introspective and non-cardinal nature of utility measurement less of an issue. Many welfare economists have delved more deeply into the philosophical foundations of equity problems, and their insights raise equity issues above simple measurement problems to include moral and ethical dilemmas. In our straightforward example, a judgement might be made that, as a matter of principle, the views of existing residents should have precedence over everything else. In this case, the development would not proceed if they were to suffer any loss.

It is not possible or appropriate here to resolve the thorny measurement and philosophical problems that are posed by a consideration of equity. Rather it should be stated that equity is a concern of modern welfare economics. Improvements in the well-being of society can come about through changes that involve redistributions of resources. Land-use changes and housing developments frequently result in such changes and a planning system can consider such changes in ways that markets cannot. A consideration of equity should thus be a significant component of an analytical approach to planning, just as it has been a significant component of an analytical approach to welfare economics.

Planning, markets and collective decision-making

The existence of a land-use planning system and of policies for the provision of housing implies an element of decision-making through some sort of apparatus of the state. It is frequently the case that the activities of the state are thought to be entirely different or even opposed to the activities of the market, but the division between markets and the state amounts to a false dichotomy. Given that markets work on the basis of property rights that are endorsed by the state, the notion of government interference in markets is misleading.

The idea of the separation of markets and the idea that government is concerned with conditions where choice is suspended are false. The view that governments do certain things and markets do other different things, and that markets are separate from and inherently superior to governments is entirely false and leads to inappropriate pro-market prescriptions. It is as wrong as the views that the state is always superior and that collective ownership of the means of production is always better than private ownership. Each of these views leads to equally false prescriptions.

Property rights in land and housing, as in all commodities, change over time as governments adapt them to changing circumstances and new policy objectives. The relationship of governments to property rights and thus markets is therefore a symbiotic relationship, the nature of which is defined by and helps to define the sort of society that exists. The relationships regarding housing determine the sort of housing system that prevails. The positions which the state adopts with respect to housing may be termed 'minimalist', 'control', 'subsidy', or 'ownership' (Oxley, 1995). These are not necessarily mutually exclusive. The terms do not describe watertight boxes but are rather labels for approximate and interrelated categories.

For planning and housing policies to exist, the decision has to have been made at some point to take collective as opposed to individual action to influence the provision of housing. Collective action, if driven by rationality, will have some aims, and the instruments to pursue those aims will have been selected with respect to the probability of them achieving the given aims. The decision to take collective action might be seen as a decision by society to act or for some sort of agent to take action on behalf of society. Policy implies the possibility of social decision-making and beneficial policy requires that the social decision-making is, in some respects, better than individual decision-making. It will be useful to make the case for social decision-making and to examine the limitations of individual decision-making. It is important to stress, at this stage, that the case for social decision making is different from the case for collective provision. Thus to argue for a housing policy and a planning policy based on some decisions taken by or on behalf of society is not to argue for society, or an agent of society, to be the owner or the supplier of the housing, nor for there to be land nationalization. There is a case that can be made for social housing, but this is not the same as the case for a housing policy with social objectives. Similarly the case for state influence over the use of land is very different from the case for government ownership of land. *Atomistic decision-making* involves lots of uncoordinated decisions being made with a view to enhancing the self-interest of the individual. Without any social controls, such a situation is one of chaos. If chaos prevails there can be no useful predictions about the outcomes in terms of individual or collective well-being. In a situation of chaos, the lack of order produces arbitrary distributions of rewards and access to resources.

It has been unusual for proponents of political economy to argue for total atomistic decision-making, for the resultant chaos is easily predicted and most often disliked. It is more common to argue for a reliance mainly on atomistic decision-making with some social decision-making. Such a situation was seen by Adam Smith (1776) to lead, by the intervention of an 'invisible hand', to one where each individual pursuing individual self-interest would maximize benefits for the society which was composed of those individuals. However, Smith saw the need for society to decide on the provision of some goods and services. If one accepts a presumption in favour of atomistic decision-making because of, say, individuals being the best judge of their own welfare, it is the exceptions to the rule which have to be justified.

In economic analysis, atomistic decision-making has been preferred and defended by economists who favour a free-market approach. Beneficial atomistic decision-making is, in fact, seen to be synonymous with a competitive market economy. There is a standard 'proof' that a 'perfectly competitive' market economy will produce an efficient utilization of resources (Winch, 1971, pp. 77–99), and in this competitive state the allocation of all productive resources and all goods and services is predicted to be 'Pareto optimal'. With this optimality there can be no improvement in the well-being of any individual without reducing the well-being of others.

Markets are social constructs; they are not 'natural phenomena'. They are also not, as is often assumed, the example *par excellence* of the operation of individual action. The decision to buy or sell, in a 'free' market, may certainly be taken by an individual, but that individual takes a decision knowing that the action is endorsed by a wider society. In a market it is not physical items that are traded, but rights. These property rights are protected by an agency acting on behalf of society. Let us, for the moment, adopt the usual convention of calling this agency the state. The state performs essential property-right enforcing, underwriting and protecting roles that allow markets to function. Without the performance of these roles, no one would engage in market exchanges for they would have no certainty of holding onto goods and services acquired through polite exchange processes. Without property-right protection, underwriting and enforcement it would be open to anyone to seek to take property from another by the use of force or other methods of persuasion that might prevail in a situation of chaos. It might be argued that the apparatus of the state may not be necessary if individuals realize through enlightened self-interest that respect for property rights is mutually beneficial, but the operationalization of this realization immediately requires a collective decision and an agent to take and apply this decision.

The question that may be immediately posed is 'can there be markets without the state?' Relatively unsophisticated markets can exist without complicated rules regarding the definition and protection of property rights. But even in unsophisticated markets it is essential that the right of the individual to benefit from the property, that has been gained through a market transaction, be recognized if trade is to occur. Thus, at least some simple form of collective agreement to recognize these rights is necessary. This agreement requires, at a minimum, a simple form of the state. With more complex markets and more complex property rights, more complex documentation, protection and enforcement of property rights may be necessary.

Property rights in housing and land bestow the opportunity to occupy, or to pass housing and land to others, often with the help of complex legal documents. The legal payment by one person to another for the right to occupy a house or a plot of land, which is supported by such documentation, is not simply an agreement between two parties. It is an agreement endorsed by the state and by society and enshrined in a system of law that has been established by collective action. Individuals take advantage of a system of laws that enable markets in housing and land, and markets in most legally obtainable items, to operate. From time to time laws are changed and property rights are moderated, and these changes influence the deals that are struck between individuals in the market. Thus laws which change the security of tenure which a tenant has relative to a landlord will change the rent which each party is willing to accept. If laws also regulate this rent the state has moderated the market considerably. Many changes in laws and regulations have subtle but very significant effects. A wide range of changes in property rights as a result of building regulations or planning requirements alter the value of the rights and influence what will be paid in the market. If a planning change gives a right to build houses in a field that was previously only available for growing potatoes, a major change in the price at which the right to use the field is traded in the market will result.

The current configuration of property rights in housing and land within any country is not necessarily the result of a careful set of decisions by the state, but the state does need to endorse that which is acceptable. The markets that follow from any configuration of property rights are thus implicitly or explicitly legitimized by the state. Hayek (1967, 1978) claimed that markets are the result of spontaneous processes rather than any particular design or plan. However, the result, whether what has gone before is spontaneous or carefully constructed according to deliberate principles, must be endorsed if it is to flourish.

Government, planning and housing

As we have used the term 'state' as an agent of society, we shall use the term 'government' to mean an agent of the state. Without the state – through its governments endorsing, protecting, enforcing and sometimes changing property rights in housing – there would be no markets in housing. Housing markets and land markets, like any markets, are not mystical happenings that are separate from the activities of the state or from governments. They are social constructs that rely on the state. It is therefore wrong to conceive of the state as 'interfering' in markets or of governments 'intervening' in markets. This is, however, the language that is frequently used to describe the activities of the state relative to markets. Even economists who support a strong and active participation by governments in housing and land markets write of the case for 'government intervention' in markets (for example Barr, 1998, Robinson, 1979). It is not a question of intervention.; it is rather one of government activity in relation to markets. Challenging the accepted language is important, for the words that are frequently used describe a separation of markets and the government, as if the market has its territory and government has its other different territory somewhere else. Sometimes the language used suggests that the territory of the market is superior to that of government, or that it is legitimate whilst the territory of government is not. Government is thus seen to 'intervene' in markets or to invade the territory of markets. The dichotomy that this language enforces is completely false. One can no more separate markets and the state than one can separate the heart from the brain and be left with a healthy body. The nature of the relationships between markets and the state, including which decisions take place atomistically through markets and which decisions are made by governments, are important but there should be no presumed superiority of one sort of decision-making over another.

If markets and governments inhabit similar and not separate territory, it is not the interference of governments in markets that should be examined, and neither should we speak of a boundary between collective and individual decision-making. We should, rather, consider how markets function and the relationship between atomistic and collective decision-making. It has been claimed that 'The entire history of political thought is driven by the great dichotomy between organicism (holism) and individualism (atomism)' (Bobbio, quoted in Rothstein, 1998, p. 31); the great mistake here is to view as a dichotomy that which is a symbiotic relationship.

The mistake is compounded by viewing individual decisions as 'free-choice' decisions which inevitably enhance the well-being of the individual and are thus always superior to collective decisions which are viewed as dictatorial or as constraining individual well-being. There is very little practical unconstrained free choice in a complex society. Freedom to do as you will is freedom to drive on the wrong side of the road, to steal and to kill. Constraints are imposed in the interests of others, since individual choices impact on the welfare of other people. The ability to exercise effective choice is also effected by the resources at one's disposal and the information that one has. What decisions to leave to the individual, which constraints to try to modify and which decisions to deny the individual are thus the important questions that must be addressed. Individuals are not in practical terms in a position to make free unconstrained choices about where they live and what sort of housing they occupy. They make constrained choices. These constraints are sometimes set by governments and almost always by the resources at the individual's disposal. More broadly, the constraints might be seen as the consequences of historical processes, acts of nature, or simply the practical circumstances in which individuals find themselves. Judgements may be made on which of these events or circumstances are of the individual's own making, or are factors for which the individual should take credit or be blamed, but ultimately the options are few. Either individual choice is accepted within the existing constraints, the constraints are modified, or collective decisions are made. Each of these options has merit in different sets of circumstances. Sometimes individual decision-making has considerable merit; there are also merits in sometimes moderating the constraints and taking collective decisions. The constraints can be moderated and collective actions can be taken through a planning system.

Conclusions

Welfare economics is about efficiency and equity. If one is concerned with an efficient allocation of resources, market failure is an important aspect of welfare economics that is central to understanding the role of land use planning and housing development control in determining an allocation of resources that is in the interests of society as opposed to only the interests of individuals. Planning and the control of land-use generally may be seen as a reaction to the failure of market forces to maximize social welfare. This failure takes several forms including, in particular, the inability to take account of external costs and benefits that accrue to those who are not party to the market transaction. This is the externality problem.

The externalities case is exemplified by housing developments that put additional pressure on infrastructure such as roads and sewers, so causing external costs. There may also be external benefits from residential development. If new higher quality housing replaces old run-down housing and this changes the nature of a neighbourhood, a range of external benefits may occur. There might be positive effects manifested in, for example, crime reductions, better health standards and an improved environment for existing residents. The concept of market failure and, in particular, the relevance of externalities is explored in depth in Chapter 4.

Markets can fail on efficiency grounds because they fail to provide appropriate means to ensure the supply of certain types of goods that may be termed 'public goods'. New housing developments might mean that more road space and more street lighting are required; these items are in part public goods that are not usually provided through the marketplace. Their provision is thus typically a result of policy and planning decisions. The relevance of public goods in a housing and planning context is developed in Chapter 4.

If one is concerned with an equitable distribution of resources it is the inability of markets to comply with any concept of fairness, other than allocation by ability to pay, that provides a possible rationale for certain types of planning and housing controls. A desire for equitable distributions of income and wealth has been a driving force behind various attempts, over the years, to design reforms, including new types of land taxation, that will redistribute the gains from increases in land values. A discussion of these ideas and the relationships between distributional justice and land markets is provided in Chapter 7.

It is unequal distributions of income that lead some individuals to have a 'need' for housing but no 'effective demand'. They thus lack purchasing power, their incomes being low relative to housing costs, and they are unable to compete effectively in housing markets. One response to this, especially in Western Europe, has been the development of some housing that is designed to meet specified needs rather than market demand. The welfare economics of this are examined in Chapter 8, which considers 'affordable' housing and planning. The role of planning systems in promoting supplies of affordable housing by placing obligations on private-sector developers is further considered in an international context in Chapter 10.

A concern to promote 'sustainable' urban environments has arisen from a desire to improve the quality of life in cities, to conserve energy and to protect the natural environment. Urban residential developments are thus now ideally contributing to a broad agenda that recognizes a host of non-marketed costs and benefits. This is again the territory of welfare economics. In Chapter 9 the links between welfare economics and housing, planning and urban renaissance are examined.

The urban renaissance agenda can be seen as a sub-set of a wider concern with 'sustainable development' that respects the extensive environmental consequences of building. Those consequences extend to the impacts on natural resources of the materials that go into new housing, the landscape into which the housing is accommodated and the resources that occupation of dwellings will consume. From roots in welfare economics, a distinctive environmental economics has developed that provides an analytical basis for examining sustainability. Environmental economics and sustainable development is the subject matter of Chapter 5. In summary, planning, and specifically the planning of housing development, can be seen as a consequence of a desire to promote efficiency and equity in the production of the built environment. Welfare economics informs the analysis of both efficiency and equity.

Chapter 4

Market Failure

There is a vast literature on market failure (see, for example, Cullis and Jones, 1998) and here only some of the essentials are set out in order to emphasize that individual decision-making and competitive markets cannot be relied on to promote an efficient allocation of resources. In general terms the concept of market failure challenges the concept of 'market success' that suggests that competitive markets result in welfare optimization. It does this by emphasizing issues that freely competitive markets fail to address; these are the circumstances in which markets may fail to provide efficient solutions to problems of resource allocation. Some aspects of market failure apply more strongly than others to housing development and planning, and it is these aspects which will receive the most attention (for further discussions of market failure and planning, including the planning of housing, see Oxley, 1975; Walker, 1980; Bramley *et al.*, 1995). Thus, the emphasis below is placed on externalities, public goods, merit goods and the concept of equilibrium. Most weight is given to externalities, and the application of externalities to housing is illustrated by reference to the impact of living conditions on health, education and crime. The ability of planning systems in principle to promote positive externalities and minimize negative externalities is discussed. Planning policy instruments are seen as one set of public-policy reactions to externalities alongside taxes and subsidies and the facilitation of private bargaining solutions.

Externalities

Externalities exist whenever the decisions of individuals impose costs or bestow benefits on others which are not reflected in market transactions. More formally, 'an externality is said to be present when the utility of an individual depends not only on the goods and services the individual purchases and consumes but also on the activity of some other individual' (Cullis and Jones, 1998, p. 31). Externalities are a wide-ranging and pervasive feature of any society; they emphasize the interdependence rather than the independence of individuals. Economists distinguish between technological and pecuniary externalities (ibid., p. 132); the former directly effect utility and production functions, whereas the latter take effect through changes in prices and wages. It is the former that are the true market failure in that the market may simply not take account of these effects. Positive externalities bring benefits and negative externalities impose costs. The production of housing and the use of land involves a wide range of positive and negative externalities. Some of these are trivial and some are of the utmost importance to the well-being of millions of people. The trivial might amount, for example, to minor disputes between neighbours; the major might involve epidemics of infectious disease that have been promoted by slum housing.

Housebuilders in a competitive economy can be expected to make production decisions on the basis of their private costs and benefits. These are the financial costs and benefits that directly affect individual firms and have an impact on their profits. If housebuilding generates external costs because, for example, it leads to a loss of green fields that are a benefit to society or it leads to increased road congestion, external costs need to be added to private costs to give social costs. If more housing is deemed to bring external benefits (because for example it improves the quality of living in society), these external benefits need to be added to private benefits to give social benefits. Whereas private-profit-maximizing output requires a balance between private costs and benefits, socially-optimum output necessitates a balance between social costs and social benefits (see Figures 4.1 and 4.2).

Planning can promote levels of housebuilding, and housebuilding in locations that maximize social welfare rather than private profits. Planning can foster decisions that take account of external costs and external benefits.

Governments tend in many parts of the world not to allow buildings of any standard, as decided by individuals, to be constructed. They do not give individuals the freedom to trade in dangerous buildings that generate external costs. Atomistic decision-making is restricted and controlled by laws that limit individual freedom but enhance public safety. The pure external effect is in this example compounded by the problem of information, and the perfect information requirement of perfect competition cannot realistically be achieved in housing and land transactions. Information about poor foundations or impending subsidence, for example, is easily concealed. Property rights cannot be exchanged efficiently if the property rights are not clearly known. Markets in this case can be

Figure 4.1 *Equilibrium output and production externalities*

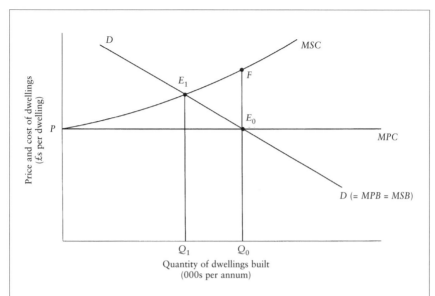

MPC = marginal private cost (the extra cost to housebuilders of building one more house)

MSC = marginal social cost (the extra cost to society of building one more house)

MPB = marginal private benefit (the extra benefit to housebuilders of selling one more house)

MSB = marginal social benefit (the extra benefit to society of housebuilders selling one more house)

With house prices at P, housebuilders will maximize profits buy building and selling at output Q_0. Private-profit-maximizing equilibrium is at E_0 where $MPC = MPB$. In this example MPC is assumed, for simplicity, to be constant (it does not vary with the quantity of dwellings built). If there are no external benefits from housing, the demand curve ($D\ D$) represents MPB and MSB. However, if there are external costs associated with housebuilding these are added to MPC to give MSC. In this case, the socially-optimal output of housing is Q_1 at a socially efficient equilibrium of E_1, where $MSC = MSB$. The production externality (external cost) creates a case for housing production below the private-profit-maximizing market equilibrium level. If output were to be at Q_0 rather than Q_1, a net social cost equal to $E_1\ F\ E_0$ would be imposed.

In this example, there is a negative production externality and no consumption externality.

helped towards greater efficiency not by governments standing back and relying on individuals to voluntarily provide information and to keep to explicit standards, but by them taking positive action. And governments do regulate for minimum standards of construction to improve information and to reduce negative externalities. Financial

Figure 4.2   *Equilibrium output and consumption externalities*

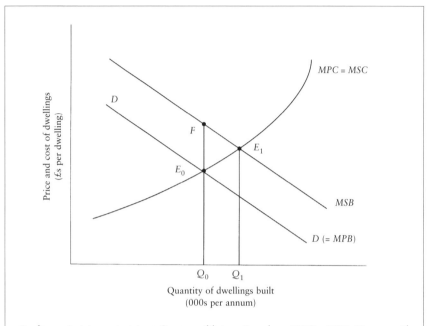

Profit-maximizing output is at Q_0 at equilibrium E_0, where $MPC = MPB$. However, if there are external benefits from housing, MSB exceeds MPB. The socially optimal level of output is Q_1 at equilibrium E_1. A restriction of output to Q_0 means that society forgoes the benefit equal to $E_0 F E_1$. The consumption externality (external benefit) creates a case for housing production exceeding the private-profit-maximizing equilibrium level.

In this example, there is a positive consumption externality but no production externality. As in Figure 4.1, socially-optimum output occurs where $MSC = MSB$.

institutions recognize the information problem by, for example, requiring surveyors' reports on dwellings against which loans are secured. Not all aspects of information deficiencies thus demand government action, but when a lack of information puts power in the hands of some at the expense of others, or contributes to an externality problem, governments may decide to act.

The construction of new housing inevitably affects the neighbourhood in which it is built. The potential negative externalities imposed by housing blocking a view or impeding light have long been tackled by planning controls. The positive externalities which well-designed and appropriately located housing can provide have similarly been promoted by planning measures. One could elaborate on many examples of housing, through its design, location, construction and maintenance, bringing positive or negative effects to individuals other than those who decide on the design, location and other matters. Where these effects are significant, governments in virtually all countries have, for many years, concluded that unfettered individual decision-making is inappropriate. This does not mean that governments make these housing production decisions themselves, but it does mean that they regulate and seek to influence the decisions of individuals.

Housing and externalities

If it can be demonstrated that housing which has particular attributes in terms of its physical standards, design and location has positive effects on the well-being of a population wider than those who inhabit the specific units considered, there is a powerful case for promoting these positive effects. Three areas in particular have received attention with respect to these wide positive externality aspects of what we will for the advantage of shorthand call 'decent housing'. The three areas are health, education and crime. The connections between these three areas and decent housing relevant to the current discussion are essentially a matter of empirical evidence. The only normative propositions here are that less ill-health is better than more, higher educational standards are better than lower standards, and less crime is preferable to more crime. The issue to be dealt with by evidence is then whether these phenomena are influenced by housing conditions. There is a growing body of empirical work in these areas that demonstrates that if there are strong cause and effect relationships there are important externalities. These externalities will not be recognized and acted upon in atomistic decision-making processes.

The health and housing connection has often been examined in the negative as well as the positive sense. That is, the proposition that poor-quality housing causes ill-health has been expounded, as has the proposition that good-quality housing promotes a healthier population. Slum housing as a breeding ground for disease was a significant fear in Victorian Britain. The case for government action to improve housing standards was promoted not only, or even mainly, in terms of the benefits to the slum dwellers, but to the neighbouring populations who would enjoy the benefits of improved health prospects (Conway, 1999).

There is a wealth of research that links specific illnesses in modern times with housing quality. The connections between poor-quality housing and health problems are not necessarily straightforward, as much of the research acknowledges, and a simple unicausal relationship between a health problem and physical housing conditions may ignore the role of other variables such as income, class and age. However, if an improvement in housing conditions can bring significant improvements in health, the quality of housing becomes not just a private but also a public matter. The nature of the public action that should be taken in the light of this finding is not determined by the finding itself. It does suggest, however, that some collective action will be appropriate if individual decisions result in a housing stock which is of an unacceptably low standard; that is a standard which contributes significantly to health problems. As with the issues of the construction and planning of housing more generally, the issue of setting standards arises. The lowest standards of housing are experienced by homeless people, and the links between homelessness and poor health have been well-documented:

> Homeless people generally suffer more health problems than the rest of the population. It is common for them to have skin ailments, respiratory infections, traumatic injuries and chronic gastro-intestinal, vascular, dental and neurological disorders. Homeless people are at greater risk of trauma, road traffic accidents and violent crime. Mortality rates are increased at least 3 fold in homeless populations. The life expectancy of a homeless person is 42 years. (Leicestershire Health Authority, 1999, p. 72)

In relation to housing and education, the first question is again an essentially empirical issue. It is whether an improvement in housing quality can bring about an improvement in educational attainment. The evidence is not as extensive as that for housing and health and the results are not as clear. A report for Shelter in 1995 claimed that thousands of children's education is undermined by homelessness (Power and Whitty, 1995). It noted the disruption of frequent school moves faced by children in homeless households and the lack of somewhere to do homework for children in Bed and Breakfast accommodation. It is not a general improvement, in the sense of an increase in the average quality of the aggregate housing stock, which may bring gains, but rather changes in the housing circumstances of a selection of the population which may bring about the necessary improvement in welfare. The problem with this approach, more so than with the housing and health connection, is that a naïve physical determinism can be substituted for more thoroughgoing analyses of the complex causal factors. One does not need to support crude physical determinism, or to be convinced by comprehensive multi-factorial analyses of the determinants of educational attainment, to accept that some changes in housing circumstances can have some positive effects on educational achievement.

The notion that certain types of crime are more concentrated in some housing areas than others is also well-documented. Again, the cause and effect relationships are less easily proved than is the case with health. Much of the literature on housing and crime focuses on 'problem estates', and it is clear that on such estates, as well as significant levels of certain types of crime, there are high incidences of unemployment and low incomes (see, for example, Page, 1993, 1994, and Power and Tunstall, 1997). The causal effects of these phenomena and the attributes of the housing should ideally be disentangled. There has been a long-running belief amongst some academics that the design of housing has an effect on behaviour and that certain types of crime are more likely with certain forms of housing than others. One does not need to accept the extremes of physical determinism that can be found in some analyses (for example Coleman, 1985; Newman, 1973) to acknowledge that some housing designs and layout may be more conducive than others to lower rather than higher rates of crime. Given that there might be no specific incentives for private decision-makers to opt for the preferable designs, there is a case for public encouragement of such designs. The weakness of individual decision-making is thus once more revealed.

The existence of significant externalities makes a case for some sort of public action, since individual decision-making in matters related to the design, construction and maintenance of housing can be inefficient. Thus some decisions may be better made by some form of government than by individuals. The options regarding these decisions will be considered later.

A planning system and externalities

If the focus of a planning system is to respond to the failure of markets to cope with externalities, the emphasis would be on stopping development where there are excessive negative externalities and facilitating development where there are beneficial positive externalities. It has been argued that 'The UK planning system is highly effective in stopping development: it is much less effective in facilitating it' (Cullingworth and Nadin, 2002, p. 12). In practice, planning systems are frequently more concerned with negative than with positive externalities. Negative externalities create problem situations; positive externalities provide opportunities. It will be useful to explore what, in principle, these problems and opportunities might be and how planning might respond. Negative externalities arise, for example, from incompatible land uses whereas positive externalities can arise from complementary land uses. The UK planning system, like most planning systems, does try to prevent incompatible land uses, but only in a limited way does it promote complementary uses.

Where land uses are incompatible, the users of land impose external costs on one another. The noisy factory with heavy lorries coming and going will have an adverse effect on the residents of nearby houses. Therefore one simple function of planning is to stop factories being developed in residential areas or, more generally, to avoid potential external costs created by the proximity of conflicting land uses.

The nature of such conflict is potentially diverse. Circumstances include a wide range of situations where pollution might occur; for example noxious substances being pumped into the atmosphere may have a harmful effect if there are houses nearby, but have little impact in an otherwise deserted landscape. Or, residential development on greenfield sites might conflict with the enjoyment of the habitat by wildlife or spoil ramblers' views. These potential losses may be seen as external costs that planning might seek to avoid.

A planning system provides opportunities for promoting positive externalities or external benefits that markets may not take into account. A coordinated approach to the provision of housing, schools and shops, for example, can bring benefits to all parties. A planning system which encourages the re-use of redundant buildings and polluted vacant urban land can promote benefits not only to developers and the owners and occupiers of the new buildings, but also to neighbouring occupants. The benefits may go wider still and extend to an improvement in the quality of life throughout a town as it becomes a more pleasant place in which to live.

If improved housing can promote better health, lower crime levels and improved educational performance, a planning system that encourages better housing can bring a very wide range of external benefits. Housing that promotes these positive changes may do so because of its design, location and quality. Some aspects of housing design and quality might be viewed as more the responsibility of building control departments than planning departments. However, it is useful to view planning in a wide context and see building regulations as part of a planning system. Such regulations typically seek to make buildings safe and of an acceptable standard, not only for the owners and occupants of the buildings, but also for a wider community. A building that collapses because of poor foundations can impose extensive external costs on those in its vicinity.

A land-use planning system clearly has the potential to influence a very wide range of external costs and benefits. However, if planning simply says 'no' to some developments and 'yes' to others, it acts as a very blunt instrument. The aim should not be to disapprove of proposals that will create external costs and approve those that bring external benefits. There should, rather, be a concern with a balance between the overall costs of a development, including all the external costs, and the overall benefits, including all the external benefits. Thus, not all developments that bring about some atmospheric pollution or spoil a view over green fields should be stopped. Nor should all new housing schemes that contribute to an improvement in the housing stock be promoted. A welfare economics approach involves a consideration of the costs and benefits to society of a given change. Conventional planning instruments need to be combined with new measures if the welfare of society as a whole is to be promoted.

Public action or private bargaining?

The prevalence of externalities related to housing and planning creates conditions where social rather than individual decision-making is required to take account of both positive and negative externalities. Externalities are important for individual and social welfare and individual action alone will often not be able to address the problems created. The Coase theorem suggests that bargaining between affected parties can produce a satisfactory solution (Coase, 1974). The bargaining can involve payments of compensation between the affected parties and these payments will reflect the positive and negative values that the initiator and the recipient of the externality place on the activity. The Coase theorem has been, over the years, the subject of much discussion by economists and there are many weaknesses that have been identified in both the essence and the practicality of the theorem; for a summary of the major criticisms see Ng (1992, pp. 182–5) and Cullis and Jones (1998, pp. 31–6). There are many shortcomings of the bargaining approach proposed by Coase which make bargaining generally inapplicable to housing externalities and to externalities associated with many land-use issues.

In practice, transaction costs are likely to be large and the affected parties will find it not only costly but impractical to negotiate. If my neighbour builds an extension to his house which blocks my view I may be able to strike a bargain with him which either allows him to build and me to receive compensation, or me to get my continued access to a view and him to receive compensation. But how we bargain will depend on the distribution of property rights. If my neighbour does not have a right to build but I have a right to a view, my hand will be greatly strengthened in the bargaining process. If he has the right to build, will he frequently threaten to construct a new extension in order to blackmail me into more compensation payments? If he is rich and I am poor, I might easily be persuaded to take a small sum of money whilst he gets a very large gain from the new construction. How bargaining works clearly depends on the initial distribution of property rights and the distribution of income between the affected parties. A claim of the Coase approach is that it takes account of the two-way nature of the externality process. In fact, as Ng argues:

> One of the basic difficulties of the bargaining solution is that no matter how we assign property rights or what liability rule we adopt, it tends to be 'one-sided' and fails to tackle the two-sided nature of the externality problem adequately. The payment of compensation only makes the payer take into account the cost he imposes on others, failing to make the receiver and prospective receivers of compensation take account of the cost they impose on the payer. (1983, p. 184)

The bargaining solution will be costly and impractical when large numbers of people are involved, as will often be the case with housing externalities. If a new housing development restricts the views of a large number of existing residents, the costs of the residents organizing themselves into an effective bargaining group may be very large indeed. It has been argued that 'bargaining will never proceed if large numbers of individuals are involved' and, 'It is not necessarily the case that negotiation will produce a Pareto optimum if both parties do not have access to all the available knowledge' (Cullis and Jones, 1998, pp. 34–5). Residents will be better able to bargain with the developer if they know the profits that are probable from the development. The developer might have strong incentives to conceal the relevant predictions.

There may be several sets of externalities involved in a given situation and many sets of parties to the externalities. The housing development might, besides having negative effects on existing residents, positively affect motorists who will be able to travel a shorter distance because of a new road which is a necessary condition for the development. Can the motorists be identified as a bargaining group and how are their benefits to be bargained relative to the resident's costs and the developer's benefits? For situations of more than one externality, the Coase theorem has been restated thus:

> the elimination of each externality is independent of the assignment of property rights so long as there is separate liability for each externality, bargaining on one externality is independent of bargaining on all others and the zero transactions cost assumption holds. (Mueller, 1989, p. 33)

The probability of these conditions holding is small. After reviewing the issues, Cullis and Jones (1998) conclude, 'The list of transactions problems . . . casts some doubt on the proposition that the market can adequately resolve the problem of externalities' (p. 36).

The bargaining solution assumes a relatively simple situation with two parties – the initiator of the external effect and the recipient – bargaining with each other. The reality of housing externalities is much more complex than this. Take, for example, the proposition that poor-quality housing has adverse effects on health, a proposition for which convincing empirical evidence with respect to specific illnesses has been amassed (see, for example, Conway, 1999). However, the answer to the question 'who has caused the adverse effect?' is not straightforward and neither is the answer to the question 'who are the affected persons?' In the case of an old damp house which is contributing to the resident's respiratory problems, if the house is rented, we may argue that is an issue for the landlord and the tenant to work out. If it is owner-occupied, what does the bargaining solution suggest then? Is the owner to bargain with himself or herself as the occupier?

Poor housing does not usually come in the form of individual isolated dwellings. In a neighbourhood of run-down housing the adverse effects might reasonably be argued to be collectively produced. There may be a multiplicity of owners, and the housing might have deteriorated over the years. There has not been a purposeful act which has led to the production of 'harmful housing'. The built environment is moulded by a complexity of agents over time and pinning the responsibility or the blame on specific agents may not be meaningful or useful. Those who will benefit from an improvement to the neighbourhood will not just be existing residents, but also future generations. Who is to bargain for them?

The prisoner's dilemma

Even if we argue that the value of a 'better quality' neighbourhood will be reflected in the market values of the improved properties, existing owners acting individually may have little or no incentive to improve. This proposition can be supported by the 'prisoner's dilemma' (Harrison, 1977, pp. 71–2; Robinson, 1979, pp. 101–3), which refers to the problem of making decisions under conditions of uncertainty caused by a lack of information about the decisions of those who can affect the outcome of the intended action. It describes a situation where coordinated informed decisions are better than uncoordinated uninformed decisions. It has been argued that:

> It is possible that a landlord (or owner) will be deterred from improving his own property because of the fear that his returns will be jeopardized by the external costs imposed on his property by unimproved adjoining ones. Because each landlord is faced with uncertainty about his neighbour's activities, no one will be willing to risk investing in maintenance and repair work. However, if they all *did* invest, both they and society in general would probably be better off (Robinson, 1979, p. 101)

If it was just a question of two landlords collaborating with each other a mutually beneficial solution might be found through cooperation, or one landlord might purchase other run-down properties and thus 'internalize' the externalities and provide a solution. However, when the numbers of properties are large such outcomes are unlikely. It has been suggested that 'Thus we may conclude that atomistic behaviour is likely to prevail and to lead to an inefficient outcome' (ibid., p. 103). In a city with a large volume of poor-quality housing in a multiplicity of ownerships, it may require much more than improvement to individual properties to raise the quality of housing. Demolition and the redesign of housing layouts may be necessary; changes in road layouts may be required. A change in the physical environment which creates new housing in conjunction with improved social infrastructure might be the only feasible way that a run-down environment can be transformed into an area of good-quality housing. It is most unlikely that individual property owners will communicate, collaborate and change the built environment in such a way.

The most serious housing externalities involving health, education and crime are complex. The parties that have 'caused' external costs are not well-defined. Those who would need to cooperate to improve the quality of the housing stock are the many owners of complex bundles of property rights. The beneficiaries of improved housing are also many but they will not all easily be identified. If improved housing conditions do have positive effects on health, education and crime, it is not just the inhabitants of specific dwellings or the residents of a given neighbourhood but the members of a much wider society who will benefit. There is some similarity between the correct application of externalities to housing and the application of the concept to environmental pollution in that adverse effects are typically collectively produced and collectively received. Tackling pollution is recognized to require action which is initiated by governments and imposed on large numbers of decision-makers, and improving the quality of the housing stock, likewise, involves many decision-makers. It does not, of course, follow that because individual decision-making fails to deal with housing externalities, state activity can inevitably and easily find a solution. Activity by the state involves costs, requires information and needs to be weighed against the probable benefits. The type of state activity also needs to be considered carefully.

Externalities and policy instruments

There is a long list of actions which economists have proposed as potential remedies for adverse external costs and for the promotion of positive externalities. It includes laws which carefully define the property rights of affected parties; the merging of affected parties into a single decision-making body; the use of regulations; taxes on those who initiate external costs and subsidies for those who promote external benefits. These options are variously suggested as means to be used as alternatives to the bargaining solution or as actions which will assist a bargaining solution. The relevance of each of the options to housing and planning depends on the specific circumstances that are considered.

The right to develop housing is limited by laws which define the boundaries to what owners may do with their physical property. Thus one does not typically have a right to build a house in a green field or to construct a large extension to one's property. Rights to a view across green fields or to freedom from the sight of an obtrusive extension to a neighbour's house could be, but are not always, defined in law. The right of a builder or a landlord to supply unsafe housing can be limited by laws, and environmental health legislation can provide occupants with some rights to healthy housing.

However, suddenly making all housing of an unacceptable standard illegal would not necesarily do anything to increase the supply of decent housing.

When landlord and tenant become one and the same through owner-occupation, it might be argued that some of the external effects of poor-quality housing become internalized but, again, the reality of the poor quality will remain without further action. The merger solution may have some significance for firms who are parties to each others' polluting outputs (Burrows, 1979, pp. 80–96), but its usefulness in housing will be severely limited.

The use of regulations, combined with related laws is, in practice, a common way of dealing with many housing and land-use externalities. The use of planning and building-control regulations can be used to limit negative and to encourage positive externalities associated with the construction and improvement of housing. Whilst regulations are unlikely to be capable on their own of promoting the transformation of problem estates or the development of new higher quality dwellings, regulations which set minimum acceptable standards are essential to a housing policy which seeks to promote decent housing.

The notion of taxes on the perpetrators of unacceptable housing is difficult to perceive. Who would be liable for the taxes? In the sense of fines on those who contravened minimum standards legislation, one can see some realism. However, as a more general proposition, taxes on those guilty of causing slum housing would be a lot more difficult to apply than taxes on an industrialist whose output exceeds some pollution-inducing level. The difficulty here is that the tax solution is usually advocated as a means of balancing the social costs and the social benefits of a variable level of production. The aim is to achieve equality between the marginal social cost and the marginal social benefit of an activity. At the optimal production level, the cost to society of an additional unit of output will be equal to the benefit to society from the output. The concept may, in this sense, be of some value in trying to find the optimum density for residential development on a given estate, but of little help in finding an acceptable level of slum housing in a country.

Subsidies are intended to encourage desirable activities. If the extra desirable activity has a value which is greater than the cost of the subsidy, the subsidy can be argued to be justified on efficiency grounds. Subsidies which lead to improvements in the housing stock which bring benefits to society, and subsidies which promote the building of housing which has social benefits that are greater than the private benefits to be received by the developer, can therefore be argued for on efficiency grounds. There is, without doubt, a significant empirical problem here. The valuation of the benefit to society will not easily be determined. This does not mean that it should be ignored or assumed to be zero. It does mean that there should be a major research effort directed at defining and measuring the wide benefits to society of an improvement in the quality of the housing stock. The efficiency case for housing subsidies is dependent on a demonstration of the social benefits of decent housing. If all the benefits of decent housing were to be reflected in the capital values and the rents of such housing there would be a much diminished case for subsidy. It is because a market system does not reflect these benefits that a case for subsidization can be made.

The prevalence of significant externalities, which cannot be simply internalized by redefining property rights or by bargaining between affected parties, is central to the argument for a positive housing policy. It is not, however, central to any case for state provision or for any particular form of housing tenure. The case for council housing or for state ownership of housing cannot be made on externality grounds. The concept of externalities provides part of the rationale for appropriate housing policy instruments, not for a particular form of ownership. Poor quality housing is not tenure-specific; it is, of course, to be found in all tenures and negative external effects will require a remedy whether they relate to social or to private housing.

Public goods

Another part of the armoury of market failure is public goods. Public goods pose a problem for markets and individual decision-making because there is no incentive for private decision-makers to demand or supply public goods. Public goods are defined essentially with respect to their technical characteristics, in particular: non-rivalry in consumption, non-excludability and non-rejectability (Barr, 1998, p. 104). A formal definition suggests that a public good is one 'which all enjoy in common in the sense that each individual's consumption leads to no subtraction from any other individual's consumption of that good' (Samuelson, 1954, p. 387). The phenomenon of public goods illustrates the point that markets work well when individual property rights are well-defined and enforceable. With public goods they are not. Private profit-maximizing entrepreneurs are thus not interested in supplying public goods. If when individual A consumes the good, the amount available for individual B is not diminished and it is not possible to provide the good for A without providing it for B, the entrepreneur cannot provide exclusive bundles of the good. There will thus be some difficulty in extracting a payment for a public good. Consumers will have every incentive to conceal rather than reveal their preferences for such goods. Once they are provided all can consume but no one will wish to pay. As with many aspects of welfare economics there is a large literature on public goods, and the essence of the technical ramifications and the associated work is summarized in Cullis and Jones (1998, pp. 45–70). There are few practical examples of pure public goods which display all of the technical characteristics set out above but many goods will display some of these characteristics.

The free market does not necessarily supply optimum amounts of these goods. Such 'quasi-public goods' are furthermore often supplied jointly with other private goods. Housing is not a public good. Dwellings can clearly be supplied exclusively. There is rivalry in consumption, and private property rights in housing are created and traded. Dwellings are, however, usually jointly supplied with quasi-public goods, so that the consumption and value of housing is enhanced by the provision of proximate quasi-public goods. For example, most dwellings benefit from access to a road and to street lighting. Roads and street lighting are quasi-public goods, and given that both of these items display some of the attributes of public goods it is unlikely that atomistic market decision-making will result in efficient levels of output. There is an opportunity cost involved in production but not in consumption. In producing the good for one household it is necessarily produced for many households. However, the lack of exclusivity in provision will make it difficult to extract individual voluntary payments; individuals are likely to attempt to be free-riders. The provision of such items therefore tends to rely on public expenditure. There is a tendency, then, for both public finance and public provision. With public and quasi-public goods the failure of price signals to suggest appropriate levels of output tends also to mean that decisions on how much to produce, and indeed when and where to produce, involve public-sector decision-making. In short, there is usually some planning involved which means that decisions are made not at an individual level but at a societal level. It follows, as a practical proposition, that decisions on the provision of quasi-public goods such as roads and street lighting have to be linked to decisions about where and when to construct housing. One could extend the examples of quasi-public goods to include sewerage and drainage and a whole range of physical infrastructure. Thus although houses are not public or quasi-public goods, their provision is inevitably closely linked to the provision of such goods, and decisions on their production cannot be made efficiently without a linkage to social decisions on the provision of infrastructure. Efficient housing production thus requires a degree of planning.

Merit goods

A further cause of market failure, well-recognized in the welfare economics literature, is the case of merit goods (see, for example, Barr, 1998, pp. 89–90; Cullis and Jones, 1998 pp. 67–8). Merit goods have been defined in this way: 'If the consumption of a good by the voluntary decisions of individuals, given their incomes, is deemed deficient/excessive not due to the existence of externalities or pricing inefficiency, it is a merit/demerit good' (Ng, 1992, p. 286). Acknowledging the existence of merit goods involves suspending the assumption of consumer sovereignty, to accept that in some circumstances the individual is not the best judge of his or her welfare. In these circumstances there are goods which individuals should consume even though they decide not to consume, or not to consume in quantities which are sufficiently large. To accept a paternalistic stance in which governments know better what is good for individuals than they do themselves involves strong normative assumptions. Whether or not a good is a public good is essentially a technical and positive issue, but whether a good is a merit good is essentially a moral and normative issue.

Why should an individual not be the best judge of whether or not to consume a good and in what circumstances might governments know better than individuals? Two sets of circumstances are sometimes cited, where one relates to a lack of information, and the other to a lack of competence. Each may require some social action but the nature of the appropriate action will be different in each case. If individuals fail to demand adequate housing because they do not have information that tells them that adequate housing will reduce the likelihood of them suffering from a given illness (which we can assume in this instance is not contagious and thus does not involve an external cost), the answer might be to improve the provision of information. If they lack competence because they lack maturity, or have a mental incapacity or their judgement is impaired by drink or drugs, the impediment is likely to relate to a range of considerations, and not just housing, and the appropriate action is unlikely to involve making only a housing-related decision. When individuals lack competence in the ways described, economic theory has some difficulties in modelling both the nature of the problem and reactions to the problem. This is because of the all-pervading assumption of rational decision-making. If individuals are not, for whatever reason, rational decision-makers the idea of their making decisions to maximize anyone's utility, be it there own or someone else's, fails to have any value.

If a drug addict fails to see the benefit to themselves of medical treatment there may be a case for arguing that the treatment is a merit good and the individual should be encouraged or forced to have such treatment irrespective of personal decisions. The proposition, and what it implies for a denial of individual liberty, is of course highly debatable and not one from which general principles should be derived.

The idea of children as incompetent decision-makers is again problematic for economic theory because it implies that they are unable to take rational decisions in their own self-interest. Economists often 'get round' the problem by considering households and not individuals to be the decision-makers, and societies tend to ascribe responsibilities for decision-making for children to someone else: parents or guardians. Only if they fail to act responsibly does society in a wider sense tend to intervene.

It is unreasonable to treat housing like drug medication or to assume a general lack of responsibility for decision-making on behalf of children. It is thus wrong to argue that housing should be treated generally as a merit good. It is equally wrong to argue that housing of some minimum standard is a merit good. This is, however, the stance of several attempts to justify social rather than individual decision-making for housing and to argue for promoting individual housing consumption above what it would otherwise be. As Barr states, without explicitly supporting the proposition, there is an argument that 'housing is such an important part of community welfare that individuals should be compelled to consume at least some minimum quantity. This is the merit good argument in its pure form' (Barr, 1998, p. 373).

Equilibrium

Before moving to equity issues, another efficiency issue should be considered. This relates to the concept of equilibrium. The welfare economics theorem which links Pareto efficiency to perfect competition seeks to show that perfectly competitive markets *in equilibrium* produce the desired result (Winch, 1971). Yet equilibrium is a complex concept. In its *general equilibrium* sense it means that there is simultaneously a balance between demand and supply in markets for all factors of production and all goods and services. But the reality of markets is that there is a constant process of adjustment which has consequences for individual utilities, and these consequences may be positive or negative. One can argue for accepting these consequences as temporary phenomena which are of little lasting significance, or one can see them as serious impediments to the acceptability of market processes. If one takes the latter view, another important challenge to market operations and to their atomistic decision-making processes is posed.

Housing and land markets can adjust towards new equilibria very slowly and with much personal cost. An increase in housing demand because of increased employment opportunities or the sudden influx of population to an area will tend to raise house prices and if the market is at work the increased prices will ultimately bring forth more supply. That is the theoretical position. If there are no barriers to increased housing production, and housebuilding resources are widely available, there is no reason to assume events on the ground will not follow the predictions of the model. But all of this may well take time – possibly a long time. In the meantime some people may pay very high prices for housing and some may go without decent housing. Problems of housing shortages, of slum housing and of homelessness can be viewed as problems of adjustment to equilibrium. If one believes that it is best to let markets work and find their way to new points of equilibrium, one will see in this situation no case for collective action, no case for social action, only a case for waiting for equilibrium. In fact to do anything other than wait for a new equilibrium can be seen as taking action which impairs the efficient allocation of resources and is thus wasteful.

Taking action which results from impatience with waiting for equilibrium does not mean replacing the atomistic decision-making of the marketplace by collective decision-making. It might mean investigation of the causes of the slowness of adjustment to new equilibria and tackling these causes. It might also mean ameliorating the consequences of short-term disequilibrium by some form of compensating action which requires collective decision-making.

Conclusions

Housing and land markets inevitably involve market failures. In particular, housing provision involves significant externalities and its provision is essentially linked to the provision of quasi-public goods.

Add to this the tendency of housing markets to linger in disequilibrium and we have important reasons to doubt the individualistic decision-making capacity of housing markets to deliver efficient outcomes. In support of efficiency one may therefore seek alternative arrangements for the provision of housing if these are likely to involve a better utilization of resources. These alternative arrangements do not necessarily involve collective provision or suspending market forces, but they do involve a variety of mechanisms which rely on social rather than individual action. The arrangements and mechanisms with some emphasis on land-use planning solutions are considered in subsequent sections.

Just as markets can fail so can governments, and there is an extensive and growing literature on government and non-market failure (see, for example, Cullis and Jones, 1998, pp. 352–73; Wolf, 1987). Government production and allocation can be inefficient and merely replacing markets by governments does not necessarily lead to improvements even if there are considerable market failures. However, governments do not inevitably fail to do better than markets, and some types of government activity are likely to be better than others. The literature on government failure should no more lead us to believe in the supremacy of the market than the literature on market failure should lead us to believe in the supremacy of governments. Rather, judgements about appropriate activity for each should be made in the light of specific circumstances. These arguments are developed in the context of 'public choice theory' in Chapter 6.

To advocate the pursuit of an efficiency objective is not necessarily to argue for the supremacy of any particular ideological perspective. In fact Barr (1998, pp. 73–7) argues that efficiency is entirely compatible with several views of society including libertarianism, utilitarianism and socialism. Barr argues that given that an increase in efficiency can raise welfare under many theories of society, 'The aim of efficiency is therefore common to all these ideologies, although the weight attached to it will vary when its achievement conflicts with distributional goals' (ibid., p. 103). The action which is taken on efficiency grounds will depend on ideological positions with respect to the redistribution of resources and the connections which are acknowledged between housing and planning issues and the distribution of resources in society.

Chapter 5

Environmental Economics and Sustainable Development

The broad objective of land-use planning is to regulate and control development in the public interest. This means that it is not just the interests of the developers and users of buildings that have to be considered, but those of a wider community. In the case of a housing development that is proposed in the countryside, the interests of all those affected by the development might ideally be considered, including those who currently walk near the site and enjoy views over green fields. If natural habitats are to be destroyed and the vitality of flora and fauna affected, should the development proceed? If the value of species is considered not just for current but for future generations, the scope of the public interest and the community that is to be considered becomes extremely broad. We might extend our considerations not only to those in the locality of the development now and in the future, but consider the national and global impacts of developments. With this line of thought we may be concerned with the materials that are used in the construction of dwellings and the disposal of waste as a byproduct of the building process. What contributions do these make to the depletion of natural resources and to the amenity value of the localities that receive the waste? What will be the energy efficiency of the completed dwellings? The geographical distribution of development will have important implications for transportation and the energy used in moving people and goods between places of dwelling, work, recreation and consumption. All of these are examples of the environmental impact of development.

In recent decades, the intensity and scope of interest in environmental issues has increased and a global concern with the use of resources in ways that take account of future generations has led to the widespread use of the term 'sustainable development'. In this chapter, the role of environmental economics in analysing environmental issues will be examined, and its contribution both to formulating environmental problems and suggesting policy responses will

85

be explored. The concept of sustainable development will be scrutinized, and the role of environmental economics in understanding the meaning of sustainable residential development and in identifying instruments to promote this will be discussed.

The meaning of environment

The use of the term 'the environment' is often confined to the natural environment. For example, it has been stated that 'By "environment", we mean the biosphere . . . the atmosphere . . . the geosphere . . . and all flora and fauna. Our definition of the environment thus includes all life forms, energy and material resources' (Hanley *et al.*, 1997, p. 1). From this definition it follows that the environment has three broad functions: supplier of resources, a sink or receptor for waste products, and a supplier of amenity. As a supplier of resources, the environment is the source of all energy and materials that are inputs to productive processes; all goods and services that are produced rely ultimately on natural resources extracted from the environment. The processes of production and consumption create waste. The byproducts of manufacturing such as gases added to the atmosphere are waste, as is the rubbish that consumers put into their bins, and, ultimately, the cars we drive, the buildings we live in and virtually everything we have produced becomes waste. If we think of this waste being sunk back into the environment, the issue of the consequences of this use of the environment as a sink for waste raises many questions. It can be argued that facets of the environment have a limited assimilative capacity, a limited ability to absorb and degrade waste. As the assimilative capacity is exceeded, the ability of the environment to supply more resources for future production is impeded. Furthermore, the assimilative capacity of rivers, oceans and atmosphere to receive waste may not be identified as some fixed volume at a fixed point in time. There may, rather, be thresholds which are approached gradually that, once crossed, create adverse and possibly irreversible reductions in the ability of the environment to supply resources and amenity. When waste products contribute to this depletion in the environment's productive capacity, we may think of them as pollutants.

Pearce and Turner (1990, pp. 35–41) suggest that ignoring the environment leads to us thinking of the economy as a linear system, but with the environment considered we can think of the economy as a circular flow. As a linear system, an economy uses natural resources to produce commodities that yield utility. The inclusion of the environment as a resource supplier, a direct source of utility and crucially a waste assimilator gives a circular flow model of activity. Waste products, which are to a greater or lesser extent recycled, are both an output and input to economic activity. Non-recycled waste goes into the environment. When we dispose of waste in ways that damage the capacity of the environment to absorb waste (that is, we exceed assimilative capacity) the economic function of the environment as a waste sink is impaired. Disposal of waste in excess of assimilative capacity also damages the ability of the environment to provide amenity.

A concern with the natural environment may focus on ecology and ecosystems. Ecology examines the interdependence between living things and their environments; an ecosystem is a system of living things in relation to their environment. Ecosystems are not static. They may respond to changes in climate and to changes in habitat induced by exogenous factors such as the dumping of waste. By affecting the environment in which flora and fauna survive, mankind can have impacts on ecosystems that change both the future of species and the benefit that mankind can derive from these species. We may suffer from the disappearance of a plant species because we no longer have the pleasure of seeing it and/or because we no longer have the benefit of consuming it.

The amenity function of the environment refers to the broad range of benefits that are derived from the recreational use of natural resources and the pleasure we derive from knowing that there are beautiful landscapes and species sharing our planet. The preservation of ecosystems might thus be desirable because of the amenity value this brings. Some analyses go much wider:

> The environment acts as a supplier of amenity, educational and spiritual values to society. For example, people in Europe may derive pleasure from the existence of wilderness areas in Northern Canada or in tropical moist forests ('rainforests'), while native peoples living in these areas attach spiritual and cultural values to them, and the flora and fauna therein. (Hanley *et al.*, 1997, p. 7)

'The environment' has in recent years become more than a consideration of just the natural environment; it has been used to describe the social and cultural contexts which influence well-being. A very wide approach suggests that

> Essentially, and in its broadest sense, the word 'environment' embraces the conditions or influences under which any individual

or thing exists, lives or develops. These surrounding influences may be placed into three categories:

1. the combination of physical conditions that affect and influence the growth and development of an individual or community;
2. the social and cultural conditions that affect the nature of an individual or community; and
3. the surroundings of an inanimate object of intrinsic social value.

(Gilpin, 2000, p. 15)

According to this view, 'environment' embraces social factors well as the natural phenomena that contribute to the quality of life, and it is this broad view of environment with a concern for the quality of life of future and current societies that has informed the sustainable development agenda.

Economic analysis of the environment

Environmental economics focuses on (1) why in decision-making processes the consequences for the environment are not taken into account in ways that might improve well-being, and (2) how institutions and policy might be improved so that environmental consequences are considered in resource allocation and consumption decisions. Environmental economics is thus concerned both with why environmental pollution occurs, and how it might be moderated. It is concerned with optimizing the use of resources in ways that take account of a wide range of intangible costs and benefits that affect the well-being of current societies and future generations. The subject matter of environmental economics is vast, embracing pollution control, climate change, protection of the natural environment, the conservation of natural resources and the evolving sustainable development agenda.

In economic systems that rely mainly on price signals to value and allocate resources, environmental items tend to be poorly valued because they are either not priced or are underpriced (Hanley *et al.*, 2001, pp. 12–33). Thus a profit-maximizing residential developer will not necessarily consider the values of a view that is obliterated by new dwellings, the natural habitats that are destroyed or watercourses that are no longer capable of supporting fish because of the dumping of construction waste. The developer might also not consider the impact on energy utilization of the insulation materials in the dwellings and the travel to work pattern to which the location of a development will contribute. All of these considerations might be ignored if they do not influence the price at which the dwellings sell or the costs that the developer has to bear.

Environmental issues can be seen as specific forms of external costs that markets ignore. Viewed in this way, environmental economics, with an emphasis on externality issues, can be seen as a distinctive branch of welfare economics. The inability of markets to value environmental items in an optimal fashion is thus seen as a specific form of market failure.

The source of market failure is a lack of clear property rights in environmental assets; and if property rights in natural resources are poorly defined, they will be poorly priced. The market system works inefficiently in allocating environmental resources because 'an imperfect specification of property rights results in a set of prices which sends the wrong signals to producers, consumers and governments' (Hanley *et al.*, 1997, p. 8). If market failure is to be avoided, markets need to be complete, and sufficient markets must exist to cover each and every possible transaction so that resources move to their optimal use. Property rights also have to be comprehensively assigned, exclusive, transferable and secure. Together, these mean that:

1   all the entitlements to the use of all resources must be known and effectively enforced;
2   all benefits and costs from the use of a resource should accrue to those to whom the property rights have been assigned;
3   all property rights must be transferable; and
4   property rights shall not be stolen or encroached illegally.

However, environmental assets tend to be subject to incomplete markets and inadequate property rights: 'The inability or unwillingness to assign property rights such that a complete set of markets can be created has provided the rationale for governments to intervene as an advocate of proper management of environmental resources' (Hanley *et al.*, 1997, p. 25).

There are opportunities for governments to influence the environmental consequences of land use by clearly specifying the property rights that are vested in the owner of any given piece of land. Thus the owner of a greenfield site that provides a habitat for a rare species of plant and from which there are uninterrupted views over a beautiful landscape may have limited rights to build houses on the land. At one extreme, there may be no rights at all to residential development. At another, there may be a right, ignoring all adverse environmental consequences, to build as many houses as the owner wishes, whatever specifications are privately chosen. In between, the rights to develop may be restricted in ways that protect the general habitat and leave the view largely intact. The resource implications of the construction and the use of the dwellings may be influenced by regulations that control the construction, materials and design. Such regulations amount to restrictions on, and clarifications of, the bundle of property rights associated with the ownership and development of the land. The implementation of regulations, through land-use planning and building controls, that moderate property rights is but one approach to resource allocation that is sensitive to environmental considerations. A more complete set of institutional arrangements and policy instruments suggested by environmental economics is considered in the next section.

Environmental strategies

Environmental economics texts have suggested a variety of instruments that might be used to achieve environmental objectives, and these instruments may be classified in a variety of ways. Hanley *et al.* (1997) consider 'economic incentives for environmental protection', including price-rationing using taxes and subsidies, quantity-rationing using marketable permits, and liability rules with financial penalties for non-compliance. Gilpin (2000) contrasts direct regulation through laws and regulations with the use of economic instruments such as taxes and subsidies which may achieve more efficient outcomes than direct regulation. Field (1994) distinguishes between 'incentive-based strategies' which use taxes, subsidies and transferable permits, 'command and control strategies' that apply standards, and 'decentralized policies' that encourage negotiated solutions by the affected parties within a framework of liability laws and property rights. It will be useful to examine the key features of these alternative strategies and to consider how land-use planning provides an approach that is compatible with, or in contrast to, the various approaches.

Financial incentives

Incentives in the form of taxes and subsidies aim to change behaviour so that the costs of damage to the environment, or the benefits of a lack of damage, become factors that producers and/or consumers take into account in their economic decisions. Emission charges, for example, are a tax on polluters levied at amounts per unit of effluent discharged. Thus toxic gases pumped into the atmosphere or waste discharged into a river would be measured and priced, and the price should ideally reflect the damage the pollution will cause. The producer is free to react to the tax in any way that is chosen. There might be a reduction in production of the item that produces the waste, or instead of using the river as a waste disposal facility the firm may arrange for the pollutants to be carted away to a more acceptable dumping place or new technologies may be employed to treat the waste so that it is no longer toxic and no longer attracts a tax as it flows into the river. The subsidy approach would offer the firm a grant, tax break or cheap loan to install new technologies to avoid producing the pollutant or provide some form of detoxification. Whether a 'polluter must pay' approach is adopted and taxes are levied or the community bears the cost through a subsidy, the outcome may be similar. That is, there will be less pollution than before. However, there may still be some pollution; the tax/subsidy approach does not necessarily aim to reduce pollution to zero, rather it attempts to achieve an optimal level of pollution. This means that the costs and the benefits of the pollution-causing activity are considered.

An alternative to emission charges that target the discharge of pollutants is product charges that take the form of fees or taxes levied on outputs or inputs that are potentially hazardous. The aim is to encourage producers and consumers to substitute more environmentally safe products or inputs. Product charges can be used when a tax on emission is impractical or costly to implement. For example, since March 2001, newly registered cars in the UK have been taxed according to the vehicle's carbon dioxide emission figure. The annual Vehicle Excise Duty (VED) varies according to the CO_2 emissions and the type of fuel that the car uses. Each make is allocated to one of four emission bands according to the grammes of carbon dioxide emitted per kilometre travelled. This approach is clearly more practical than having a device in each car that continually measures the output and attracts a tax bill with complicated collection requirements. The CO_2-related system of VED raises the price of running a more heavily polluting car relative to that of a less polluting car.

One can imagine taxes being used as an alternative to planning regulations in controlling the density at which a site is developed. A profit-maximizing housebuilder will wish to develop a site until the additional benefits of housebuilding, reflected in the revenue received from sales, is equal to the additional costs of housebuilding. If extra houses on a site are expected to add more to revenue than to costs they will be built. If they are expected to add more to costs than to revenue they will not be built. If extra dwellings impose environmental costs associated, for example, with less wildlife or more road congestion, these external costs when added to the housebuilder's private costs equal the social costs of housebuilding. If the external costs can be estimated they may, in the form of taxes, be reflected in the housebuilder's costs. The tax should ideally reflect the external costs of each extra dwelling on a site; the total cost might be small at low numbers of dwellings but bigger with a larger number of dwellings. The taxation ideally encourages the housebuilder to restrict the number of dwellings on a site to a socially optimal number, where the social costs of development equal the social benefits of development (see Figure 5.1).

Financial incentives may be linked to liability rules, which entice producers to follow acceptable practices: 'Liability rules attempt to reduce the level of shirking on environment pollution control by raising the costs of misbehaviour' (Hanley *et al.*, 1997, p. 79). Incentives can take the form of non-compliance fees, performance bonds and deposit refunds. Non-compliance fees fine a producer if his or her actions lead to a level of pollution that exceeds a set standard. For example, noise on a construction site below a given decibel level for a given number of hours or in specific time periods may attract no fine at all, but on exceeding the thresholds that have been set constructors may become liable for heavy fines.

Performance bonds involve payments made by producers before activities commence, with the value of the bond depending on the potential environmental damage of the producer's actions. The potential damage therefore has to be evaluated in advance. If the damage does not materialize, or does not materialize in full, the producer at some future specified time is reimbursed. The burden of proof for the scale of damage rests with the producer rather than society. Rather than taking legal action to prove the producer was liable for damages, the producer must prove that no environmental hazards have occurred to avoid forfeiting the bond. For example, a developer seeking to build houses on a site with environmentally valuable habitats might thus post a bond on the granting of planning permission and redeem this bond after the completion of the project as long as the habitat is still intact. Performance bonds might also be used to ensure that agreed materials are recycled or disposed of in acceptable ways. In principle, bonds offer the opportunity for flexibility with respect

Figure 5.1 *The socially-optimum number of dwellings on a site*

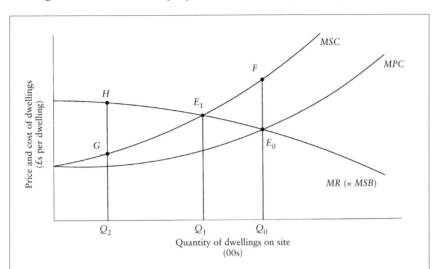

MR = marginal revenue (extra revenue from selling one more house)
MPC = marginal private cost
MSC = marginal social cost
MSB = marginal social benefit

The private-profit-maximizing volume of dwellings on the site is Q_0 where $MR = MPC$. MR slopes downwards on the assumption that the greater the number of dwellings on the site the lower the price at which they will sell. MPC slopes upwards on the assumption that the extra costs of production rises due to site constraints. Production greater than Q_0 is unprofitable because it adds more to costs than to revenue.

If dwellings built on the site produce environmental effects that impose an external cost (e.g. wildlife is diminished and/or local road congestion increases) MSC is greater than MPC. With these external costs considered, the socially-optimal number of dwellings on the site is Q_1 where $MSC = MSB$. (There are external costs at Q_1 but the marginal costs to society – including external costs – are balanced by the marginal benefits to society.)

It is assumed that the social benefit of the houses is fully reflected in the MR. There are thus no external benefits from the dwellings and $MR = MSB$. If the number of dwellings on the site is Q_0 rather than Q_1, there is a net cost to society equal to the area $E_1 F E_0$. If the external costs are known in advance of development, a tax equal to this cost could be imposed on the developer so that MSC represents the developer's post-tax MPC. The imposition of the tax should thus achieve output level Q_1.

Alternatively, if this optimum output level Q_1 is determined in advance of development, a planning regulation may simply determine that Q_1 is the maximum number of dwellings that may be built on the site. If the regulation was too severe and restricted output to Q_2, housing equal in volume to $Q_1 - Q_2$, where $MSB > MSC$, would not be built and net benefits to society equal to the area $H E_1 G$ would be forgone.

A complete elimination of the externality would mean no housebuilding at all on the site. The diagram emphasizes the point that an environmental economics approach involves a balance between MSC and MSB rather than an elimination of external costs.

to the specific circumstances of a development. They do, however, require that the potential hazards can be identified and valued in advance of the development.

Deposit refund systems require that the purchasers of potentially polluting products pay a surcharge that is refunded when the product or its container is returned to an approved depository for recycling or disposal.

Lafferty and Meadowcroft (2000, pp. 381–4) suggest that there is a growing recognition in advanced economies that a varied portfolio of instruments must be deployed to tackle environmental problems, and there has been growing interest in tax-based policy instruments. They point to cautious steps to extend environmental taxes and changes and suggest that the Netherlands, Sweden and Norway have led the way in introducing new forms of environmental taxation. These include water effluent charges, hazardous-waste fees and sulphur emissions and pesticides taxes.

Transferable permits

Transferable permits create new property rights. The holder has the right to emit a specific quantity of pollutant, and permits that allow a total volume of emissions within a region are distributed to all producers in the region. The permits can be traded so that a market in permits will exist between producers. The aim is that the total permits issued in a region should allow a pollution level below the current level of emissions. The scarcity of permits creates an incentive to reduce emission levels and an incentive to trade. Producers in receipt of permits that allow less than current emission levels have three choices. They can take actions that reduce their level of pollution to that allowed by the permit; they can buy more permits to allow their current level to be maintained or exceeded; or they can reduce emissions below that allowed by their permit and sell the surplus permit capacity to another producer. The total effect of the permits will be a reduction in pollution but the distribution of the reduction will depend on the actions of the producers. Hanley *et al.* (1997, p. 136) suggest that the USA has made more use of tradeable permits for the control of pollution than any other country. They show, for example, how sulphur emission permits have been used in the pursuit of clean-air policies, suggesting that marketable permits facilitate market solutions:

> Regulators must however have sufficient knowledge to design the market. This includes knowing how to establish the time frame of

the permits, such as weekly or monthly; knowing the kinds of information required to allocate permits efficiently and fairly; knowing how monitoring data will be obtained and tested; and knowing what the inspection schedule should be. (Ibid., p. 88)

Transferable permits for pollution control are paralleled in the USA by the use of Transferable Development Rights (TDR) initiatives as land-use planning tools. In America development rights rest first and foremost with individual owners rather than the central state, as is the case in the UK (this contrast is examined further in Chapter 10). TDR programmes, which are used in a variety of forms by communities in the USA to restrict growth in some areas and encourage it in others, sever the development potential of a site from its title and make it transferable to another location. The owner of a site in a transfer area retains property ownership but not the right to develop. The owner of a site in a receiving area may purchase transferable development rights which allow development at a higher density than without TDR. The preservation of farmland and areas of natural beauty have been promoted by shifting development to urban locations by local governments promoting TDRs. The authorities designate 'sending areas' and 'receiving areas' and specify development incentives for purchasers in receiving areas.

Whilst TDRs have been successful in many parts of the USA, they have sometimes been impeded by obstacles that include (1) lack of public support for higher-density development in receiving areas, and (2) difficulties in calibrating values for development rights in sending and receiving areas to insure a market for the rights (Lane, 1998). An analysis of the potential for marketable development rights to improve the preservation of American farmland and open-space is provided by Thorsnes and Simons (1999). The arguments about transferable and marketable development rights are taken up in context of a public-choice perspective of planning in Chapter 6.

Standards

All economic incentives to promote environmental objectives require 'an adequate information base and administrative capacity; a strong legal structure; competitive markets; administrative capacity; and political flexibility' (Hanley *et al.*, p. 95). Without feasible valuations of environmental hazards, and the costs of reducing these hazards, markets will not be moderated in ways that promote efficient solutions to environmental improvements. Direct regulation that applies standards through the application of laws and regulations is the most common method for implementing environmental policy. This is the approach that has been called the 'command and control' strategy in the USA. Three types of standard can be identified: ambient, emission and technology.

Ambient standards set targets in respect of the receiving environment. These might, for example, set limits on the maximum concentration of sulphur dioxide in the atmosphere, maximum levels of noise, or maximum concentrations of nitrates in drinking water. Emission standards set limits on the quantities of emissions that may be discharged into the environment. For example, in the UK the 'MOT test', required annually for cars over three years old, checks the roadworthiness and the hydrocarbon and carbon monoxide emissions from the vehicle. If the emissions exceed prescribed limits, the vehicle fails the test and may not legally be driven on public roads. Emission standards are a type of performance standard that require a given result to be achieved. Technological standards require that specified equipment or practices are in place to prevent pollution. Thus the requirement that cars have efficient exhaust systems and catalytic converters is a technological standard.

The standards set are ultimately determined through political and administrative processes. Standards change over time as knowledge about the consequences of pollutants and the technical means to influence these levels changes. To be effective, standards have to be policed and enforced, which involves costs, which must be justified in terms of the environmental benefits. Much of the environmental economics literature argues that because of the bluntness of their operation, and the problems of balancing costs with benefits, standards are an inefficient environmental policy instrument.

Standards can be seen to have an all-or-nothing quality. If they are not met the implication is that they should be, regardless of the cost. If they are met, the implication is that it is not necessary to do better even though the cost of improvement may be low (Field, 1994, pp. 211–25). Standards have to be set and enforced by governments.

Decentralized approaches

A more decentralized approach involves governments setting a framework and then allowing individuals who are party to pollution to find their own solutions. One approach is to use liability laws that make polluters pay compensation to those who are adversely affected by their actions. The purposes of liability laws are to dissuade would-be polluters from adverse actions and to give affected parties a right to sue for compensation if pollution occurs. In simple cases where, for example, one firm dumps toxic waste in a river and another firm is prevented from using clean water in production processes, the liability laws may work well. The two parties reach an agreement within the given framework of law. When many parties are involved, as for example when aircraft noise adversely affects thousands of households in the vicinity of an airport, the high transaction costs and the difficult practicalities of civil agreements between polluters and households makes such an approach unfeasible. This approach is thus of limited value:

> We may rely on private liability arrangements to identify efficient pollution levels when relatively few people are involved, causal linkages are clear, and damages are easy to measure. These conditions may be met in some localized cases of pollution, but for most cases of environmental externalities they are not. (Field, 1994, p. 194)

A decentralized approach can in principle mean that governments specify clear property rights and then stand back and let individual firms and households work things out for themselves. In specifying property rights, governments need to ensure that rights do not conflict. Firm A cannot have a right to dump toxic waste into a river and firm B have a right to use clean water downstream of firm A's dumping. However, if either firm A has a right to dump waste or firm B has a right to use clean water, a privately bargained solution may be possible. B might be willing to make a payment to A to compensate A for a reduction in its right to dump waste. Alternatively, A might pay B for a loss of B's right to clean water. The solution might not be 'zero dumping' or 'maximum dumping', but some negotiated position between the two with money changing hands between A and B. The direction of payment and how much is paid depends on the initial distribution of property rights, and the values to A and B of dumping and clean water. According to the 'Coase theorem', (see also chapter 4) clearly defined property rights over environmental assets with bargaining among owners and users will result in efficient levels of effluent irrespective of the initial distribution of rights (Coase, 1960). The implication of the Coase approach is that 'By defining private property rights (not necessarily individual property rights because private *groups* of people could have these rights), we can establish the conditions under which decentralized bargaining can produce efficient levels of environmental quality' (Field, 1994, p.

197). The Coase approach has had much appeal amongst market-orientated economists and politicians. Its appeal lies in the non-bureaucratic decision-making process that follows from the initial specification of policy rights and the idea that policy-makers can keep clear of the detail of the costs and benefits of alternative outcomes. Indeed, the outcome will be determined by the interested parties and not by governments.

However, this approach will, in practice, face a number of difficulties. For a property rights and bargaining approach to work three main conditions (ibid.) must be met:

1   Property rights must be well-defined, enforceable and transferable.
2   There must be a reasonably efficient and competitive system for interested parties to come together and negotiate about how these environmental property rights will be used.
3   There must be a complete set of markets so that private owners may capture all social values associated with the use of an environmental asset.

These conditions will not hold other than in very simple circumstances. Environmental externalities can involve many parties: dozens of firms dumping waste into a river and dozens wanting to use clean water, not just A and B. The parties to pollution may be in different countries: power stations in one country can damage air quality in several other countries. Or, more fundamentally, those suffering the adverse effects of pollution may not be born yet. Whilst one can postulate complex bargaining arrangements between many parties and countries to engage in environmental treaties, negotiating with future generations stretches the imagination somewhat. Even in the feasible circumstances, negotiation costs may be very high. Property rights that capture the complexities of time, space and natural habitats present imponderable intellectual and practical challenges.

Whilst the decentralized Coasian bargaining solution may have limited practical application, clear specification of property rights will be an essential adjunct to incentive and regulatory strategies. Where property rights can be specified with reasonable precision, this will assist the efficient implementation of taxation and subsidy policy and the clear definition and enforcement of standards. Clearly defined and enforceable property rights are an important facet of effective land-use planning approaches to environmental externalities. This point will be elaborated once some measurement issues have been set out, which is our task in the next section.

Valuation, time and the precautionary principle

If an environmental strategy is to involve economic incentives such as taxes and subsidies that will change behaviour in ways that provide environmental benefits, valuation of environmental costs and environmental benefits is necessary. Given that there are typically no markets in items to which the costs and benefits are attached, monetary valuations are difficult. The costs of atmospheric pollution, the loss of natural species and the obliteration of views over green landscapes, for example, pose conceptually and practically complex problems. Equally, measuring the value of the benefits of clean air, the preservation of natural species and the retention of scenic views set arduous conundrums about the valuation of intangible items.

When an item is traded in a market, the price offered gives a starting point for measuring the value placed on it by the consumer. In fact, if I pay £30 for a new shirt, my valuation of the shirt might well be £40. My maximum willingness to pay (WTP) is £40 and by buying it at £30 I get £10 worth of 'consumer surplus'. Given that a view over the hills in a national park is not for sale, I cannot even offer a payment and far less determine my maximum willingness to pay. By enjoying the view I do not necessarily spoil it for other people. Thus it is not just what I might pay but what many thousands or millions of others might pay that is relevant to the value of the view. Furthermore, millions of those who might enjoy the view are yet to be born. How can we estimate how future generations might value a view which once destroyed cannot be recreated? If we conclude that the value of all pleasant views is infinite because of the millions who may benefit now and in the future, we might argue to stop all development that destroys pleasant views unless we can argue that the benefits of the development are also infinite. Despite the problems, if some balance is to be achieved between alternative courses of action, some sort of valuation of environmental costs and benefits must be undertaken.

A range of techniques for valuing environmental factors have been developed, from direct methods that seek to infer individual preferences for environmental features by asking people questions about what they might do in hypothetical situations to indirect methods that seek estimates of WTP by observing behaviour in related markets (Hanley *et al.*, 1997, pp. 383–424). Both techniques are applied within the framework of cost–benefit analysis (CBA) that attempts to value and compare the costs and the benefits to society of alternative courses of action (Gilpin, 2000, pp. 173–98).

The principal direct method employs the contingent valuation method (CVM) to value environmental goods. Surveys seek to ascertain an individual's maximum WTP for an improvement in environmental quality or their minimum willingness to accept compensation (WTAC), which may be quite different, to forgo such an increase or accept a reduction in environmental quality. Hanley *et al.* (1997, p. 386) split a CVM exercise into five stages: (1) setting up a hypothetical market, (2) obtaining bids, (3) estimating mean WTP and/or WTAC, (4) estimating bid curves, and (5) aggregating the data.

The first stage involves describing a proposal to respondents, stating how it will be financed and how a decision will be made. The relevant population might, for example, be told that a new housing development in countryside near them is planned and the effects of the development on the local environment would be described. In the second stage, interviews are conducted to ask either how much people would be prepared to pay to prevent the change (WTP), or how much compensation they would require to accept the change (WTAC). The third, fourth and fifth stages involve a systematic analysis of the responses to arrive at an aggregated value that represents the affected population. A large volume of complex theory and application has developed around CVM which has been used in America and Europe for estimating the value of a wide range of environmental factors including forests, waterways, noise and atmospheric quality. Hanley *et al.* (pp. 383–424) examine both the advantages and the pitfalls of the approach.

A major problem with the approach is that people may find it difficult to both realistically imagine the proposed change in advance of its implementation, and to honestly assign values to a WTP or WTAC. Their values will be influenced by their understanding of the change, their experience of similar changes, their income levels and whether they really expect to pay or receive compensation. Identifying the relevant population to question is also highly problematic. Should just local residents whose environment will be changed be questioned, or should visitors now and in the future also be questioned? How will this wider population be identified? Such problems lead some economists to prefer indirect methods of valuation that infer values from behaviour in related markets. For example, travel costs have been used as a proxy for the value of recreational sites such as forests and national parks (see for example the review in Fletcher *et al.*, 1990), and Willis and Garrod (1991) have used the method to obtain estimates of the consumer's surplus for UK forests.

Values for environmental characteristics may also be inferred by the use of hedonic pricing (Hanley *et al.*, 1997, pp. 411–16). That technique attempts to explain the value of a commodity as the sum of the value of the bundle of characteristics that make up that commodity (see Chapter 2). It has, in particular, been applied to housing where the individual features of the house (for example number of bedrooms, terraced or detached) and the neighbourhood (for example proximity to shops, crime rates, proximity to country-side) are seen to contribute specific sums to the overall value for which the property might be exchanged.

A large volume of data on the prices at which houses have been sold and the characteristics of these dwellings and their neighbour-hoods is needed to estimate the hedonic prices of the diverse attrib-utes that contribute to value. By inferring the additional amounts that consumers are prepared to pay for houses in environmentally desirable locations (for example nearness to public parks), we may assign values to the benefits derived from the environmental factor. In this way hedonic pricing has been used widely to estimate the impact of the environment on house prices. For example, Smith and Huang (1993) reviewed 37 studies of the impact of air pollution on house prices, and the effect of noise on property prices has been esti-mated by several studies (O'Byrne *et al.*, 1985). Whilst a great deal of sophistication has developed in the statistical methods that accompany hedonic pricing, isolating the effect on property prices of single environmental variables remains extremely difficult. Even if we do obtain estimates that appear reliable, we will know only how house purchasers over a given period of time value some environ-mental factors. Also, the relevant population may include many who do not own dwellings in the vicinity, since it is not only those who own houses near a park that may value its benefits.

If by some direct or indirect method of valuation estimates of environmental costs and benefits of development are obtained, they will need to be placed within a wider cost–benefit framework that compares the benefits to society with the costs to society of the proposal. Thus, for example, the benefits of the flow of services provided by new housing need to be viewed broadly. The positive impact of the new housing on health, crime, employment levels and income generation may be estimated as well as any detrimental envi-ronmental effects. Cost–benefit analysis may attempt to measure the external costs and benefits to society of new housing, including envi-ronmental effects, as well as the private costs and benefits that impact on the firms involved in development and the households that occupy the housing. There are no hard and fast rules about what costs and benefits to include, just as there are no conclusive rules about how to value the items. There is thus an inevitable element of judgement involved, and it has been argued that

> The hope that CBA provided a method by which all the conflict-
> ing values involved in environmental decision-making could be
> transformed into commensurable numbers and slotted into a
> universal calculus must be disappointed. It is now clear that, even
> though some environmental goods may be valued in money terms,
> many of the most important are not commensurable in this way.
> Effects of irreplaceable and large-scale environmental goods, like
> those on human life, must be judged directly . . . there can be no
> mathematical short-cut to the "correct" solution . . . ultimately
> such choices must be a matter of judgement, not computation.
> (Jacobs, 1991, p. 219, quoted in Gilpin, 2000, p. 180)

A cost–benefit approach accepts that a development will result in a flow of costs and benefits over time. Some of the costs and bene-fits will accrue many years into the future, but need to be expressed in terms of their present value. Thus future costs and benefits need to be discounted at some rate that reflects the fact that future values are different from values experienced now. The net present value (NPV) to society of the development may thus be estimated by taking account of the streams of costs and benefits over time. If the NPV is positive, the development might be deemed to be a worth-while investment.

The present value of a sum to be received (or a cost to be incurred) in the future is the amount that will with compound interest equal the future sum. Thus:

$$PV = \frac{1}{(1 + i)^n}$$

where PV = present value, i = the discount rate and n = the number of years.

For example, if i = 5 per cent, the value now of £1,000 to be received in five years' time is £784. The value of £1,000 to be received in 50 years' time is £87. If a higher discount rate is used so that i = 15 per cent, the value of £1,000 to be received in five years' time is £497 and the value of £1,000 to be received in 50 years' time is only £1.

Thus the higher the discount rate, the less we value costs and benefits to be paid and received in the future; and the further we look ahead, the lower the values we assign to the future costs and benefits. High discount rates may thus disadvantage future generations and we may tend to undervalue the costs and the benefits received some distance into the future. So, for example, if a development is expected to result in environmental damage in say 30 or 40 years' time, this cost may be of little significance compared with the benefits to be obtained over the next five years.

The discount rate that is chosen is thus crucial. There is, however, no agreed single rule governing how the discount rate should be determined, although there are two main schools of thought. One favours the social rate of time preference, corresponding to society's preference for present as against future consumption. Another favours the social opportunity cost of capital, corresponding to the rate of return elsewhere in the economy (Gilpin, 2000, pp. 180–4).

Low rates of discount may favour future generations in that they will bear lower costs. Summers (1993) has, however, argued that there is no sound case for tackling environmental issues by using abnormally low discount rates. It is suggested that 'We can help our descendants as much by improving infrastructure as by preserving rainforests, as much by educating children as leaving oil in the ground, as much by enlarging scientific knowledge as by reducing carbon dioxide in the air' (quoted in Gilpin, 2000, p. 184). If we can, however, improve infrastructure and educate children whilst still preserving rainforests and leaving some oil in the ground, we might enhance the well-being of present and future generations.

There may be a temptation to undervalue the future costs and benefits on the grounds that we do not know what the future holds in terms of scientific developments and technological advances. In some cases, the evidence of the effects of environmental change may be less than certain. To guard against adverse environmental decisions on such grounds, some environmental economists have argued in favour of the 'precautionary principle' which states that 'where there are threats of serious or irreversible damage to the environment, lack of full scientific certainty should not be used as a reason for postponing cost-effective measures to prevent environmental degradation' (Gilpin, 2000, p. 102). It might, for example, be argued that the exact relationship between carbon dioxide emissions and global warming has not been specified in precise detail even though some general cause and effect relationship is generally accepted. The argument for reducing carbon dioxide emissions before uncertainty is removed and precise relationships are specified is essentially that the costs of inaction may be higher than preventative action given the possible irreversibility of the environmental consequences.

Sustainable development

In the last 20 years it has become fashionable to argue that good development is 'sustainable', and that on a worldwide, national and local basis governments should promote 'sustainable development'. Despite several authoritative attempts at definition, there is much confusion over what sustainable development means and what actions are necessary to promote it. The starting point of many discussions of the concept is the often-quoted definition in the Brundtland Report: 'Sustainable development is development that meets the needs of the present without compromising the ability of future generations to meet their own needs' (WCED, 1987, p. 49). Blowers (1993, p. 5) suggests that 'There has been a tendency to use sustainable development as a device for mobilizing opinion rather than an analytical concept for developing specific policies'. Cullingworth and Nadin (2002, p. 198) suggest that 'Sustainability and sustainable development are not capable of precise scientific definition. They are instead social and political constructs used as a call to action but with little in the way of practical guidance'.

In an attempt to expand on the basic definition, Blowers (1993, p. 6) suggested that sustainable development is intended 'To promote development that enhances the natural and built environment in ways that are compatible with:

(1)   The requirement to conserve the stock of natural assets, whenever possible offsetting any unavoidable reduction by a compensating increase so that the total is left undiminished.
(2)   The need to avoid damaging the regenerative capacity of the world's natural ecosystems.
(3)   The need to achieve greater social equality.
(4)   The avoidance of the imposition of added costs or risks on succeeding generations.'

The goals of sustainable development are then seen as:

1   *Resource conservation*: to ensure the supply of natural resources for present and future generations through the efficient use of land, less wasteful use of non-reusable resources, their substitution by renewable resources wherever possible, and the maintenance of biological diversity.
2   *Built-environment quality*: to ensure that the development and use of the built environment respects and is in harmony with the

natural environment, and that the relationship between the two is designed to be one of balance and mutual enhancement.

3 *Environmental quality*: to prevent or reduce processes that degrade or pollute the environment, to protect the regenerative capacity of ecosystems, and to prevent developments that are detrimental to human health or that diminish the quality of life.

4. *Social equality*: to prevent any development that increases the gap between rich and poor and to encourage development that reduces social inequality.

5. *Political participation*: to change values, attitudes and behaviour by encouraging increased participation in political decision-making and in initiating environmental improvements at all levels from the local community upwards. (Ibid., pp. 6–8)

The inclusion of social equality and political participation goals in the sustainable development agenda widens the perspective significantly beyond a concern with the natural environment. This is, however, in line with the approach of the Brundtland Report (WCED, 1987) in linking poverty and environmental degradation in developing countries. Protecting environmental resources might thus mean that some redistribution of resources in favour of poorer countries was necessary in order to ensure that present needs in poorer countries were satisfied even though their natural resources were not exploited to maximum potential. Such maximum exploitation might be to meet demands in richer nations.

Hanley *et al.* (1997) argue that 'Within the field of environmental economics, it is now widely recognized that the goal of sustainable development is principally an equity, rather than an efficiency issue' (p. 425). They suggest that achieving sustainable development involves achieving equity both within and across generations. The promotion of both intra-generational and inter-generational equity involves redistributive judgements that provide challenges to political systems that are concerned only with a current localized national constituency. Given the international dimensions to the need for coordinated environmental and distributive policies, it has been suggested that 'The sovereign power of the nation-state appears to be a major obstacle to sustainable development' (Blowers, 1993, p. 13).

The most significant environmental policy initiatives have, in fact, involved international agreements. The UN Conference on Environment and Development (UNCED) in 1992, which is usually known as the Rio Summit, was a landmark event. From this came 'Agenda 21' which set out a comprehensive worldwide programme for sustainable development in the twenty-first century (Cullingworth and Nadin, 2002, pp. 200–7). The UK government has responded with a series of policy statements, noteably *Sustainable Development: The UK Strategy* (1994) (CM2426) and *A Better Quality of Life: A Strategy for Sustainable Development in the United Kingdom* (1999) (CM4345).

The 1999 strategy sets four main objectives: social progress, protection of the environment, prudent use of natural resources and maintenance of high levels of economic growth. A total of 147 sustainable development indicators are identified, a baseline position established and a commitment to ongoing monitoring established. Through 'Local Agenda 21', each local authority has been required to prepare and implement a local sustainable development strategy.

The policies and directives of the European Union (EU) have been highly influential in determining environmental action taken in the UK. The 1987 Amsterdam Treaty made sustainable development a fundamental objective of the EU and there is an ongoing commitment to ensure there is environmental appraisal of community initiatives. EU directives give particular prominence to spatial planning as an instrument to promote sustainable development (see Cullingworth and Nadin, 2002, pp. 208–10).

Environmental assessment of significant proposed developments is now an established aspect of land-use planning in Europe, as a consequence of European Union directives (see Rydin, 2003, pp. 115–33 and 227–52, and Cullingworth and Nadin, 2002, pp. 221–3). Environmental Impact Assessment (EIA) is required for specified large projects, for some projects in environmentally sensitive locations and some projects that may have potentially adverse environmental effects. The process involves providing detailed evidence on the potential environmental consequences of a development, and the planning authority has regard for this evidence in considering relevant planning applications. As a consequence of an EU directive which extends environmental assessment to 'plans and programmes', Strategic Environmental Assessment (SEA) procedures are to be adopted by all member states. These procedures will involve the preparation of an environmental report on development plans and statements on how environmental concerns have been addressed within the plan.

Sustainable development is now a recognized objective throughout the world. The American Planning Association has argued that the objectives need to be taken more seriously in the USA, arguing that:

Most Americans consume wastefully, using our limited resources inefficiently and inequitably. People need to acknowledge that we are an interconnected part of nature. Policies and actions must reflect the important linkages among a healthy environment, a strong economy and social well being. (APA, 2000)

Environmentally and socially destructive residential development especially suburban sprawl is seen as a key component of the problem. The shift in favour of more compact development that APA urges is consistent with the urban renaissance agenda which is discussed in Chapter 9.

Whilst planning systems are changing in an attempt to reflect environmental concerns, discussions of housing policy issues typically avoid the environmental agenda. It has been suggested that

Recent housing debates, in Britain at least, have remained silent on issues of environmental sustainability . . . but . . . ecological thinking forces us to look at housing historically, and pose the question of what role the individual, market institutions and the state can play in minimizing negative impacts. (Bhatti, 2001, pp. 39–40)

If sustainable residential development is to meet the needs of the present without compromizing the needs of future generations, and if it is to be compatible with the environmental and social objectives of sustainable development, it must indeed be viewed holistically. Residential development must be seen as related to economic, social and environmental processes.

An environmental economics perspective on sustainable residential development confirms the need for some form of planning to achieve societal objectives. It also suggests a range of policy instruments that might be integrated with a land-use planning approach to promote these objectives.

Conclusions

By identifying environmental issues as specific forms of market failure and viewing environmental costs and benefits as particular types of externalities, environmental economics provides a clear case for some sort of governmental response. In the broadest sense of the term 'planning', it shows that some form of planning is necessary. Environmental economics offers property rights and pricing ideas that might be a part of the planning process.

Redefinitions of existing property rights such that environmental hazards are restricted might be complemented by planning permissions that carefully define the rights to use land and property in ways that protect environmental interests. The limitation of a right to develop might be totally restrictive, as, for example, in prohibiting a development where species of flora and fauna are endangered. Alternatively, a limitation might be conditional, and in such cases an evaluation of the consequences of the development for flora and fauna would have to be balanced with an evaluation of the benefits of the development. A right to build houses might also be conditional on the specification of the building materials used, the source of the materials and the 'environmental performance', including the energy efficiency of completed dwellings. Restrictions might extend to the construction process, including matters related to waste disposal, the generation of noise and traffic from the site, and the timing of the work.

Whilst many such restrictions are already in operation, a more radical set of changes would involve a larger role for financial incentives and the price mechanism in promoting environmental objectives. The use of non-compliance fees, performance bonds and deposit refunds in influencing the behaviour of developers offers new methods for achieving environmentally beneficial development.

More explicit use of monetary valuations in the environmental impact not just of individual developments but of the planned development of towns and regions offers an improved information base on which to judge the merits of development and of alternative forms of development. It is a more holistic evaluation of the proposed location and interactions of residential development over a period of time that offers the most significant opportunity for improved environmental evaluation. Clearly some patterns of development generate more traffic, use more energy and have bigger impacts on the countryside than others. We do, however, lack explicit evaluations of the social costs and benefits, including the environmental consequences of alternative future patterns of developments. There has nevertheless been a growing preference for more compact development with more housing developed on brownfield sites. This has been coupled with arguments for an urban renaissance with an improved quality of urban living and higher density development. Environmental arguments have been to the fore in promoting this agenda, which we address in Chapter 9.

Chapter 6

Public Choice Theory, Planning and Housing

In answer to the question 'why do we need planning?', earlier chapters have argued that planning is needed as a response to the failure of markets to achieve specified efficiency and equity objectives. Markets may, at varying levels of complexity, fail to deal with incompatible proximate land uses, inadequate poor-quality housing, the provision of parks and open spaces, environmental pollution and the preservation of endangered species. A possible reaction in each case is to conclude that some form of land-use planning is necessary. Support for planning from this market failure viewpoint can be termed the 'liberal interventionist' perspective. In this chapter we recapitulate the basic tenants of this perspective and examine the challenges posed by the contrasting 'public choice theorists' view of the world.

It will be shown that public choice theory raises a series of important questions about the ability of land-use planning to respond efficiently to market failure. Public choice theorists have argued that public-sector planners do not have the information to make choices that will compensate appropriately for market failures. Furthermore, they do not have the motivation to act in the broad public interest – they will, rather, follow narrower self-interest objectives. The costs of planning will not necessarily outweigh the benefits, especially when the failures of the public sector are set against the failures of the market. Public choice theory has been used to develop a so-called 'positive theory of planning', the conclusions of which we shall summarize. The chapter will explore ideas for changes in planning that emanate from the public choice school of thought, focusing on bringing market principles to bear more directly on the allocation of land and the resolution of land-use disputes, but also including a case for 'private land-use planning' (Pennington, 2002a, 2002b). It will also be shown that public choice theory can be applied to an evaluation of the processes of housing policy, and the implications of such an approach will be examined. The challenges of public choice theory will be reviewed and the strengths and weaknesses of the perspective evaluated.

The liberal interventionist perspective

The liberal interventionist perspective starts from an assumption that markets work well in determining the production and consumption of a wide range of goods and services. They fail, however, to deal satisfactorily with the production and allocation of specific goods and services because of a given distribution of income and wealth. This failure can be compensated by various forms of government activity, including some form of land-use planning, and there is potential for the net effect of this government activity to improve well-being. Public choice theorists, in contrast, argue that the effect of government activity is likely to make things worse, and that the so-called failures of markets can be addressed by encouraging markets to work better rather than replacing them by government activity such as land-use planning.

Liberal interventionists take a comparatively benign view of the activity of governments. They assume that both central and local governments have the desire and the potential to improve welfare and that a land-use planning system, as part of the overall activity of governments, can usefully address some market failures. The principal market failures that a planning system is expected to address are 'externalities' and 'public goods'. As explained in Chapters 3 and 4, the inability of markets to take account of external costs and benefits and to allocate optimum levels of resources to the provision of public goods results, arguably, in inefficient outcomes if markets are left to their own devices. Inefficiencies, according to this analysis, arise from the failure of individual decision-makers (such as housebuilders or households) to take account of the impact of their actions on the welfare of others who do not trade directly in the markets in which they express their demands. Thus housebuilders in an uncontrolled market will not be concerned about the impact of development on road congestion or the need for school places as long as these do not unduly reduce the price at which they can sell houses. The wider and longer-term impacts on the environment such as the loss of amenity from greenfields or the increased energy costs of dispersed development will, similarly, not necessarily enter the housebuilder's decision-making calculation. On the external benefits side of the coin, the private developer may have no reason to consider the urban regeneration advantages of new housing in run-down areas or the increased revenues for local shops as more housing is built. Through influences on the location and density of housing development, planning can – arguably – seek to reduce external costs and increase benefits, thus bringing about net benefits to the community. By considering the interactions between impacts of new housing, schools, roads and shops, for example, planning can perform a coordinating role that maximizes social benefits.

The dispersed nature of atomistic decision-making in the market-place makes efficient coordination through the market unlikely. The market will (so the liberal interventionist perspective goes) fail to supply optimum quantities of public goods and quasi-public goods such as parks, open spaces and roads because of the absence of an opportunity to sell these goods to individual consumers at prices that reflect their value. Planning therefore tries to ensure an efficient volume and locational distribution of such goods.

Equity and distributional arguments form another set of reasons for government activity. Markets make no judgements about the rights or wrongs of income and wealth distributions; if a lack of adequate financial resources means that households cannot demand housing of some sort of minimum standard, the market outcome is that these households occupy housing below this standard or they are homeless. Governments, if they wish to react to this unmet housing need, may do so in a variety of ways. They might for example decide to redistribute incomes, to subsidize the provision of housing for households on low incomes, or get involved directly in the provision of housing. They might also decide, with or without such measures, to use the land-use planning system to influence the provision of housing for low-income households. The use of the planning system in relation to the provision of so-called 'affordable housing' in England is discussed in Chapter 8 and in a broader international context in Chapter 10.

We may, from a liberal interventionist viewpoint, identify two separate propositions:

1   Planning, as part of a wider system of government activity, has the potential to make people better-off by compensating for the inefficiencies and inequities of a market-determined system of land use; and
2   Planning does in practice make people better-off.

Both of these propositions are challenged by the public choice school of thought.

The challenges of public choice theory

Public choice theorists such as Downs (1957), Buchanan (1968) and Mueller (1989) have challenged the welfare economics that underpins the liberal interventionist perspective, questioning the motivation and competencies of governments and emphasizing the positive aspects of markets. They provide a wide-ranging critique of the role of markets and of the public sector in promoting economic success. They also cross the boundary between economics and politics, applying economic analysis to the operation of government. Other public choice theorists such as Wolf (1987) have categorized and emphasized the idea of 'non-market failures' to parallel the idea of 'market failure'.

Hayek (1948) has provided the inspiration for much of the public choice thinking. Hayek believed that because values and knowledge are subjective and information diffuse and uncertain, government-inspired planning is unlikely to succeed. Planners, he suggested, could never perceive and respond to as many instances of dis-coordination as individuals who have the freedom and motivation to express their desires in the market. In this view the prices at which goods are exchanged in competitive markets are an indication of individual values that cannot be bettered by the judgements of government planners. Government should not and does not need to plan because the market is, according to Hayek, viewed as a form of decentralized social planning.

The major influence on the application of public choice theories to land-use planning has been the work of Coase (1960), whose analysis, in particular, raises the idea of voluntary solutions to externality problems. Efficient bargaining solutions can, according to Coase, in specific cases be reached by the individuals who are party to externalities. Government can facilitate efficient bargaining solutions by establishing a clear system of property rights.

Drawing in particular on the work of Coase, Webster (1998) very usefully draws out five strands of the public choice arguments and their contributions to planning theory:

1   There are major problems in measuring the costs and benefits associated with externalities and public goods. These are by definition unpriced items and there is no completely satisfactory way of measuring their value. As shown in Chapter 5, surrogate willingness-to-pay and contingent valuation approaches have been used to measure the value of environmental attributes but there is no general agreement on the most appropriate methodology. Pennington (2002a, pp. 44–5) argued that:

> from a Hayekian point of view, *none* of the relevant 'experts'
> may know the 'optimal' policy response, because the range of
> interconnected variables that contribute to the quality of
> urban life may be far too complex to rely on in a conscious
> attempt to 'integrate' the land-use system . . . the costs and
> benefits associated with environmental externalities are inher-
> ently subjective. The informational problems of government
> land-use planning . . . stem primarily from the difficulties of
> attributing values to a variety of land-use externalities without
> a competitive market process and the comparative price
> signals that such a process produces. In the absence of such
> prices, attempts to create an 'optimal' mix of land uses are
> likely to be arbitrary, reflecting the subjective valuations of the
> planners concerned.

The impossibility of accurate measurement leads the public
choice school to seek alternative analytical frameworks.

2   Welfare economics emphasizes 'outcome efficiency' at the
    expense of 'process efficiency'. The process of planning will be
    inefficient if the costs of operating planning exceed the gains
    from 'correcting' market failures. The argument is that the costs
    of implementing policy are typically ignored: 'A public choice
    theory of development control would want to extend the search
    for inefficiency to look at the costs of alternative forms of inter-
    vention. This leads to a consideration of transaction costs'
    (Webster, 1998, p. 61).

3   The related point is thus that 'the market failure approach
    assumes zero transaction costs' (ibid.). In reality, of course, there
    may be high private and public costs of planning controls, and
    without the costs of government intervention brought into
    consideration there can be no certainty that resource-allocation
    efficiency has been improved by public actions.

4   Traditional welfare economics assumes static property rights. A
    public choice perspective questions society's preference for alter-
    native property rights and seeks an analysis of the efficiency of
    alternative systems of property rights: 'Public choice analysts
    seek to endogenize the analysis of property rights; to *close the
    system* and to address the question of society's preferences for
    alternative systems of legal use, ownership, compensation and
    betterment rights' (ibid.). A crucial challenge of Coasian and
    other public choice analysis is 'to seek to conceptualize and to
    measure the relative costs of alternative planning constitutions,
    policies and procedures' (ibid.).

5   Welfare economics ignores the welfare-maximising motives of government itself. Public choice theorists argue that inevitable inefficiencies are introduced by the actors in the planning system pursuing their own objectives. As Poulton has stated 'Public choice theory rejects any belief in the altruism or potential altruism of governments' (1991b, p. 266). Pennington claims that planning works in the interests of expansionary bureaucrats and special interest groups who have 'captured' planning to promote their own ends. The special interest groups cited include amenity groups who have sought to prevent development 'in their backyard', and large housebuilders:

> The local amenity lobby is not the only set of special interests to have benefited from the operation of the planning system. Evidence suggests that the corporate housebuilders have also been important beneficiaries. The granting of planning permission confers a *monopoly right* on developers, as other potential development sites are excluded from the market . . . the larger corporate developers prefer a controlled system providing permission to develop their own land while restricting access to development land for potential competitors. (Pennington, 2002a, p. 64)

Without detailing the evidence, Pennington asserts that 'The reality of land-use planning in Britain has often been one of institutional sclerosis and special-interest capture. Benefits have been concentrated on interest groups and bureaucrats with costs dispersed across an invisible mass of taxpayers and consumers' (ibid., p. 71).

A positive theory of planning?

Building on the public choice perspective, Poulton (1991a,b) develops what is termed a 'positive theory of planning'. The starting point is that 'planning theory is lost' and this is largely because it has focused on the wrong questions. It is claimed that a positive theory is needed to explain why planning is the way it is, how it may or may not be used and what the outcomes are likely to be. 'The positive theory that I pursue is based on the axiom of the applicability of individual self-interest in trading-like situations. This axiom underlies mainstream microeconomics and public choice theory' (Poulton, 1991a, pp. 225–6). It follows, according to this premise, that in a democracy 'consumers as voters desire planning insofar as they perceive it as improving their personal well-being; planners, as advisors and administrators, seek to maximize their personal return from employment; and politicians seek to utilize planning as a means to help attain or retain political power' (Poulton, 1991b, p. 266). A series of propositions about how land-use planning will function as a government activity are derived from these assumptions, and the propositions relating to municipal planning include:

1   Planning will seek to protect the quality of existing neighbourhoods and existing residential property values because homeowners are the largest single interest group supporting planning;
2   Planning will be used to general revenue for a municipality to benefit local residents and municipal employees. It will thus be used to attract net revenue-generating activities;
3   Planning will tend to be discretionary, exploiting the bargaining position of the municipality to extract communal benefits from new developments;
4   There will be little interest in long-range planning and it will rather be short term and *ad hoc*. This is because short-range plans tackling specific current problems are more likely to appeal to specific interest groups and politicians who seek to gain popularity;
5   Planning will be consensus building, seeking dialogue with existing interest groups and on controversial issues tend to adopt a value-neutral stance. (Ibid., pp. 267–8).

Whether or not this public choice-orientated 'positive' view of planning reflects reality depends on (a) the extent to which the axiom of self-interest is valid, (b) the extent to which the motivation of self-interest will lead to the outcomes suggested, and (c) the powers, resources and responsibilities that are bestowed upon a local planning system. The axiom of self-interest is based on a particular interpretation of individual behaviour. Poulton suggests that:

> The basic axiom of positive economics is that people act in their roles as consumers, employees, or entrepreneurs to promote or maximize their own welfare. If this axiom of self-interested behaviour of individuals bent on maximising their own welfare holds for economic relations, it would be downright bizarre to hold that it is not true in other bargaining relations. (Ibid., p. 264)

Actually it is somewhat bizarre to suggest a transferability of individual behaviour in markets to collective public behaviour. To reject the axiom of self-interest we have to believe that individuals are capable of acting with something more than their own selfish individual gain as motivation. We have to believe that individuals might just raise their sights to see a perspective that stretches beyond their own narrow horizon. Public sector organizations, be they central government departments or local planning authorities, do not usually function on the bases of individuals making crucial decisions in isolation. Collective decisions are made which seek to achieve some sort of collective, not individual, objective. If individual bureaucrats did seek to maximize their own status or salary within an organization in any appropriately governed organization this would be done by promoting the objectives of the organization as a whole. Thus, if a planning authority does have objectives that do work against some special interest groups, are long-term and don't maximize local revenue, individuals seeking personal reward will work to support these objectives.

The objectives that are pursued through planning depend on the political process within which planning operates. If some form of democracy is in operation it is reasonable to assume that there will be some public support for at least some of the aims and methods. The special-interest capture proposition of public choice theorists is an inevitability only if there is a weakness in political structures that subjugates the wider public interest. Rather than viewing Poulton's 'positive' theory of planning as describing inevitable outcomes, we might more usefully view them as warnings of what might happen if planners were allowed to act according to the axioms suggested. Appropriate governance of a planning system must ensure that the public interest and collective objectives are defined, valued and promoted.

Institutional reforms and property rights

Rather than using public choice theory to emphasize the likely failures of a publicly administered land-use planning system, it is possible to use the theory as a basis for suggesting institutional reforms that will make planning work better. Several constructive ideas have been built on the property-rights propositions of Coase (1960). Coase suggested that the case for the public sector stepping in to resolve externality problems rests on the proposition that individuals cannot resolve external cost disputes efficiently when property rights are ill-defined and the transaction costs of private resolution are high. Voluntary bargaining according to this approach is often costly because resolution will require complex negotiation and then enforcement might require detailed monitoring and policing. Voluntary solutions are more likely to be successful when property rights are clear. Governments should, so the argument goes, seek to structure property rights so that voluntary solutions to externality issues are encouraged. Land uses will not then inevitably be imposed by planning controls. The more voluntary solutions are encouraged, the more efficient land-use allocation will be, because the greater will be the weight of individual evaluations of the costs and benefits of a given configuration of land uses. Following this approach, it has been suggested that a key question which anyone wishing to carry out an economic evaluation of land-use planning has to address is: 'How far does the land-use planning system allow for the possibility of allocative efficiency improvements through voluntary trading in development rights?' (Corkindale, 1999, p. 2060).

Easements and covenants have been suggested as examples of the outcomes of voluntary negotiations:

> Users of land generating nuisance in the form of pollution and so on, might be required to purchase easements from neighbouring land owners, thereby internalising the externality. The neighbouring landowners would be compensated for the loss in the value of their land, and prospective purchasers of the neighbouring land wishing to use it for a purpose which required a cessation of the nuisance-generating activity would have to buy back the easement. Covenants, on the other hand, can be used to register publicly a restriction on the use of land. A party sensitive to the use to which a neighbour might put his or her land could purchase from the second party the right to do what would otherwise be lawful. A party seeking a restrictive covenant would be likely to want it to 'run with the land', that is to be binding on subsequent owners. (Ibid.)

Such arrangements are seen to be compatible with land-use zoning as operated in much of the USA. Within a zone, regulations limit the land uses that are allowed. The ownership of land confers the right to develop, provided that there are no adverse effects on the property rights of others; the right is limited by the law of nuisance and by easements and restrictive covenants. This is not a system of zero planning, rather, it is a different sort of planning in which there is a different distribution of property rights than in the UK, where development rights are nationalized. 'In most US jurisdictions . . . land-development rights are held as private property but the exercise of those rights is subject to regulation by the land-use planning authorities' (Corkindale, 1999, pp. 2060–1). If development rights rest with property owners rather than the state, it follows that these rights might be traded. Corkindale (1999) discusses the use in the USA of transferable development rights (TDRs) and a variant termed the habitat transaction method (HTM). With TDRs, development rights allocated to landowners may either be used by those landowners or sold to others (see also the discussion in Chapter 5). Development is restricted in 'conservation zones' in which TDRs cannot be exercized. With HTM all land can, in principle, be developed but land is classified according to its relative habitat value based on ecological criteria. Land with the highest habitat values is effectively more expensive to develop than land with lower habitat values. TDRs and HTM are in line with the ideas about the application of economic policy instruments in environmental planning that were discussed in Chapter 5.

Pennington (2002a, pp. 78–81) is critical of both options because, in the allocation of permits and the classification of the values of different bundles of land, much power is vested in planners. Pennington wants to see the preferences of individual consumers given more weight than either of these systems allow. It is suggested that this might be done by combining a system of compensation with the auctioning of development rights. The possibility of direct financial compensation for those adversely affected by development would be an incentive for negotiated solutions to disputed development proposals. Local authorities would allocate sites for potential development and sell the rights to the highest bidder which might include those who object to the development. Objectors could thus bid and if their values were greater than the developer's value the land would not be developed. It is claimed that, 'The greatest advantage would be that since people would have the potential to bid for the relevant sites, the resulting land allocations would be more likely to be reflective of consumer preferences' (ibid., p. 83). These preferences as expressed in the market would also, of course, reflect the relative financial resources and organizational abilities of the competing bidders.

Although seeing some merits in auctioning development rights, such a change would not go far enough for Pennington because planners would have to decide which sites should attract bids, and the bulk of development rights would remain with the State. More fundamental changes in property rights would be necessary to achieve more wide-sweeping reforms, leading ultimately to a system of 'private land-use planning'. Changes in property rights would create markets in externalities so obviating the need for further government intervention (ibid., pp. 85–103). Rather than planning and regulating, governments would seek to create systems of property rights that facilitated bargaining solutions and they would promote a legal system that effectively adjudicated disputed property rights. Developers would create restrictive covenants that restricted the use of open space and controlled changes in the local environment. In doing so they would seek to maximize the value of the properties they sold. In deciding where to live, households could choose developments with a given bundle of environmental characteristics preserved in restrictive covenants, as long as they were prepared to pay the enhanced property values. Pennington argues that

> Ultimately, the key to the property rights approach is that a *price must be paid for the exercise of controls over other people's property*. Those who wish to restrict development in order to preserve amenities have to compete directly in the market for land with others who value the land for alternatives uses – and vice versa. (2002a, p. 90)

An elaboration of the restrictive-covenant model is the concept of a 'propriety community' in which people would enter into voluntary contracts to sacrifice complete control over decisions relating to their property to a 'central community landlord'. In a fully privatized system of 'proprietary governance', development rights would be held collectively by all property owners in a given locality that was encompassed by a 'recreation and amenity company'. Development rights would become a form of collective private property rights; all profits and losses attributable to development decisions made by the company would be shared between property owners. It is interesting that ultimately some form of collective decision-making is seen to be necessary, in this case by the board of the company rather than by a planning authority. The driving force behind the decisions of the recreation and amenity company board would, however, be

> the likely effect on community asset prices. Decisions to prevent any development in the locality would be based on knowledge of the *opportunity cost* of such decisions – that is, the forgone financial gains from allowing new developments to proceed. Likewise, decisions to allow inappropriate development and to lower the quality of life within the locality would be taken at the risk of lowering company asset values. (Pennington, 2002a, p. 109)

Institutional reforms of the sort suggested by Corkindale (1999) and Pennington (2002a and 2002b) and founded on the property rights and bargaining analysis of Coase (1960) are intended to internalize externalities by bringing external costs and benefits into the decision-making framework of the affected parties. A major problem with this approach is the practicality of encompassing the relevant externalities on anything other than the smallest of scales. One can imagine two neighbours bargaining with each other over a property extension, but is far more difficult, whatever the configuration of property rights, to imagine the thousands or millions adversely affected by new airports or motorways bargaining with the beneficiaries. It is even more difficult to imagine bargaining with future generations about the environmental pollution generated by more dispersed, rather than less dispersed, patterns of residential development. The notions of self-interest and consumer sovereignty that are attached to private bargaining solutions do, moreover, ignore any problems of income and wealth distributions. It is an ability to demand amenity in the market that drives private-property-rights solutions to environmental issues. This demand, as with all other demands, depends not just on the desire to pay but also on the ability to pay. Issues of principle will stop those who consider equity as well as efficiency to be important from pondering too long the merits of fully privatized development rights before they begin to dwell on the practicalities.

Coasion reforms have been suggested as methods to tackle externality issues. One of the suggestions, auctioning planning permission may, however, have more relevance to tackling the 'betterment' issue that is addressed in Chapter 7. The betterment, or enhanced land value that might reasonably accrue to the community upon the granting of planning permission, might be captured not through taxation, as is frequently suggested, but rather by selling planning permission to the highest bidder.

Whilst Pennington (2002a) has used public choice theory to argue for 'private land-use planning', alternative applications of public choice theory show that property rights that are consistent with the British planning system can, under certain conditions, meet efficiency criteria. Using computational techniques to simulate outcomes from varying planning systems, Webster and Wu (2001) tested Coasian propositions on development control, by comparing two planning regimes. In one, the community has property rights in development and uses planning mechanisms to influence outcomes. This is seen to be a theoretically simplified version of the British development control system. The simplifications relate to an assumption of perfect knowledge and a single objective of optimising locational externalities. In the alternative simulation, developers have the right to develop but the community is allowed to make, rather than take, compensatory payments to achieve required outcomes. Webster and Wu claim to show

> the theoretical superiority of a British-style development control system compared with a market-orientated system in which identically efficient local development decisions are achieved through perfect bargaining between developers and the community . . .' and a system of property rights such as the one in place in Britain, which holds polluting developers liable, will give rise to greater total (social and private) product in the urban land economy as factors are deployed in locations with lower social costs. (2001, pp. 2043–4)

Webster's and Wu's conclusions are based on an analysis which considers not just the immediate and initial outcome of single-case negotiations, but the wider temporal and geographical ramifications. They thus consider the redeployment possibilities for factors that might be employed in non-compatible uses and the opportunity costs of alternatives. In essence this means that an oversimplification of the Coasian bargaining solution on a single-case basis can miss the wider impacts and opportunities that arise from broader perspectives. Whereas Coase suggested that the direction of compensation between polluter and affected parties did not matter for the efficiency of outcomes, Webster and Wu argue that 'pollution liability will, other things being equal, make less polluting locations more attractive to developers and lead to a greater social product' (ibid., p. 2052).

Market information in planning

Instead of concluding on the basis of a public choice perspective that planning will inevitably fail or that wholesale institutional changes are needed to introduce 'private land-use planning', one might decide that the appropriate lesson is that better use can be made of existing markets. This might mean using price information more effectively in the planning process and deploying planning policy instruments such as taxes and subsidies that adjust markets in an effort to produce better outcomes.

Research by Monk and Whitehead (2000) concludes that in the

British context there is scope for a wider use of land and housing prices in the planning process. Prices, it is suggested, can be used in policy-making, implementation, monitoring and evaluation. In assisting planning, price is seen to be an indicator of market preferences, a measure of opportunity cost and a provider of the implicit values of market and administrative decisions. Prices of different types of houses and houses in different locations can be used as an indicator of the relative values that consumers place on such houses and such locations. Variations in land prices will also reflect what developers think different locations are worth to them and to consumers. If land might be used for housing development or agricultural use, but is constrained by planning to be kept in agricultural use, its opportunity cost is its value in housing use. The loss of land value from the planning constraint can be seen as an implicit value of the benefit of no development (ibid., p. 17).

Price information may be used at national, regional or local levels. Monk and Whitehead suggest that:

- At national level, changes in land and house prices in real terms can be compared with the economic cycle to show how expectations of future planning constraint is reflected in prices. Price information can also be used to compare regional growth or decline and hence general pressures of relative demand.
- At the regional level, prices help to establish the extent to which regional planning strategies are following or steering the market. They can also help to assess the strategy's success.
- At local level, prices reflect the demand for different types and sizes of dwellings, and can be used to assess what types of housing are required to meet future housing requirements at the local level. At site-specific level, they show the economic viability of a particular site compared with another, whether a site level density policy is likely to succeed, and the extent of potential gain for affordable housing. (2000, pp. 7–8)

An evaluation of the consequences of proposed affordable housing policies in London has made extensive use of house price and building cost data. The Spatial Development Strategy for London gives the Greater London Authority (GLA) the opportunity to set a London-wide target for the provision of affordable housing from planning, and in order to inform the choice of a target level, the GLA commissioned an appraisal of the economic viability of developing varying levels of affordable housing in all the London boroughs (Oxley *et al.*, 2001). This analysis involved the development of a model that estimated the expected revenues and costs from specimen housing developments across London, based on manipulations of house price and building cost data together with information on a range of variables such as planning and subsidy levels that would influence the commercial viability of development. Market data were thus used to inform policy choices. The need for affordable housing policies to be guided by market data is now widely accepted, and the value of house price data, in particular, in assisting understanding of the affordability of housing from the household's perspective and the profitability of construction from the developer's viewpoint is increasingly appreciated by local planning authorities. There is more information on achieving affordable housing through the planning system in Chapter 8.

House price and building cost data can be used to examine the economic viability of housing development in the context of urban capacity studies (examined in Chapter 9). Urban housing capacity studies have conventionally focused on the physical availability of land for housing development, and whether or not sites identified in such studies are attractive to developers and might be commercially developed depends on market variables. House prices can be used to forecast the revenue that developments might yield, and when compared to the costs of housebuilding the residual value of land to the developer may be calculated. The relationship of the developer's value to the price at which the land can be acquired indicates the economic viability of development. Such information can potentially transform urban capacity studies from studies of 'land availability' to studies of 'development viability'.

If price information is to perform an enhanced role in planning it should be done with a clear understanding of what prices show and do not show. House prices are an indicator of preferences, but more fundamentally they are an indicator of ability to pay; low-income households will have less power in the housing market than high-income households, and variations in house prices will reflect variations in incomes as well as preferences. Households unable to afford housing will be unable to express their preferences through the market. If house prices are comparatively higher in rural than in urban locations this may reflect a strong desire for living in the countryside. However the prices offered might not reflect the environmental costs of building on greenfield sites. Prices reflect demand; they do not reflect needs or external costs.

If planning is to respond to demand, price information is important, and if planning is to continue to have social objectives that transcend market forces, price information will need to be combined with indicators of need and environmental effects. The use of house and land price data should, furthermore, be accompanied by an understanding of the determinants of prices including the possible impact of the planning system on these prices. The extent to which prices reflect preferences, planning and the social opportunity cost of the use of resources will not be clear without an investigation of the specifics of particular markets. If price data is used with both an understanding of the determinants of market values and the complexities of interpreting what those values represent, the data will provide a very useful additional source of evidence to support both the formulation and implementation of planning policies.

Economic policy instruments

In response to market failures, planning systems in mixed economies have typically developed allocation systems such as land-use plans that assign particular uses to particular locations. Such plans are then implemented by responding to market forces. Market forces are thus taken as given, and demands for particular land uses are steered towards desired locations and away from protected locations. The use of economic policy instruments enables a planning system to work in a different way by moderating market forces and working through market processes. Economic policy instruments such as taxes and subsidies change the prices and costs of given land uses and thus try to promote land-uses and possibly land use patterns that are socially desirable.

In *Modernising Planning* (DETR, 1998) the British government signalled its desire to explore the advantages of an increased use of economic policy instruments to support the planning system. Such instruments were to supplement rather than replace the existing planning framework. Subsequently several changes in taxation to promote brownfield development were announced–these changes in VAT and taxation concessions are discussed in Chapter 9 in the context of the 'urban renaissance' agenda. The government has also mooted the idea of 'tariffs' on certain types of development with the proceeds being used to support affordable housing; this proposal is discussed in Chapter 8. The use of tax concessions to promote more environmentally friendly development is examined in Chapter 5.

Economic policy instruments either (a) tax demand, (b) subsidize demand, (c) tax supply, or (d) subsidize supply. Given that the subsidies frequently take the form of tax concessions, rather than grants, the term 'fiscal policy instruments' is often used. By changing prices and costs, such instruments can change behaviour. If the policy instrument also raises revenue this may be used to promote social objectives. In principle, one would expect demand and supply that produced negative externalities to be taxed and demand and supply that produced positive externalities to be subsidized. The effectiveness of such measures will depend on how consumers and producers react to changed prices and costs. Knowledge of the relevant demand and supply elasticities will help to predict the required rates of tax or subsidy. Political and planning decisions will decide which activities to promote and which to suppress and the degree of change in demand or supply that is desirable. The market will then be used to effect the required changes. Such economic policy instruments do not, therefore, necessarily meet the major objections of public choice theorists to the problems of measuring external costs and benefits, but they do promote a significant role for the positive choice and resource-allocation aspects of market mechanisms.

Public choice theory and social housing provision

Public choice principles have been applied to the operation of public sector bureaucracy generally, and land-use planning is but one of many applications. Boyne and Walker (1999) have provided a public choice evaluation of the post-1980 reforms in the provision of social housing in England and Wales, and their interpretation of public choice theory suggests that, 'If appropriate market structures are created in the public sector then the behaviour of bureaucrats will be steered towards the general welfare of society rather than their own selfish objectives' (1999, p. 2238). Low levels of public sector success and significant inefficiencies are seen from this perspective to be a function of monopolistic structures in public services, the absence of valid indicators of organizational performance and the large size of government agencies. A public choice prescription for improved efficiency thus involves:

1 competition between public sector agencies with consumer choice between alternative public sector providers;
2 improved information on the performance of public agencies to enhance the basis on which consumers choose; and
3 the division of large public-sector agencies into smaller organizational units.

Boyne and Walker argue that the changes in the provision of social housing in England and Wales have to a large extent followed public choice principles: the size of local authority housing departments has been reduced through the right to buy and through the transfer of stock to housing associations; more competition has been introduced through an enhanced role for housing associations, and tenants are systematically provided with more information and have more choice of landlord and location. Three criteria are established to evaluate the effect of the changes: the 'technical efficiency of service provision'; 'consumer satisfaction'; and the 'equity or fairness in housing provision' (ibid., pp. 2240–1). On the basis of the available evidence, it is concluded that efficiency and responsiveness to consumers' demands has improved, but the degree of equity has declined. This decline in equity is seen to reflect the increased residualization of public housing with the least well-off left in a stigmatized tenure of last resort with insufficient levels of support.

This conclusion emphasizes a general point about public choice perspectives: there is a concern for improved efficiency but no particular concern with equity. It might be reasonable to argue that redistributional changes to support equity objectives can best be achieved through taxation and direct subsidy measures rather than particular structures of service provision. This is true whether the service is planning or housing. However, arguments for improved efficiency through market processes need to be accompanied by arguments for effective redistributions through non-market processes if equity as well as efficiency objectives are to be promoted.

Conclusions

A liberal interventionist approach to housing and planning stresses the problems of market failure, particularly the inability of markets to cope efficiently with externalities and public goods. There is also concern for the inequities that arise from distributions of resources that confound principles of social justice. This approach suggests that government activity such as planning and housing-market policies can lead to more efficient and more equitable outcomes.

The public choice perspective issues a series of warnings against government activities that do not consider the costs and negative outcomes of policies and the benefits of market forces. The warnings emphasize the problem of measuring externalities, the problems of government failure including interest group capture, and the costs of bureaucracy borne by the private as well as the public sector. The relevance of property rights and a consideration of alternative systems of planning and intervention are stressed.

The prescriptions that emanate from the public choice school are varied, depending on which aspects of public choice analysis protagonists decide to promote. At one extreme are arguments for replacing public land-use planning with private land-use planning, characterized by property rights in development that are no longer vested in the state. At the other extreme are arguments for a more informed use of market data with the prevailing system left intact. In between are ideas about reforms that make the institutions of planning and housing more receptive to consumer preferences and encourage governments to make more use of economic policy instruments.

No version of public choice theory suggests that externalities, public goods and distributions of income and wealth do not matter. All versions show the problems of tackling these issues without giving proper weight to property rights and efficiency issues. Constructive application of lessons learnt from public choice warnings indicates that with appropriate understanding of how market processes work and what market values mean, markets can be encouraged – through policy instruments which change prices and costs – to work for social, and not just individual, objectives.

Chapter 7

Distributional Justice and Land Markets

This chapter examines the relationships between distributional issues and planning, building on the concept of equity introduced in Chapter 3. There equity was considered to be concerned with notions of fairness in the distribution of resources and rewards in society, and planning might be seen as sometimes reacting to an inequitable or unfair distribution of such resources. If it is viewed in this way, promoting a more equitable or fairer distribution of resources sits alongside promoting a more efficient distribution of resources as an aim for a planning system. The implementation of planning does, however, change land uses and redistribute wealth and income, and if these redistributions are deemed to be unfair, planning may be seen as a cause of, as well as a response to, inequities.

The relationship between planning and land values will be explored with the aid of a theory of land-value determination, and the arguments about the increased values that follow from planning permission being the object of some sort of taxation will be examined. Both the theory and the history of special taxes on land will be considered, as well as the roles of 'planning gain' in Britain and 'value capture' in the USA.

Planning and redistribution

Planning has sometimes been advanced as a means to promote a more equitable distribution of resources. It has been seen as an instrument for social change, redressing inequalities and working for the benefit of disadvantaged groups (Gans, 1991). It is possible to view the growth of a concern with land-use planning in late nineteenth century and early twentieth century Britain as a reaction to the poor living conditions of workers and their families that arose from rapid industrialization and urbanization (Rydin, 2003, pp.

12–14). Thus the desire for improved housing conditions through physical planning may be viewed as a desire for a better distribution of resources in favour of the less well-off. There were of course also efficiency reasons; better-housed workers in better-planned communities would be more productive workers and contribute even more to economic growth. *(meet the ever growing sustainability challenges).*

A desire for improved living conditions for reasons of distributional justice is a desire based on a belief that it is right that the living conditions of the poorest sections of society are improved. It is, moreover, founded on a belief that such improvement is desirable, fair and equitable, even if it means that the poor gain at the expense of the better-off. The desirability of redistribution thus depends essentially on beliefs about what people deserve or have a right to. However, the realms of equity and distributive justice are the realms of beliefs and of imprecision; precise definitions of 'poor' and 'better-off' are extremely difficult to elaborate, and rarely confronted.

In recent decades, planning has arguably made a very limited contribution to a reduction in urban poverty (Cullingworth and Nadin, 2002, pp. 24–6); urban deprivation, poor housing, and deindustrialization have posed problems well beyond the scope of planning. It has become clear that economic, social and physical measures need to be implemented in an integrated way if such problems are to be tackled. Planning has a role, but only as part of a larger package of measures that redistribute and reorganize resources. The limited role of planning in relation to the provision of 'affordable housing' is considered in Chapter 8, and planning's role in promoting improvements in the quality of urban living is examined further in relation to 'urban renaissance' in Chapter 9.

If underlying problems of the poor physical quality of housing are issues of unemployment, low incomes and social exclusion, planning cannot be expected to solve the problems. A much more sophisticated analysis of the distributions of income and wealth is required than one which assumes a large degree of physical determinism. In relation to the much narrower issue of the income and wealth of landowners, there is a more straightforward set of cause-and-effect relationships with planning. As planning influences land uses, so it also influences land values, and there are gainers and losers from changes in land use. Planning has redistributional consequences. Whether or not gainers should be taxed and losers compensated has been a cause of much debate and much legislation for over a hundred years. The relationship between land value and planning has to be examined in the context of a broader analysis of the determination of land values, and it is to this analysis that we now turn.

Land values

The value of land is a measure of what it is worth. However, what it is worth to whom and in what circumstances are complex issues. Land in a public park that is never likely to come onto the market has a value to the community that uses the park, but use of the park may be free and assigning a monetary value to the parkland in these circumstances would be very difficult. Land that changes hands in the marketplace between a private seller and private buyer will, in the absence of any controls, be traded at a price that reflects the use to which the land can be put. The price or value in exchange for a plot of land that can be used to build houses is likely to be many times the price of a plot that can only be used for growing vegetables. Land can also be viewed as a factor of production, as one of several inputs to a productive process, combined with other factors such as labour and machinery to produce outputs.

The demand for factors of production is derived from the demand for the commodities they help produce. If the only commodity that a plot of land can help to produce is potatoes, the demand for the land will be derived from the demand for potatoes, and the price offered to buy and use the land will reflect the demand and price for potatoes. If the plot of land can be used to build houses, and there is a demand for houses at this location, the price offered for the land will reflect the demand and price for houses. And the value of the land for housing development is likely to be many times its value for growing potatoes. In locations where houses demand high prices, developers are likely, other things being equal, to offer higher prices for development land than in locations where house prices are lower. Prices paid for land on which to build houses will reflect the demand for houses and the supply of land on which houses can be built.

Historically, it has been argued that the supply of land is fixed and this fixity of supply distinguishes land from other factors of production. In the sense that the total volume of land within a country, in the absence of land reclamation and land falling into the sea, is fixed, it is true that there is a fixed amount of land. This is, however, not a fixed supply in the sense that supply is used in market economics; it is rather a fixed stock of land. The amount of land supplied in the sense of being available on the market at any point in time is variable. The availability of land for a particular use in a particular location will vary considerably from time to time, and from one location to another (see Figure 2.6).

Thus the supply of land for housing development is not fixed; it is highly variable through time and from location to location. This was true before planning controls were introduced and is true with the existence of planning controls. Without planning controls, land will have several potential uses and it might be supplied in several markets. It might be supplied for potato growing, housebuilding, office building, shopping development, or any one of many other potentially competing uses. The total supply offered for housebuilding will be influenced by the prices offered by housebuilders compared with the price offered by farmers, office builders and shopping developers.

The price of housing development land is thus a function not only of the demand and price of houses, but also of the supply of development land, and this supply is influenced by the demand for land from competing uses. With the existence of a planning system, this supply of land for housing development will be further influenced by the availability of planning permission. More restrictive planning regimes will tend to result in a lower aggregate supply of development land than less restrictive planning regimes. This is, however, a wide generalization – the effect of planning on the supply of housing development land at specific locations depends on how the planning system curtails or promotes land being used for housing compared with it being put to other uses. Before delving further into the effect of planning on the demand and the supply of development land in aggregate, it will be useful to consider the more simple issue of the demand, supply and value of individual plots.

The individual plot of land

Imagine a plot of land on the edge of a town. Currently, it is a green field in agricultural use; it is owned by a farmer. Let us consider the potential demand for this land to have houses built upon it and the potential for it being supplied for this use. The demand for this plot as residential development land will depend on all the factors influencing the demand for new houses in this locality. New housing demand at this location is likely to be affected by such factors as local employment, incomes, demographics and the availability of alternative housing at other locations. Strong growth in local employment, higher household incomes, local population growth and a desire by households to move into the area will all tend, other things being equal, to increase local housing demand and, unless there are already plenty of houses available, this will tend to contribute to a demand for this edge-of-town plot to be used for housing. Thus there might be a strong demand for the agricultural plot to be developed for housing. However, if unemployment is high and household incomes are falling, there may be outmigration from the area resulting in lots of empty houses in the location and the demand for the plot to be used for housing development will be much weaker.

If demand for new housing at the location is strong, will this lead to houses being built on the plot? The short answer is: only if housing developers are willing and able to build on the site and the farmer is willing and able to allow the land to be developed. The willingness of the developer to build will be influenced by what the completed houses might sell for and how many houses can be built on the plot. These will determine the expected revenue from sales. The developer will also consider the costs of construction and the reward required to make the enterprize worthwhile. From a consideration of such financial variables, the developer may take a view on what it is worth paying the farmer for the land. The farmer will then decide whether or not it is worth selling to the residential developer in light of the current valuation put on the land and any competing offers from other potential land users. If there is a better offer for the land from a developer who wishes to construct an out-of-town shopping precinct, the farmer may well wish to sell to the shopping developer rather than the housing developer.

We can assume that, if there is no planning system and narrow financial considerations are driving developers and the farmer, the land will go to the highest bidder and the land will be developed according to its highest value use. If there is a planning system in place that deems that permission is required before the land can change use, then clearly there is an additional constraint to consider. This is very different from arguing that planning determines the use and thus the value of the land.

The demand for the land to be used for housing or any other use will be only indirectly influenced by a planning system. Only if one argues that planning has a strong and direct influence on such factors as employment and incomes would one argue to the contrary. However, a planning system is likely to have a more direct influence on the use or uses for which the land can be supplied. If agricultural use is the only permitted option then, despite residential development demand, the land will be supplied only for the farmer's use. If planning allows the land to be used for a shopping development, but not a residential development, the housing development use is again frustrated. From this point of view, there is an argument that planning acts as a constraint on land use and therefore land values. It does not, however, determine land use and land values. The granting of planning permission for the agricultural plot to be used for residential development would be of no consequence, assuming that development is to be carried out by private-sector profit-orientated developers, unless there is sufficient demand for new housing.

Land use and redistribution

In the previous example, we envisaged one plot of land that might be used for housing development but was currently in agricultural use on the edge of a town. Now let us consider the possibility that there are four such plots, each in separate ownership, on the edge of the town. There is potential for any one of these plots (but not all of them in the near future) to be demanded for housing development, but there is insufficient demand locally for new housing for all four plots to be developed.

If planning permission for housing development exists for plot A, but for the other plots B, C and D only permission for agricultural use is forthcoming, it is likely that A would be developed for housing, whilst the other plots would not. The owner of plot A would see the land value increase from its agricultural use value to its residential development use value. The owners of plots B, C and D would not receive any gain. In an alternative scenario where there are no planning restrictions, assume that it is the owner of plot B that is most keen to sell to the residential developer. This owner will accept a lower price than the owners of the other plots, and the housing developer would find that higher bids were necessary to secure plots A, C and D and would thus buy plot B and build houses. The other plots would remain in agricultural use.

Without planning, the owner of plot B sells to the residential developer. With planning, the owner of plot A sells to the residential developer. An effect of planning is to redistribute wealth between the owners of plots A and B. Both the pattern of land use and the pattern of wealth distribution are affected by planning.

If the owner of B has lost wealth and the owner of A has gained wealth as a consequence of planning, should the former be entitled to some sort of compensation and the latter be subject to a 'betterment' tax? This has been a significant long-running issue in the UK and many other countries with strong land-use planning systems, and we will return to this debate. First, though, it is necessary to examine the concept of 'economic rent'.

Economic rent

It has been argued that land can be viewed as a factor of production. Classical economists divided the rewards of factors of production into two elements: transfer earnings and economic rent (Prest, 1981). According to their analysis, transfer earnings are necessary to ensure the supply of a factor for a particular use; they are the minimum payment necessary to stop a factor being used for the production of some alternative commodity. Thus if the farmer can sell a plot of land for £100,000 to another farmer, he will not sell for less than this to a residential developer. The residential developer will need to offer the farmer at least £100,000 to secure the land (see Figure 7.1).

'Economic rent' is a payment over and above transfer earnings. It is a payment above that which is absolutely necessary to secure the

Figure 7.1   *Economic rent and transfer earnings of land*

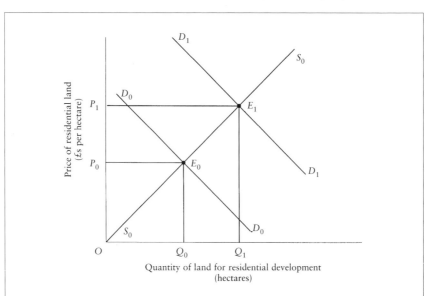

Within a given area, $D_0 D_0$ shows the initial demand and $S_0 S_0$ the initial supply of land for residential development. If each hectare of residential development land changes hands for P_0, the total payment for this land is shown by the rectangle $O P_0 E_0 Q_0$. Of this total, $O P_0 E_0$ is economic rent and $O E_0 Q_0$ is transfer earnings. Transfer earnings are necessary to ensure supply. Economic rent is a payment over and above transfer earnings. If the demand for residential development land rises to $D_1 D_1$, the total payment for such land rises to $O P_1 E_1 Q_1$. Of this new total payment, $O E_1 Q_1$ is transfer earnings and $O P_1 E_1$ is economic rent. The increase in demand thus increases economic rent by an amount shown by the area $P_0 P_1 E_1 E_0$.

use of a factor of production for a given productive purpose. Assume that the residential developer offers the farmer £500,000 for the land and this sum is accepted. As long as an offer above £100,000 was made, the farmer would have accepted, but if £500,000 is received a large part of this is economic rent. Economic rent is a surplus which, according to the classical argument, can be taxed away without any effect on supply. Thus the farmer could be taxed £399,000 and would still sell to the housing developer because the farmer would be better off than in the case in which the land was retained for agriculture.

An obvious question in relation to this example is why does the developer offer £500,000 for the land when it could be prised from the farmer for, say, £101,000. The residential developer will not offer £500,000, we assume, unless this can be afforded on the basis of expected house prices and construction costs. However, why does the developer not offer £101,000 and have £399,000 extra profit, rather than leave the farmer with a large amount of economic rent? A possible reason is that the residential developer believes that £500,000 will have to be paid to ward off bids from competing residential and possibly non-residential developers.

If it is known that the maximum amount that another residential developer will offer is £400,000, this is the minimum payment necessary to ensure the supply of the land to our residential developer. The transfer earnings are at least £400,000 in this case and not £100,000. If a retail developer is willing to offer £450,000, the minimum payment necessary to secure a given use is higher still. It clearly depends on what alternative uses are under consideration. On this basis, there is not a straightforward answer to the question 'How much economic rent does the farmer receive if £500,000 is paid for the agricultural plot?' The answer could be as much as £400,000 if agriculture is the only alternative use, or as little as £50,000 if retail development is the alternative use.

The negotiating strengths and skills of the farmer and the residential developer will influence how much actually changes hands for the plot. This might be anywhere between £100,000 and £500,000. If the developer obtained the plot for only £101,000, it can be argued that an additional potential economic rent of £399,000 has been captured by the developer in the form of a super-normal profit. This is a profit over and above the minimum that the developer would require to proceed with the scheme.

How much of the payment for land is in practice economic rent is crucial to arguments about taxing, or taking for the community, increases in land values that arise from the granting of planning permission. Also central to the arguments is an answer to the question 'What is the cause of increased land values?' If the farmer sees the value of his land increase from £100,000 to £500,000, is the cause simply 'the granting of planning permission', or is it 'a significant increase in the demand for housing'? It might also be due to the land achieving housing development potential because of new roads and drainage installed at public expense. Within a given area, an increased demand for housing may lead to an increased demand for housing land, and this demand may, without any controls on land supply or price, lead to an increase in the price of housing land. The total payments for housing land both before and after the increase in demand can be seen as comprising transfer earnings and economic rent. After the increase in demand, the extra payment to land will be, in part, an extra payment of economic rent (see Figure 7.1). Alternative explanations for rising land values need to be remembered as we examine first the theory and then the history of betterment.

Land values: theory and thinkers

Economists from Adam Smith (1723–70) onwards argued that land values were determined differently from other factors of production and other goods and services. This different process that gave land value did, moreover, make land an ideal case for special taxation. The development of planning in the twentieth century led to further ideas about how land values were determined and what part planning played in this process. It also led to many (usually short-lived) attempts to impose some kind of special tax on land.

In *The Wealth of Nations* (1776), Smith distinguished between the part of the rent for a house that was a payment for the use of the building, and the part that was for the use of the land. The latter was a 'ground rent'. The general payments for the use of land of all types he called the 'ordinary rent of land'. He stated that:

> Ground rents are a still more proper subject of taxation than the rent of houses. A tax upon ground rents would not raise the rents of houses. It would fall altogether upon the owner of the ground rent, who acts always as a monopolist, and exacts the greatest rent which can be got for the use of his ground. Both ground rents and the ordinary rent of land are a species of revenue which the owner, in many cases, enjoys without any care or attention of his own. Ground rents, and the ordinary rent of land are, therefore,

perhaps, the species of revenue which can best bear to have a peculiar tax imposed upon them. (Smith, 1976, pp. 843–4)

Adam Smith saw taxes on rents as efficient in that they would be neutral in their resource-allocation effects and equitable in that it was fair to tax away surpluses that were due more to extraneous circumstances than to individual effort. He argued that rental values were partly due to good government, and that people should pay for government actions and services that are to their advantage.

David Ricardo (1772–1823) identified an element of land rent which he called 'economic rent' that was 'due to the original and indestructible powers of the soil' (Ricardo, 1951, p. 67). Ricardo was more concerned with agricultural land than urban land. He introduced the concept of 'derived demand', declaring that the rent of corn land was high because the price of corn was high. It was not the case that the price of corn was high because land rents were high. The economic rent was a surplus payment to a factor of production over and above what was necessary to keep it in its present use. Ricardo argued that land supply did not depend on market price; higher prices do not lead to larger quantities being supplied and falling prices do not reduce supply. The supply price (or transfer earnings) is the minimum reward necessary to keep a factor in its current employment; any surplus above this is an economic rent.

J.S. Mill (1806–73) argued that rents were 'created by circumstances' and could thus justifiably be appropriated. Of landlords he declared 'They grow richer, as it were in their sleep, without working, risking or economizing. What claim have they, on the general principle of social justice, to this accession of riches?' (Mill, 1909, p. 818). Mill did, however, acknowledge that whilst some of the landlords' rewards were due to circumstances that might occur in their sleep, there was also an element of land values that was due to private endeavour. The practical difficulties in distinguishing between value due to 'endeavour' and value due to 'circumstances' were recognized by Mill and these difficulties constituted a significant barrier to swingeing taxation of landlords. He did, furthermore, have some concern for the present owners of land who had purchased, perhaps recently, at market values expecting a given return. There would be some injustice in depriving them of what they expected. To get round these problems, Mill proposed that the present value of all land should be ascertained and future increases in value should be taxed unless they could be shown to be the result of 'endeavour'. It was therefore a tax on windfall gains that Mill saw as the appropriate way of confiscating the unnecessary and unjust rewards of landlords.

Marshall (1842–1924) demonstrated that the same principles applied by Ricardo to agricultural land also applied to urban land. Urban land values, just like agricultural values, were a function of the demand for what was supplied from the land. Land was a distinct factor of production in that it was fixed in supply and the whole of the return of it was a surplus. Thus, as it has been put in the most authoritative survey of land-value theory:

> Marshall argued that the taxation of site value (or public value, as he called it) was analogous to the taxation of monopoly profits in that there was a surplus which could be tapped without any dele-terious effects on resource allocation. Taxes on site values would reduce these excess profits of owners but that was all. (Prest, 1981, p. 15)

Pigou (1877–1959) provided what Prest (1981, p. 19) has called a synthesis of the views of Marshall and J.S. Mill. Pigou distinguished between taxes on site values and taxes on windfall gains, but he favoured both. Site value taxes would be neutral in their effects on resource allocation, whilst on windfall increments his view was that 'if increments arose which were neither foreseen nor due to effort on the part of the recipient they were ideal objects of taxation from a resource allocation viewpoint and also distributionally commend-able' (Prest, 1981, p. 18).

One of the most influential proponents of land-value taxation was the American, Henry George (1839–97). In *Progress and Poverty* (George, 1879) he argued for a single tax on land and the abolition of all other taxes. Rather like other nineteenth-century economists, George believed that land rents and land values were the result of natural and social forces and not individual effort. He asserted that landlords had no moral right to land values and one could justify a tax of 100 per cent of annual rental values.

George went further than other advocates of land-value taxation in arguing for a single tax upon land values as the sole source of government revenues, replacing all existing taxes. Such a tax, as a tax on economic rent, following the arguments of Ricardo, would not be shifted to others and would not affect resource allocation. The elimination of all other taxes, including those on buildings, would stimulate construction and economic growth. Also, a single land tax would have the added advantage of being simple to admin-ister (Lichfield and Connellan, 1997, p. 9). Henry George visited

Britain five times in the 1880s and his popularization of Ricardo's ideas on rent was arguably a major influence on the Fabian Society and Trade Union movement. He has been credited with 'being the most potent single instrument in the conversion of both individuals and the working class itself to trade unionism and socialism' (ibid., p. 10). The effect of Henry George's arguments did, however, go much wider: 'The influence of George on a worldwide scale can be seen from the fact that the Library of Congress Division of Bibliography was by 1913 able to publish a list of 180 references to books and articles advocating the Single Tax' (Prest, 1981, p. 65).

Marx (1818–83) in his vast works on capitalism and the structure of society developed many provoking ideas on the causes of value. Building on a labour theory of value he developed a theory of rent which saw rent as a form of surplus value (Blaug, 1997, pp. 215–76). He thought that landowners had no right to their properties or to land rents which were surplus values (Prest, 1981, p. 12). However, Marx had no time for special taxes on land; he sought more radical solutions. Marx had a low opinion of Henry George and his ideas, writing: 'The man is utterly backward. He understands nothing about the nature of surplus value'. Marx claimed that George was amongst those who wished to 'leave wage labour and therefore capitalist production in existence and try to bamboozle themselves or the world into believing that if ground rent were transformed into a state tax all the evils of capitalist production would disappear of themselves' (Marx, 1881).

Land values: history and policy

The principle of special taxes on land has a long history. The Romans appointed surveyors to measure land for the purposes of taxation which 'would have been a normal part of imperial taxation in Roman Britain during four centuries of occupation' (Litchfield and Connellan, 1997, p. 12). There are many examples over the years of local levies for the benefit of public works. For example, legislation in 1427 imposed taxes on those benefiting from land drainage and sea walls and in 1662 a levy sought to recover a proportion of the increase in property values arising from street-widening schemes in London. In the late nineteenth century there were many attempts by local authorities to allow parliament to grant them powers to impose charges on property owners for infrastructure improvements. Nine London County Council Improvement Acts from 1885 to 1902 gave the authorities powers to impose a levy on the annual increase in property values due to road improvement schemes. However, these resulted in much litigation and relatively small yields (Ratcliffe, 1976, pp. 40–1; Prest, 1981, pp. 70–1).

The first significant attempt in Britain at a comprehensive measure to tax increases in land values came through the Housing and Town Planning Act of 1909. This was the first Act in the UK to bear the term 'town planning'. Local authorities were given new powers to promote healthier housing and an improved environment, and a 50 per cent levy on increases in land values due to planning schemes was introduced. To balance this charge, landowners could claim compensation for losses resulting from the consequent restrictions on development. There was thus an explicit recognition that planning redistributed wealth and that compensation and taxation should ameliorate these changes.

The principle of land taxation was taken further in the Lloyd George Budget of 1909 which eventually resulted in the 1910 Finance Act. Four kinds of land tax were introduced: a 20 per cent tax on future capital gains; a small annual tax on the site value of undeveloped land; a 10 per cent reversion duty to be paid on the value of reversions at the end of a lease; and a 5 per cent per annum levy on the value of mineral rights. The politicians of the day echoed nineteenth-century economists in defence of the proposals. Lloyd George argued about the evil whereby a 'community has always to pay a heavy duty to its ground landlords for putting up the value of their land', and Winston Churchill spoke of landlords who grew rich as society prospered but they did nothing: 'In fact you may say that the unearned increment . . . is reaped by the land monopolist in exact proportion not to the service, but to the disservice done' (both quoted in Prest, 1981, pp. 72–3). The aims were not achieved however, because of challenges in the courts and problems of valuation and implementation; there was a low yield and in 1920 the legislation was repealed.

Another attempt at a betterment levy came in the 1932 Town and Country Planning Act. The 50 per cent tax on increased value introduced in the 1909 Act was raised to 75 per cent, but the tax proved difficult to collect. The difficulty of proving that value increases were due to planning made the tax 'virtually inoperative' (Prest, 1981, p. 76). Local authorities were liable for compensation when planning permission was refused, and as a result much more residential development than was needed was granted permission. It is claimed that

Between 1909 and 1939 . . . in order to avoid onerous compensation payments . . . only 143 planning schemes having been formally approved, enough land was designated for development to accommodate approximately 290 million people against an actual population of around 40 million, and in respect of the betterment provisions, only three occasions of charge were recorded. (Ratcliffe, 1976, p. 42)

A significant landmark in the history of policy on land taxation came with the 'Report of the Expert Committee on Compensation and Betterment' in 1942. This became known (after its chairman) as the Uthwatt Report. The committee proposed that with good planning, land would be put to its most suitable use irrespective of the value of individual plots. The problem of compensation and betterment was seen to arise from an individualistic approach to land ownership, and this approach had to be challenged if fundamental reform was to be achieved. The committee proposed that:

1   All development rights in land outside of built-up areas should be vested in the state.
2   Compensation for the acquisition of these rights would be at market values on 31 March 1939.
3   Land to be developed would be acquired by the state, using compulsory purchase powers if necessary, and leased back to private developers at full open market value.
4   Land in built-up areas could also be purchased for development if redevelopment of a whole area was necessary.
5   A betterment charge was to be levied at 75 per cent of increases in land values (except for agriculture uses).
6   Central government grants would enable local authorities to redevelop central urban areas.

The committee's conclusions were influenced by their concern with their enunciated concepts of 'floating' and 'shifting' value. It was suggested that given the potential for development within an area, the hopes of all landowners in the area would be raised but only some of them would actually realize an increase in value as the result of the development occurring on their land. There was thus a floating value which would settle somewhere but which would not actually be known. If all potential gainers were compensated, except for the actual gainers, the compensation bill would clearly exceed any actual increase in value.

The concept of 'shifting' value refers to cases where the refusal of planning permission in one locality caused value to 'shift' to another where permission was given. Compensation claims might thus be faced by one local authority but the proceeds of betterment would accrue to another.

Such ideas persuaded the committee of the impracticality of ongoing comprehensive compensation for the refusal of planning permission. The committee also made a distinction between (a) the case for compensation for compulsory acquisition by the public sector, and (b) the case for compensation for a limitation of use imposed by the public sector. The former was deemed worthy of compensation because it was an interference with basic property rights. The latter was deemed not worthy of compensation because there was a long-standing tradition of laws being obeyed for compliance with public health and building regulations, for example, without any payment for compliance.

The Uthwatt proposals have been seen as both pragmatic solutions to difficult issues (Ratcliffe, 1976, p. 43) and conclusions that 'flowed from the ignorance and/or neglect of elementary economic principles' (Prest, 1981, p. 79). Prest suggests that 'elementary economic price theory played no part whatsoever in their reasoning; it was a pariah as far as the committee was concerned' (ibid.).

Prest viewed both the concepts of floating and shifting value as flawed. The floating value concept suggested that landowners would assume that development would occur on their land even if the statistical probability was low. In practice, many landowners would be disappointed and if all of these were compensated, the costs would be very high. As Prest says:

> The simple proposition that a site is worth an inflated value because the owner thinks it is will not stand up to the slightest scrutiny; it takes two to make a bargain and in the last resort the site will not be sold if the buyer does not think it worth the asking price but the seller refuses to lower it. (Ibid., p. 133)

Shifting value implies that the refusal of development in one locality would lead to development elsewhere and values would shift accordingly. There is no reason to assume that the demand and supply conditions and hence the land price at one location will be the same at another. A refusal of planning permission in the UK might mean development in another country so no shift in value within the country occurs (ibid., pp. 132–3).

The Uthwatt proposals were, in part, implemented in the Town and Country Planning Act 1947 in which all development rights were vested in the state. Planning permission was now required for all development, and no compensation would be paid (in most cases) if permission were refused. A 100 per cent development change was introduced on increases in land values that resulted from planning permission. A fund was established to make payments to landowners who could show that they had lost development value on the day the Act came into force (Cullingworth and Nadin, 2002, pp. 160–1).

The Conservative government that came to power in 1951 was determined to abolish the development charge introduced in 1947, and in 1953 legislation was enacted to repeal it. The 1954 Town and Country Planning Act restricted compensation for compulsory purchase to the existing use value. There was thus a dual market in land with one set of values if the state acquired land, and another set of values if land was sold in the open market. Those who sold privately now received the full development value of the land with no obligation to pay any development charge. The 1959 Town and Country Planning Act abolished the dual market, which was seen as inherently unfair, and restored market value as the basis for compensation for compulsory purchase. Whilst all development rights remained nationalized, there was now no provision for either compensation for loss of value or betterment taxation for any increase in value.

The Labour government elected in 1964 declared that it wanted to ensure (1) that the right land was available at the right time for the implementation of national, regional and local plans, and (2) that development value created by the community was returned to the community. A Land Commission was established in 1967 to promote these objectives, and the Commission could acquire land for development either compulsorily or by agreement. A betterment levy, set initially at 40 per cent, was introduced, so that when the Commission acquired land it paid market value less the levy. Owners who sold privately paid the levy directly. The Commission assessed the supply of land for house building and made it clear that it would use its powers of acquisition to enhance this supply where necessary. The Commission did not long survive the election of a Conservative government in 1970, and by the time of its demise in 1971 it had collected far less than anticipated in betterment taxation. Its effectiveness in promoting the supply of development land is difficult to assess for several reasons. It was unable to exercise powers of acquisition unless planning permission existed, and the absence of permissions may have been a significant barrier to development in areas where local authorities were keen to limit growth. It did not, furthermore, last long enough for its procedures to become accepted as fixed and its consequences evaluated (Cullingworth and Nadin, 2002, pp. 163–4; Prest, 1981, pp. 93–5; Ratcliffe, 1976, pp. 44–5).

In the early 1970s, large increases in property values spurred the Conservative government to announce in 1973 new taxes on development land gains. These were to take the form of the application of marginal income tax rates to gains by individuals and corporation tax rates to gains by companies. In addition, some unrealized gains, especially those from the first lettings of non-residential buildings, were to be subjected to new taxation.

These measures were in fact introduced in 1974 by a Labour government that saw them as a stop-gap before more fundamental reforms could be enacted. In the 'Land' White Paper (1975), two objectives were stated: (1) to enable the community to control the development of land in accordance with its needs and priorities, and (2) to restore to the community the increase in value arising from its efforts. Ultimately, this was to be done by public acquisition, at current-use values of all land destined for development and then disposal to developers at market value. The development gain would thus be acquired by the community without any special taxation. Until such a scheme was fully operational, a development land tax would capture a proportion of development value. The Community Land Act (1975) and Development Land Tax Act (1976) provided the legislative framework for these proposals. Development Land Tax was set at 80 per cent on all non-exempt development value over £150,000 (the rate was 66⅔ per cent below this threshold).

Like previous attempts at taxing betterment, the 1975/6 legislation was short-lived. In 1979, the newly-elected Conservative government stated that it would scrap the Community Land Act (whose full provisions had never come into effect) and change Development Land Tax. The value of exempt gains was raised from £10,000 to £50,000 and a unified 60 per cent rate was introduced. Development Land Tax was subsequently abolished in 1985.

Planning gain

It would be incorrect to claim that in Britain the transfer of 'betterment' from developers and landowners to the community ceased with the ultimate repeal of the Community Land legislation. A form of 'betterment taxation' continues through the imposition of planning agreements or planning obligations, which allow local authorities to obtain benefits in kind or monetary payments in lieu of specific facilities being provided as a condition of planning permission. Such agreements have been possible since the 1930s but their use to extract 'planning gain' has been both extended and debated more rigorously in recent years (Cullingworth and Nadin, 2002, pp. 166–8).

The extraction of 'planning gain' means that some of the profit from the development process, which would otherwise go to the developer or landowner, is used to provide social infrastructure either on or off the site. Thus at least some of the costs of providing a road to improve access to a site or a school in the neighbourhood might be borne by the development process. A significant bone of contention has been the demands by local authorities for social housing to be provided by developers, as a condition of planning permission. The issue of planning and affordable housing is addressed directly in Chapter 8.

The statutory provisions relating to planning agreements were modified by the Planning and Compensation Act 1991. 'Agreements' have become 'obligations' which can be unilateral. Thus a developer can offer to resource specific improvements in facilities without the local authority agreeing, and such offers might be taken into account at any subsequent inquiry into the refusal of planning permission. Official policy on planning obligations (DETR, 1997) states that planning obligations should be directly related to the proposed development and be necessary to make the proposal acceptable in land-use planning terms. There is of course room for much debate over what is really necessary and how direct the connection is between the obligation and the permission. The Royal Institution of Chartered Surveyors (RICS), in a statement of its position on planning obligations, argued that they provided 'the most practical method of ensuring that the development industry mitigates the impact of their developments'. However, it made a distinction between obligations 'to require developers to meet the cost of remediating the adverse impacts of their developments', of which it approved, and obligations being used to reduce profits, of which it did not approve: 'Planning obligations should never be used as a means of securing for the local community a share in the profits of development' (RICS, 1998). However, it is difficult to see how developers might make a contribution to the costs of remediation without reducing their profits. What the RICS statement appears to suggest is that the case for planning obligations to deal with an external cost problem is accepted, but the case for their use to tackle redistribution or equity problems is not. This implicit distinction between an efficiency and an equity motive is important to the evaluation of theory and practice on land values.

Value capture

In American literature the term 'value capture' is used to describe the extraction of betterment through a variety of processes. A succinct definition states:

> value capture refers to the process by which a portion of or all land value increments attributed to 'community effort' are recouped by the public sector either through their conversion into public revenues through taxes, fees, exactions and other fiscal means, or more directly in on-site improvements for the benefit of the community (Smolka and Amborski, 2000)

Property taxes perform a value-capture function only if they are specifically related to value increments. Property taxes that take a simple annual proportion of value or tax transactions in property do not necessarily do this. However, impact fees can have a value-capture component. As used in the USA, these are related both to the infrastructure and other public facilities required of new development and the land-value increment. As the American Planning Association explains:

> Impact fees are payments required by local governments for the purpose of providing new or expanded public facilities required to serve that development. The fees typically require cash payments in advance of the completion of development, are based on a methodology and calculation derived from the cost of the facility and the nature and size of the development, and are used to finance improvements off site, but to the benefit of the development. Local governments throughout the country are increasingly using impact fees to shift more of the costs of financing public facilities from the general taxpayer to the beneficiaries of those new facilities. As a general matter, impact fees are capitalized into land values, and thus represent an exaction of the incremental value of the land attributable to the higher and better use made possible by the new public facilities. (APA, 1997)

Impact fees, as well as having a value-capture function, have been used to finance 'public goods' or 'quasi-public goods' (see Chapter 4). Their most widespread use is for sewer and water facilities, parks and roads, but they are also being used for schools and libraries.

Value-capture regulations usually lead to developers providing benefits 'in kind', but they can instead result in a contribution to the public purse. In such cases the amount is typically negotiated with the authorities. The 'in-kind' provision involves the direct creation of new infrastructure or other public assets by the developer. It is claimed that 'the idea that new residential development should pay for the infrastructure costs that it generates (the benefit principle) has been broadly embraced by high-growth jurisdictions in the US and Canada' (Smolka and Amborski, 2000).

Planning obligations, impact fees and economic rent

In examining the theory and practice of planning gain, value capture and economic rent it is useful to distinguish six sets of circumstances (which may not be mutually exclusive):

1   There is a general increase in demand in a community that leads to increases in land values but no new development.
2   New infrastructure, for example a new tram line, is provided from the public purse and nearby land values rise as a result. No new development occurs.
3   Permission to develop is given on specific sites and the value of these sites increases as a consequence.
4   New development on a site is not economically viable until new infrastructure, for example a new access road, is provided. If the infrastructure is provided land values rise. The infrastructure may be funded by the public purse, the developer or both. Once provided, property values rise.
5   New development imposes a need for a new facility that is directly relevant to the new development. For example, a new school is needed because of new housing. The new facility may be funded by the public purse, the developer or both. Once provided, property values rise.
6   A community needs a new facility irrespective of whether any new development happens or not. For example, more affordable housing is needed for low-income households.

In situations 1, 2 and 3, land values rise because of community effort. In situations 4 and 5, land values rise due to community effort if the public purse covers at least some of the costs of the infrastructure or facility. In situation 6 there is no necessary connection between any land value increment and the community need.

In situations 4 and 5, measures such as planning obligations and impact fees clearly have the potential to extract funds, infrastructure or facilities for the public sector as a consequence of a link between new development and public costs. There is also potential in situation 3 if public costs are imposed as a consequence of the permission to develop.

The public costs are not the same as the land-value increment. If, however, the public sector is successful in recovering some of these costs there must be sufficient 'surplus' in the development for the developer to be able to afford the cost imposed. To the extent that the developer can afford the cost imposed by the public sector because the cost is passed on to the landowner, the public action is a 'tax' on the economic rent of land. The more the public payment is negotiated, rather than a blanket payment regardless of the economics of the development, the greater is the chance of the tax being only a tax on economic rent and not a tax on transfer earnings which stifles development.

In situations 1 and 2, economic rent may accrue but it is not taxable using planning obligations or impact fees. In situation 6 only if there are rules which allow developments to cross-subsidize schemes that are not directly necessary for their implementation, will there be a potential for an effective tax on economic rent to finance a facility such as affordable housing. Whilst this is the essence of affordable housing through planning in Britain, such cases are generally outside of the spirit and detail of impact fees in the USA. Inclusionary zoning ordinances can, however, effectively require or encourage developers to support affordable housing out of development profits in return for incentives such as higher density development. This procedure is discussed in Chapter 10.

Conclusions

Our review of land-value theory shows that a strong theme running through the literature has been that land is fixed in supply. From this flowed the idea that the earnings of landowners were 'economic rent' and thus that surpluses could be taxed away without any effect on supply. Such a tax would therefore be efficient. Given that land values increased because of the efforts of society as a whole rather than individual landowners, their gains were 'unearned increments' and could thus, on grounds of distributional justice or equity, rightly be confiscated and put to use for the good of the community. The modern reality is much more complicated than this. Land supply for any given use is variable and influenced both by market considerations and the availability of planning permission. Some of the earnings of landowners may be economic rent, but some is necessary to ensure supply. If all the increase in land value contingent on the granting of planning permission is taxed away, there is no incentive to develop. However, some of the increased value may well be economic rent that could be taxed without reducing supply. The practical question is 'How much of the land value or the change in land value is economic rent?' If it were always 100 per cent or 40 per cent, simple uniform-rate taxes would work. They have been tried and they don't work, largely because the size of the economic rent element in any land transaction varies with the specifics of each development. It is, moreover, more useful to think of a potential surplus arising from the whole of the development process rather than simply a gain to the landowner. What the landowner receives depends on what the developer is willing to pay. This depends, in turn, on the developer's expected revenues and costs. If the developer expects a large surplus of revenues over costs, a large payment may be offered and accepted by the landowner and the developer might retain more of the surplus as additional profits. The relative bargaining positions of the parties is significant in determining how the surplus is 'shared' between developer and landowner.

One of the benefits of a system of planning agreements, planning obligations or mutually agreed value-capture arrangements is that it gives local governments the opportunity to negotiate about some of this surplus being used for the community. In principle, this allows for the possibility that the value of the economic rent which may be transferred to the community is not some fixed percentage of land values or development profits, but is something that varies from case to case depending on the specific costs and revenues relating to any given development opportunity. From this perspective, a negotiated deal between developers and representatives of the community has the potential to be more efficient in identifying and taxing economic rent than does a universal percentage tax.

The important downsides of this system are the uncertainty, the perceived arbitrariness, and the costs of negotiation that are imposed. The skills, knowledge and bargaining positions of the parties will, moreover, have a significant impact on the outcomes. Clearer guidelines and more informed negotiations with more information provided by planners and developers can potentially address these issues. It would be better to acknowledge that the process involves a 'negotiated tax' than to pretend that it does not.

It would be useful to recognise that the objective of such a negotiated tax regime is to extract some potential development surplus for the use of the community. The size of the tax payment would then clearly be related to what the development process could afford, and it would effectively be a tax on economic rent. It would not, necessarily, be related to (a) the external costs of the development, or (b) what the community needed. Different policy instruments would be required if development taxation were to be related to the objectives of covering or contributing to external costs and/or community needs. In Chapter 8 we consider a particular form of 'negotiated taxation' that has grown in recent years; this concerns the provision of 'affordable housing'.

Chapter 8

Affordable Housing and Planning

The term 'affordable housing' has become a synonym for housing provided at sub-market prices to households on low incomes. In Britain, the production of such housing has in recent years been supplied in large measure by housing associations, and similar non-profit organizations supply affordable housing throughout Europe. The suppliers also include, in some countries, private- sector organizations who, in return for fiscal concessions or other forms of support, supply housing at low rents to low-income households. This is the case in Germany, for example. It is also the dominant model for affordable housing supply in the USA where both profit and non-profit organizations play a role in affordable housing provision. Such accommodation, especially when rented, is often called 'social housing', but affordable housing also embraces various forms of low-cost home ownership and partly-rented, partly-owned dwellings. Affordable housing involves some sort of explicit or implicit subsidy, and as explicit subsidies in the form of grants or soft loans have declined, attention has focused on the role of the planning system in facilitating the development of new affordable housing.

The mechanisms through which the planning system promotes the supply of affordable housing typically involve a form of cross-subsidy from private-sector developers or landowners. Private-sector residential development might thus be granted planning permission, in certain circumstances, only if a proportion of affordable housing is provided on- or off-site, or a payment in lieu of direct provision is made to the local authority. This is the model in Britain. In the USA, developers can be encouraged or required to contribute to the affordable housing stock in return for enhanced development rights, including the opportunity to develop at higher than normal densities. In its consideration of institutional arrangements, this chapter concentrates on the system in England. In Chapter 10 there are comments on the use of 'inclusionary zoning' to promote affordable housing through planning in the USA. However, the discussion of principles in this chapter has a general application. The provision of affordable housing through planning has, on both sides of the Atlantic, been controversial. In both academic and practice circles, many questions have been raised about the practicality and efficiency of such provision, and, more fundamentally, the question 'Is it right to use the planning system to provide affordable housing?' has been asked. Thus the equity of the redistributive mechanisms has been questioned. In this chapter, critiques of the efficiency, legitimacy and equity of delivering affordable housing through planning will be considered, and the operation of planning and affordable housing mechanisms in England will be reviewed. The links to the economic viability of housing development will be examined and ideas for reform of the current system in England will be discussed.

Planning and affordable housing provision

The processes by which planning has been used in England to secure low-cost housing have been surrounded by much confusion, with official policy often following rather than leading current practice (Gallent, 2000). The 1971 Town and Country Planning Act gave local authorities the opportunity to negotiate additional returns for the community from planning permission. By the 1980s agreements were being used widely to negotiate the inclusion of an element of low-cost housing in private-sector developments. There were concerns from developers, however, that agreements were being used to unreasonably impose additional taxes, and it was not until 1991 that central government tried to clarify and more effectively control the negotiation process. In Circular 7/91: *Planning and Affordable Housing* (DoE, 1991), it was made clear that a 'community's need for affordable housing is a material planning consideration which may properly be taken into account in formulating local plan policies'. However, the circular posed something of a conundrum by declaring that 'planning conditions and agreements cannot normally be used to impose restrictions on tenure, price or ownership', although 'they can properly be used to restrict the occupation of property for people falling within particular categories of need' (ibid.). The circular acknowledged that a practical way of ensuring long-term control over ownership and occupation was to involve registered housing associations in the provision of the new affordable housing created through planning conditions.

An attempt to provide further clarity on this issue was made in Circular 13/96 (DoE, 1996). More detailed guidance on the assessment of housing need, the use of conditions and the involvement of regis-tered social landlords was provided. Thresholds were introduced for site sizes below which it would be inappropriate to seek affordable housing, the thresholds varying with location. Outside London, only sites above 40 units were to have affordable housing quotas, whereas in Inner London sites with more than 25 units were appropriate. These thresholds were subsequently deemed to be too high and a restriction on affordable housing development. In Circular 6/98, developers are expected to provide affordable housing on develop-ments above 25 dwellings or more than one hectare, except in Inner London, or other areas where a robust housing needs assessment provides support, where the threshold is set at 15 dwellings or half a hectare. In rural areas, local planning authorities may additionally sanction the use of land that would not otherwise have obtained planning permission for development as social housing. In settle-ments of 3,000 persons or less, dwelling sites of any size might accommodate affordable housing.

Through DETR's Planning Policy and Guidance Note 3, *Planning and Affordable Housing* (1999d), the government attempted to encourage a more consistent approach that facilitated speedier and more effective negotiations on affordable housing. There is, however, a potential and real conflict between consistency and local flexibility. Locally negotiated solutions allow developers and local planning authorities to, in principle, promote development that recognizes local housing needs and local market circumstances. A major criti-cism, however, has been that the interpretation of needs, market circumstances and policy advice has varied considerably from authority to authority and developers face unreasonable uncertainty regarding the outcome of negotiations.

Should planning be used to provide affordable housing?

Critiques of planning and affordable housing policy can be divided into (1) arguments about whether, in principle, planning should be used to support the supply of affordable housing, and (2) arguments about the inconsistent application of policy. The arguments about principles will be considered in this section and the arguments about practice in the section following.

By agreeing to a proportion of affordable housing on a site, a developer is accepting a cost that equates to the lower level of profit to be made on the development. If the developer knows about this reduced profit in advance of buying the land, less might be bid for the land and some of the cost thus transferred to the landowner. The affordable housing that is built might additionally receive subsidy in England in the form of a Social Housing Grant through the Housing Corporation. An important question of principle is whether all of the subsidy for the production of affordable housing should come from public funds channelled through an agency such as the Housing Corporation, or whether it is acceptable for there to be an element of subsidy from the developer and landowner.

The Joseph Rowntree Foundation's (1994) *Inquiry into Planning for Housing* said 'We do not think it any more reasonable to expect suppliers of new private housing to house the homeless than to make farmers responsible for feeding the hungry' (1994, p. 3). The Inquiry concurred with the views of Healey *et al.* (1993) that it is reasonable for the planning system to require development schemes to bear (1) the costs of their implementation such as additional infrastructure, and (2) the costs of adverse impacts on the community whether these arise at or away from the site being developed. It is, however, 'unreasonable to require a developer to contribute on an *ad hoc* basis to wider community objectives, such as social housing, *unless* it can be justified in terms of the specific development' (Joseph Rowntree Foundation, 1994, p. 33).

Linking the need for a new road or school to a specific development is much easier than linking the need for new social housing. It is difficult to construct an argument that building more private housing for sale does of itself create a need for more low-cost housing. If this link cannot be established, on what grounds might a cross-subsidy from private development be justified?

In the previous chapter, the arguments for taxing development gains that amount to 'economic rent' were elaborated. The taxation of economic rent, it was shown, should have no effect on the type or volume of development. If such taxation is acceptable, it might be argued that extracting affordable housing contributions from developers and landowners is a means of implementing this form of desirable taxation. If one acknowledges that affordable housing contributions from developers and landowners are a form of betterment taxation, there are five sets of issues that have to be addressed. These relate to:

(1)   the principle of hypothecation;
(2)   the nature of an equitable redistributive process;
(3)   the *ad hoc* nature of the taxation;
(4)   the problem of measuring economic rent; and

(5)   the contradictions in policy between betterment taxation and affordable housing delivery.

Each of these will be considered in turn.

Affordable housing contributions through the planning system, negotiated on a site-specific basis, are a form of hypothecated taxes. It is a long-established principle of British taxation that hypothecation, whereby the proceeds of specific taxes are earmarked for specific types of expenditure, is undesirable. The yield from any single tax is likely to be variable and uncertain, and the volume of funds available for the earmarked need will thus be difficult to predict. If funds from the tax are not available, the need goes unmet. If the need is sufficiently merit-worthy, the satisfaction of the need should not be contingent on the yield from a single tax. When the need is linked to the activity that triggers the tax, the position is different. If a new housing development brings about the need for a new road, a tax on the development might usefully and reasonably help to pay for the road. The market housing and low cost housing link will inevitably be tenuous.

Hypothecation implies that there are some needs that are so superior that they warrant their own dedicated form of taxation. This argument has occasionally been applied to the National Health Service in Britain, with some politicians arguing (unsuccessfully) for extra taxes to specifically fund more healthcare. Society will always have competing needs; the need for more hospitals, more schools, more roads and more affordable housing will vie for public funds. What good reasons are there for 'more affordable housing' having a claim to the proceeds of a tax on development that is superior to all other competing claims? Development taxation might reasonably be used to meet a variety of needs. In fact this is often the case as local planning authorities sometimes secure contributions from a given development for a variety of needs. The desirability and the degree of hypothecation in the case of affordable housing are in practice determined by local government officers and local politicians. The acceptability and the size of the specific link between private- sector housing development and affordable housing development remain key policy questions.

This linkage may also be considered from the perspective of the type of development that is to be taxed. Why should only private-sector residential development be taxed to support affordable housing? Contributions from office, industrial and retail development might also be considered. Without this, one form of development, residential development, is receiving less favourable treatment than other forms. If linkage between need and the development that is taxed is a primary criterion, it will be easier to make this link for many forms of local employment-creating developments and affordable housing than it is for residential development. Additional employment opportunities arguably create a need for more housing, and some of this housing may be housing for those on lower incomes.

Turning to the nature of an equitable redistributive process, one may question whether a variety of alternative means are better than the planning system at addressing housing needs. The key questions are: Is general taxation a better way to provide for those in need? Is such redistribution likely to be more equitable than taxing development and is housing need better met by supplementing low incomes rather than offering provision in kind? These questions concern fundamental issues about the nature of social housing and the appropriateness of alternative redistributive mechanisms.

The *ad hoc* nature of the taxation that occurs through affordable housing negotiations is a challenge to both the equity and the efficiency of the processes. The contributions that occur are the result of local negotiations between planning authorities and developers. Whilst these negotiations take place in a framework of national policy guidance and local planning statements, the range of the bargaining can be very wide, and the outcomes are typically very uncertain. The variability in outcomes from site to site and from local authority to local authority results in a range of unequal outcomes for developers. There is thus a lack of consistency in the cost of the affordable housing contribution whether this is measured as a proportion of gross development value or developers' profits, and the uncertainty is a source of inefficiency. Developers will lack knowledge of how much it is worth paying for a site and what volume of resources it is worth dedicating to the negotiation process.

In the previous chapter it was argued that a betterment tax was ideally a tax on economic rent, but it was also shown that economic rent is difficult to measure. If tax collectors attempt to extract more than economic rent, development will not take place. If they accept less than economic rent, opportunities to benefit the public sector are lost. Economic rent is the surplus that exists in the development process. It is a surplus that can be taxed away whilst still leaving the developer with sufficient profit to build houses and the landowner with sufficient reward to accept the sale of the site to the developer. The size of this surplus thus depends on the detailed economics of individual developments, including all the revenues and the costs associated with delivering the completed development. There is therefore some advantage in a tax on economic rent being determined on a site-by-site basis, since there is a better chance that a site-specific approach will capture economic rent than a nationally imposed single-rate tax on development or land value. However, the site-specific estimation still imposes a considerable challenge; an understanding of the economic viability of individual developments is needed by those engaged in the negotiation process. This problem is considered in more detail later in this chapter when the connections between viability and affordable housing delivery are explored.

There is a contradiction in policy between betterment taxation and affordable housing delivery. It has been argued in this chapter that affordable housing contributions through planning are an *ad hoc* tax on development. However, this concept of affordable housing contributions is not accepted in central government's planning guidance. The principles governing planning obligations, which are typically used to formalize affordable housing contributions secured through planning, are set out in Circular 1/97 (DETR, 1997). This states that 'planning obligations should never be used as a means of securing for the local community a share in the profits of development, that is as a means of securing a "betterment levy" '. This is, however, exactly what affordable housing planning obligations do. If they do not 'secure a share of the profits of development' they have no source from which to provide the subsidy for affordable housing. Planning obligations therefore impose a tax on betterment. It has been argued that:

> affordable housing obligations, even if regulated, are a crude and inefficient method of levying such a tax. A community will have many needs, including perhaps a shortage of affordable housing. But why should the tax on windfall gains be paid only on affordable housing units, ruling out any opportunity to prioritize the community's needs and meet other non-housing requirements? (Stewart, 2001)

Planning and affordable housing policies in practice

Whilst there are national guidelines on securing affordable housing through planning, local practice varies widely. This variation in practice might variously be seen as a lack of clarity in the national policy framework; the useful flexibility that the framework provides; or mainly a consequence of varying housing needs and local housing markets. However, the local variations can be a source of confusion for developers. Local authorities usually use so-called Section 106 agreements as part of the process of delivering affordable housing. These agreements between the planning authority and developer set out the details of the volume of new houses on a site that are to be 'affordable' and how these houses are to be provided; planning permission will be given subject to a satisfactory Section 106 agreement being negotiated. Again, variations in local authority practice on what they require from such agreements may create uncertainty for developers.

A large majority of local authorities in England have policies in place to secure affordable housing through the planning system. Surveys have estimated that between 89 per cent (Joseph Rowntree Foundation, 2001) and 95 per cent (Bishop, 2001) of authorities have affordable housing policies in their local plans. Where there is no such inclusion, the principal reason given by local authorities is a lack of proven need for additional affordable housing. In recent years about 10 per cent of all new housing given planning permission (around 15,000 dwellings) has been affordable housing secured through planning. Nearly half of this has been in London and the south-east, with comparatively small volumes in the north of England. There is also regional variation in the type of affordable housing provided. In areas of high housing need, especially in the south of England, rented housing predominates. Shared ownership housing and low-cost market housing are more common in the north. Low cost market housing is sold at less than the full market price. On sites where affordable housing is approved, the proportions range from 11 per cent in the north-east to 27 per cent in the south-east. However, it is only a minority of sites on which affordable housing is approved, with many sites being too small for mixed 'market-sector'/'affordable' developments. It has been shown that there is not a clear correlation between the degree of housing need in an area and the amount of affordable housing secured, but the following factors have been shown to be important:

- 'Where there are constraints on the overall release of land for housing, the small number of sites available means that there is little opportunity to secure additional affordable housing. However, these are often areas with a high housing need.
- In contrast, some areas with a plentiful supply of housing land are characterized by a lower level of need.
- Political priorities towards planning and affordable housing issues, and local authority officers' understanding and experience

of operating the system, also affect the amount of affordable housing that is secured' (Joseph Rowntree Foundation, 2001, p. 3)

The difficulties of policy implementation have been identified in research reports. For example,

> Local authorities identify a lack of clarity in the policy framework set by central government as the main problem in achieving affordable housing through Section 106 agreements. More detailed problems in implementing the policy include: difficulty in determining the level of financial contribution developers should be expected to make, estimating what the developer can afford to provide from a particular site, and securing sufficient Social Housing Grant for sites that come forward. (Ibid.)

The local link between subsidy in the form of Social Housing Grant and the economics of affordable housing through planning is explored further in the next section.

Another research report places the problems of long and costly negotiations over affordable housing squarely at the local level:

> Protracted Section 106 negotiations largely stem from unclear, planning-led affordable housing policies. Without clear local policies, the granting of planning permission 'subject to a Section 106 agreement' has proved in some cases to be the granting of little more than the right to enter into lengthy, legal and costly wrangling. (Bishop, 2001, p. 3)

Central government policy requires local authorities to negotiate with developers over the amount of affordable housing provided, and most negotiations take place around a local authority's target figure. Where housing need and demand are relatively low, local authorities are typically more prepared to accept a lower level of contribution.

Government policy encourages a mix of market and affordable housing on the same site; the objective is more 'balanced communities'. On small sites, this may be particularly difficult to achieve, even if the affordable housing takes the form of low-cost market housing. Because of the effect on the prices that may be achieved for market housing, developers may prefer to make 'payments in lieu' (sometimes called 'commuted sums') to the local authority. However, there is much variation in practice in the willingness of local authorities to accept this option. In some cases this will be very acceptable to the local authority, and the sums might be used to assist in off-site provision or improvements to the existing stock of social housing. In other cases, local authorities may press strongly for on-site provision of social housing in line with the preferences of government policy.

One study of local authorities found that 45 per cent of responding authorities had accepted either off-site affordable housing provision tied to the affordable site in question or commuted sums. It found that the reasons for accepting off-site provision included:

- local reaction against social housing provision;
- unsuitable site location and configuration;
- other secured affordable housing sites but with insufficient resources to develop; and
- little need for additional affordable housing when compared to other affordable housing priorities, such as house condition issues (Bishop, 2001, p. 20).

Where commuted sums are accepted, the methods for calculating the amount to be paid vary widely. For example, a fixed price per unit of housing or proportion of the site value might be claimed.

Local authorities are required to underpin affordable housing strategies with evidence of local housing needs, but the nature of the evidence varies considerably. It has been claimed that 'The analysis and forecasting of particular local housing needs, and what these households can afford is in its infancy' (ibid., p. 3). Various forms of postal household surveys, desk-based analyses of market data, and interviews are used to assemble data on needs. Most local authorities commission consultants to do the work, and sometimes needs surveys usefully cross administrative borders. The variability in the practice and use of housing studies relates to a lack of clarity about what is being measured. In general terms, those in housing need are defined as being unable to compete for housing in the marketplace; that is, they cannot afford market prices or rents. What this means in practice, however, is open to a variety of interpretations. Logically it requires some measure of minimum acceptable quality to be considered, but this is rarely attempted. Without clear definitions it is not surprising that 'there is considerable variation, and little apparent consensus, in approaches to quantifying affordability, many of which have important limitations. Central government approaches to clarifying affordability have been of little practical help' (ibid., p. 16).

It has been suggested that 'some three-quarters of housing

provided by affordable policies is either for social rent or shared ownership' (ibid., p. 14). This provision usually involves a housing association, whose involvement helps to ensure that the dwellings will remain 'affordable' and 'available to meet needs' as time goes by. However, about half of local authorities do not specify how occupancy is to be controlled.

The financial viability of affordable housing through planning

The financing and subsidy provisions for affordable housing from planning are complex and varied, with much variability in the contributions that come from landowners, developers and housing associations. The extent to which Social Housing Grant is available to support affordable housing also varies considerably.

In response to a survey of housing departments 'Almost two thirds (63 per cent) indicated that as a matter of policy, their local authorities required private sector (land owner, development or conceivably RSL) subsidy into the affordable housing identified in particular schemes' (Bishop, 2001, p. 30). However, even if there is not an explicit cross-subsidy from the private sector, there will be an implicit cross-subsidy:

> Some developers are clearly of the view that the affordable housing provisions of local planning policies of themselves prompt private sector subsidy because of the opportunity cost. This takes two forms. First, land developed for affordable housing rather than housing for open market sale is less profitable. Second, open market sale housing juxtaposed with affordable housing will command a lower sale price, fewer economies of scale, and lower profits than if the affordable housing was absent. In effect, so the argument runs, developers and/or landowners are subsidizing affordable housing developments at least to the tune of the difference between the profits. (Ibid.)

Whilst the availability of Social Housing Grant can, in its initial impact, be seen to boost viability, it can also raise land prices; the availability of grants tends to increase what developers are prepared to pay for land. Thus part of the effect of the grant ends up with the landowner. The relationship between the developer's profits and what is paid for land is central to the financial viability of affordable housing. The developer's return before paying for land can, in principle, be divided into two elements. These are 'normal profits' and 'supernormal profits'. The normal profit is necessary to reward the developer for entrepreneurship and, without this minimum level of profit, development will not be commercially worthwhile. Normal profit can be viewed as a standard cost of production. Supernormal profit is, in principle, a variable surplus that has no effect on the decision to develop.

The maximum that the developer will be prepared to pay for land is equal to expected revenue from house sales minus all costs, including normal profit. How much the developer will actually pay for land, in a market situation, depends on the relationship between the developer's willingness to pay, what the landowner is prepared to accept, and their relative bargaining positions and bargaining skills. What the landowner is prepared to accept will be influenced by the value of the land in alternative uses.

Any policies that attempt to get affordable housing must, if they are to be effective, ensure that what the developer is prepared to pay for land remains positive and is equal to or greater than what the landowner is prepared to accept. These values might, however, be skilfully manipulated, with appropriate knowledge, to keep the actual surplus from the land transaction to a minimum and to use the potential surplus to provide affordable housing. The combination of supernormal profit and potential land surplus is a residual. An elaboration of the concept of residual value as applied to the viability of affordable housing development on a site is given in Figure 8.1.

Policy can influence the revenue from house sales, and thus influence what the residential developer is prepared to pay, by impacting on the number of houses that can be sold at market prices on a site. It can also influence the relationship between the developer's bid for land and what the landowner is prepared to accept by determining the alternative permissible uses for a site. A key point is that the impact of relevant factors will be site-specific, and any rules about which policies are going to maximize affordable housing production and/or total housing production will be misleading if they do not take account of the specifics of particular developments. However, without digging into the specifics of particular developments it is still however possible to make an assessment of the probable influence of policies of different sorts, in varying market circumstances, on developer surpluses and the potential for directing these surpluses to affordable housing outputs. What the land is worth to the developer, in varying circumstances, and the relationship of this to what the landowner is willing to accept from the developer, need to be understood if policies are to be effective.

Figure 8.1   *Affordable housing and residual value*

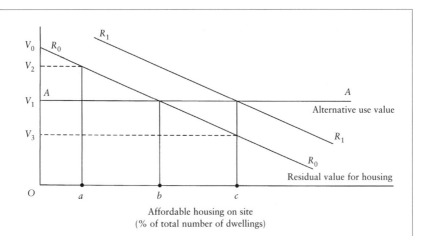

Figure 8.1 relates to an individual site of a fixed size on which affordable housing development is being considered. The residual value of the site for housing development depends on the revenue from housing minus all the non-land costs of housing development. If the site is developed 100% for the sale of private dwellings at market value, the residual value is V_0. If the percentage of affordable housing on the site is 'a' residual value falls to V_2; at 'b' it is V_1 and at 'c' it is V_3. Residual value is thus assumed to fall as the percentage of affordable housing on the site increases (because affordable housing is assumed to give the developer less revenue than dwellings sold at market value and the non-land costs for developing affordable and market housing are assumed to be equal) and this is shown by $R_0 R_0$. The alternative use value, for example the value of the site for office or retail development, is shown by $A A$. (The relevant alternative use for the site will be influenced by what the planning system allows). The residential developer has to pay at least V_1 to prise the land from an alternative use. If no affordable housing is required on the site, the developer could afford to pay as much as V_0 but anything greater than V_1 should be sufficient to prevent the land going to the alternative use. If only V_1 is paid to the land owner, the developer receives a surplus or supernormal profit equal to V_0 minus V_1. If V_0 is paid to the landowner, an economic rent of V_0 minus V_1 is received by the landowner. How the surplus shown by V_0 minus V_1 is split between the developer and the landowner will depend on their relative bargaining strengths and skills. If a percentage of affordable housing equal to 'a' is to be developed on the site, the surplus available for distribution between the developer and landowner is V_2 minus V_1.

With residual value $R_0 R_0$, the maximum percentage of affordable housing that can viably be developed on the site is 'b'. At proportions greater than 'b', alternative use value exceeds the residual value for housing development.

Several factors may cause the residual value for housing development to rise, shifting $R_0 R_0$ to $R_1 R_1$. The shift might occur because, for example, house prices rise, the density at which the site is to be developed increases or building costs fall. With residual value for housing development at $R_1 R_1$, the percentage of affordable housing that may viably be developed on the site rises to 'c'.

Variations in the number and type of houses on a plot, the prices that houses can be sold for and the cost of building houses will all have an effect on a developer's profits. What landowners are prepared to accept for a site is crucial. All these factors need to be understood by local authorities when they negotiate over affordable housing provision. They need, in short, to understand the concept of economic rent and to have some estimate of how much potential economic rent exists in a particular development proposal. This requires a set of skills and a body of data that are usually absent.

Affordable housing in London

The Mayor of London, Ken Livingstone, has proposed that 50 per cent of all new housing developed in London should be 'affordable'. His Housing Commission (a group of experts) proposed that there should be a London-wide target of 50 per cent, comprising 35 per cent for social renting aimed at households on low incomes, and 15 per cent for new intermediate housing aimed at households on moderate incomes (GLA, 2000). The Commission's proposals were based on an assessment of housing need in London. In the late 1990s most London boroughs were seeking around 25 per cent affordable housing through planning.

Private-sector developers have complained that a 50 per cent target is not achievable and that attempts to impose it will result in less housing development with both market and affordable housing production declining as it becomes less profitable to build (Minton, 2000, 2001). Disagreement on the issue is characterized by the following quotations: the land-buying director of a large developer said 'Anything near 50 per cent will have a serious impact on the market. I would rival it with the development land tax – and that showed that the last time the government tried to tax the development of land, the market responded by not doing any business'. The planning policy officer at the National Housing Federation responded by saying: 'developers give you this sort of story a lot and occasionally when sites are unviable they move away. But what we're more likely to see is a period of market adjustment where the currently artificially inflated land values will start to fall. Housebuilders cannot buy sites at prices that don't reflect their wider community responsibility' (both quotes are from Minton, 2001). The alleged consequences for land values produced provocative journalistic copy: 'Ken Livingstone's plan to make half of new housing in London affordable will reduce land values by 70 per cent', said

Geoff Marsh of London Residential Research (Coppin, 2000). The research on which this quote was based suggested that increasing the social housing element from 25 per cent to 50 per cent on a 100,000 sq ft site in central London reduced the amount that the developer could afford to pay for land from £8.75m to £2.5m.

The effect on land use of this lower bid from developers does, however, depend on the attitudes of landowners and what the planning system allows. Landowners may try to sell for alternative higher value uses, but if planning permission is only available for housing and not for, say, offices then sale and development for residential use may occur at lower values. In this scenario, land values will be lower, but houses will still get built and landowners will receive less, but housebuilders' profits may not be affected.

A detailed analysis of the financial viability of delivering affordable housing across London showed that the consequences for developers' profits before paying for land varied considerably from borough to borough (Oxley *et al.*, 2001). In central London boroughs where house prices and density are very high, developers' profits and their ability to bid for land would remain high, even after 50 per cent of a site is developed for social housing, whilst in outer London with lower prices and lower densities, profits would be lower and the ability to bid for land lower. The profitability of housebuilding in some central boroughs was estimated to be sufficient to deliver 50 per cent affordable housing without any additional public subsidy. In other boroughs with lower levels of profitability, it would be difficult to deliver 50 per cent affordable housing and make a profit even if there was public subsidy available at the going rate. Thus 'There are 12 boroughs where 50 per cent affordable housing provision is not a realistic option and a 35 per cent affordable housing target would be more achievable' (ibid., p. vi).

The 'affordability of affordable housing' thus varies with the profitability of housebuilding and developers' ability to acquire land at prices they can 'afford'. The need for affordable housing may not coincide geographically with the viability of delivery, and there is thus a case, particularly in London, for cooperation between localities so that payments in lieu collected in one local authority can be used to provide housing to meet need in another.

The need to provide housing for so-called 'key workers' who are essential to the functioning of the local economy has been an essential part of the policy debate in London. These 'key workers' are seen to include nurses, teachers, policemen and other public-sector employees whose incomes are too low to allow them to buy or rent market-sector housing. Without affordable dwellings, it is argued that there will be prolonged shortages of labour. However, the suggestion that labour-market shortages should be resolved through subsidies from housing developers is, of course, highly contentious. Many other remedies are possible, including increasing the incomes of workers, providing more housing through general public subsidy and, if developers are to be taxed to provide housing, taxing all developers and not just housing developers.

Reforming planning obligations

Planning obligations (also known as Section 106 agreements) are the principal means through which affordable housing is secured. More generally, they are a means of ensuring that developers contribute towards infrastructure and local services that are necessary to facilitate developments. In December 2001, the government stated that it was fundamentally dissatisfied with the operation of planning obligations in England and proposed radical changes that were designed to achieve social, economic and environmental objectives. The proposals were set out in *Planning Obligations: Delivering a Fundamental Change* (DTLR, 2001).

It was argued that an effective planning obligation system should enhance the quality of development and the wider environment, provide social, economic and environmental benefits to the community, and 'help to provide an increased supply of affordable housing, the provision of public spaces, and the facilities and infrastructure needed to accommodate growth'. It was argued that 'An effective planning obligation system should be transparent to all stakeholders in the planning process, including the community. It should provide greater certainty to those contemplating development and enable agreements to be concluded quickly'. It should also promote economic prosperity and 'not impose unacceptable burdens on developers'. However, 'our present planning obligation system falls short of our objectives' (DTLR, 2001, paras 1.3–1.6). Several criticisms of the existing system were acknowledged:

- the absence of predictable limits on the scope or total cost of a planning obligation has led to charges that, on the one hand, planning permission is being bought and sold and, on the other, that developers are being held to ransom;
- planning obligations are time-consuming to agree, can slow the development process down and are expensive in legal costs;

- negotiations are often conducted in private, leading to charges of impropriety and lack of transparency; and
- there is a lack of accountability, with contributions not necessarily being used for the purposes for which they were originally sought. (Ibid., para 3.7)

The government also questions

whether, under the present system, planning obligations are falling unequally – and possibly unfairly – on some developments but not others, and whether this is biasing investment decisions. The common practice, which we encourage, of seeking affordable housing contributions on larger residential developments may, for example, cause developers to favour commercial development rather than housing, greenfield developments may be preferred to re-using land within our towns and cities. (Ibid., para 2.5)

To overcome the objections to the existing system and to achieve the broad social, economic and environmental objectives of sustainable development, it was suggested that a system of tariffs be introduced:

We have developed the proposal that local authorities should set standardized tariffs for different types of development through the plan-making process ... tariffs would contribute to meeting a range of planning objectives, including the provision of affordable housing. We propose that negotiated agreements should only supplement or substitute for the tariff where these are clearly justified to deliver, for example, site-specific requirements. (Ibid., para 1.11–1.12)

The consultation document goes on to state:

We propose that local authorities should have discretion to determine the types, sizes and location of development on which the tariff would be charged and how it would apply in different circumstances, subject to national policy considerations. We also propose that there should be local discretion about how receipts from the tariff are spent, again subject to national policy guidance. We envisage a wider range of developments being subject to a tariff than is currently subject to planning obligations. (Ibid., para 4.6)

Whilst there would be some local discretion, it was envisaged that there would be central guidance on how a tariff might be set and that variations in the rate of the tariff would be used to encourage some types of development and discourage others: 'Some locations would attract a higher tariff than others: Greenfield development would almost certainly have a higher tariff than brownfield developments, which may be exempted altogether' (ibid., para 4.11).

The exact method by which a tariff would be determined was not proposed in the discussion paper, but several broad options were identified. Thus it was suggested that it might be set as a cost per gross floorspace or a cost per dwelling or a proportion of development value or some combination of these.

It is clear that the government sees tariffs as a new way of financing the supply of affordable housing. Local authorities would define the proportion of the tariff to be used for affordable housing and 'depending on the local assessment of the needs of the area and regional policies, the affordable housing element may represent a large proportion of the overall tariff' (ibid., para 4.19). The tariff supporting affordable housing would be paid by both residential and commercial development schemes. It might be paid in the form of houses delivered on or off-site, or in the form of money. The money might be used to develop new dwellings elsewhere, including possibly in another local authority area, if local authorities had chosen to pool contributions. It is also proposed that 'tariffs should be used not only to develop new property but to convert existing buildings and to buy empty property back into affordable residential use' (ibid., para 4.25).

Although the government's discussion paper did not explicitly acknowledge that a tariff would be a new form of betterment taxation, this is in fact what it would be. If it were to be successful, it would have to set out rates for individual developments that taxed only economic rent (see the discussion in Chapter 7, where economic rent is defined as a surplus that can be taxed without affecting production decisions). If the tariff was set at too high a level, it would be greater than economic rent and would result in a decision not to develop. Finding the right level, however, is very difficult, requiring planners to have information about the economics of different sorts of development in different locations and to appreciate what levels of taxation will achieve planning objectives and what levels of taxation will stifle development. Taxation levels that achieve planning objectives at one level of property values and building costs may not provide the desired results at another level of values and costs. Tariffs might thus need to change as circumstances in the property market change. Tariffs that yield large sums of money for affordable housing at higher levels of profit may, with a property-market slump, result in less commercial development and less money for affordable housing. Predicting the incidence of the taxation imposed through tariffs will also be difficult. Depending on circumstances in the markets for land and for completed properties, the tax might be shifted, at least in part, to the landowner or the purchaser of the property.

The revenue from tariffs according to the government's 2001 proposals (DTLR, 2001) was to be used for specific and well-defined purposes, including the provision of affordable housing. Several other items such as local schools and roads might also be financed from tariffs. Tariffs would thus be a form of hypothecated taxation. The purposes to which the taxation proceeds were dedicated would be determined by local authorities with central government guidance. Tariffs would have all the disadvantages of hypothecation identified earlier in this chapter. In November 2003 the government revised its proposals on tariffs and suggested that they might take the form of an 'optional planning charge' as an alternative to negotiated planning obligations.

Conclusions

Private-sector residential developers and landowners have subsidized the provision of affordable housing by providing either dwellings or payments in the form of commuted sums as a condition of planning permission. The degree of subsidy has been a consequence of negotiations between developers and planners. The implementation of affordable housing policies has varied widely from area to area with differences in the definition of affordable housing, the level of contributions expected from developers and the clarity of the negotiation process differing from authority to authority. The principles and the practice of affordable housing delivery have been criticized, and as is clear from our discussion, the imposition of an *ad hoc* and uncertain tax on residential developers can bias development outcomes.

Improved clarity, greater certainty and lower negotiation costs are likely outcomes of an alternative system of tariffs. If imposed on all types of development, tariffs would be more equitable. As a tax on betterment they will be effective if they do not exceed the economic rent on individual developments. It would, however, be difficult for tariffs to tax economic rent unless there was some site-specific flexibility, which poses a conundrum in that this flexibility is likely to clash with the greater certainty expected of tariffs.

As a form of hypothecated taxation, tariffs would provide a variable volume of funds that are not necessarily linked to the severity of the needs they are designed to meet. This variability will be from one location to another and also from time to time. The ability of a tax to effectively deal with a betterment problem will be different from its ability to provide a sum of money to meet housing needs. We return to affordable housing through planning in an American context in Chapter 10.

Chapter 9

Housing, Planning and Urban Renaissance

In Chapter 5 it was shown that sustainable development is a key planning objective throughout the world. In advanced economies, and in Europe and America in particular, less urban sprawl and more compact energy-saving residential development have been viewed as important components of this environmental agenda. In this chapter we review ideas about combining compact development with an improved quality of urban living. These have been objectives of 'urban renaissance' in Britain and 'new urbanism' and 'smart growth' in America. The essence of these concepts will be examined, with an emphasis on the aims and instruments of urban renaissance.

In Britain, the government-appointed Urban Task Force, in its report *Towards an Urban Renaissance* (DETR, 1999a), set out a vision for improved urban living. This vision, in which towns and cities provide a high quality of life and accommodate an increased proportion of new housing development, was endorsed by the White Paper *Our Towns and Cities: The Future: Delivering an Urban Renaissance* (DETR, 2000a). In this chapter the meaning and implications of urban renaissance are reviewed. Three related issues are then be examined: promoting brownfield residential development, the role of urban capacity studies, and the low demand for housing in some urban areas.

More development on previously used or brownfield land is now an objective in many advanced countries. In Britain, achieving 60 per cent of future housing development on brownfield sites by redeveloping previously used land and buildings is a key government target. The role of economic policy instruments such as new taxes in promoting this target will be examined, and the connections between economic policy instruments and the planning system will be explored. Urban capacity studies are required to assess how much new housing can be accommodated in towns and cities, and the methodology and the implications of these studies will be examined. In some inner-city neighbourhoods in England urban renaissance has

171

been threatened by low and falling demand for housing; the reasons for this and possible responses will be examined.

What is urban renaissance?

In short, urban renaissance is about making towns and cities better places in which people want to live and work. Much of the discussion of urban renaissance involves broad generalities about the desirability of urban living and the means by which cities might become more attractive locations for existing and future inhabitants. The mission statement of the Urban Task Force said:

> The Urban Task Force will identify causes of urban decline in England and recommend practical solutions to bring people back into our cities, towns and urban neighbourhoods. It will establish a new vision for urban regeneration founded on the principles of design excellence, social well-being and environmental responsibility within a viable economic and legislative framework. (DETR, 1999a)

The Task Force agenda was driven by demographic forecasts that suggested there would be around 3.8 million more households in England in 2016 than in 1996. The location of these extra households is a significant policy and planning problem. The essential question being faced by the Task Force was therefore 'How can we improve the quality of both our towns and countryside while at the same time providing homes for almost 4 million additional households in England over a 25 year period?' (DETR, 1999b, p. 4).

The Urban Task Force endorsed the government's target that 60 per cent of new dwellings should be built on previously developed land. It was claimed that:

> Achieving this target is fundamental to the health of society. Failure to do so will lead to fragmentation of the city and erosion of the countryside. It will also increase traffic congestion and air pollution, accelerate the depletion of natural resources, damage biodiversity and increase social deprivation. (Ibid.)

Environmental issues are thus a key driver of urban renaissance. More housebuilding in existing urban areas is deemed to be desirable because of the environmental benefits that will follow. There is an assumption that more compact, higher density urban living will use less natural resources than more dispersed development on green-field sites. The environmental benefits are assumed to be greater than any costs associated with more people living in towns and cities, and there is also an assumption that it is advantageous to provide new dwellings by converting existing buildings to residential use or building new dwellings on previously used land where redundant buildings have been demolished.

It may well be true that the environmental cost of urban compaction is less than the environmental costs of more building on greenfield sites. The case for urban compaction is, however, more usually assumed than argued through; the case is rarely supported by detailed evidence. If a particular pattern of development (more urban compaction, less greenfield development) and a particular form of production (more recycling on brownfield sites, less new building on greenfields) are superior in terms of environmental costs, it would be useful to have some more research findings to clearly support the propositions (some of the limited evidence on the merits of the compact-city concept is reviewed in Adams and Watkins, 2002, pp. 67–90). Intuitively it might seem that the preferred pattern of development and form of production should use less energy and destroy less of the natural environment, but in the absence of strong evidence such intuition does not go unchallenged. It has, for example, been argued that

> The idea that somehow urban land is environmentally good is, at best, an oversimplification and, at worst, a distortion of the truth . . . it is surely far more important for land-use planning policy to concentrate on the optimal use of land than on maintaining the largely artificial distinction between urban and rural land. (Corkindale, 1999, pp. 2064–5)

The urban renaissance agenda, however, suggests that more brownfield and less greenfield development represents an optimal use of land.

This optimality in the arguments used in the Urban Task Force report is strongly influenced by the energy consumption, and specifically car usage effects, of a more dispersed population. It is claimed that 'There is a proven link between urban densities and energy consumption. Urban sprawl contributes significantly to energy consumption due to the increased dependency on car use' (DETR, 1999a, p. 36). Belief in a scenario in which more housebuilding in existing areas results in less travelling and a lower level of energy consumption than a more dispersed pattern of development is thus a strong driver for urban compaction.

The protection of the countryside argument for more urban development should, according to some observers, be seen in the context of the highly urbanized pattern of existing development in Britain and the relatively small amounts of rural land lost to housing each year. For example, Stewart (2002) states 'Anti-development groups often claim housebuilders are "concreting over the countryside". This highly emotive soundbite is completely false ... loss of rural land to new housing amounts to an additional 0.02 per cent every 50 years'. Nevertheless, the Urban Task Force stated that:

> To enable the Government to meet its 60 per cent target for accommodating new dwellings on previously developed land, we must make best use of derelict, vacant and under-used land and buildings before we develop on greenfield sites. To achieve this, we should limit greenfield land releases and channel development into redeveloping urban brownfield sites. (DETR, 1999b, p. 5)

The Urban Task Force report argues for urban regeneration on economic and social grounds as well as arguing for the environmental benefits. It is claimed that:

> Maintaining and improving the economic strength of our towns and cities is ... critical to the competitive performance of the country as a whole. The future economic success of urban areas is itself dependent upon their ability to carve out a competitive role within a knowledge-based economy. This means providing an attractive location for investment. (DETR, 1999a)

The social benefits of urban regeneration are argued in very broad terms. There is a desire to 'create beautiful places that are socially cohesive, avoiding disparity of opportunity and promoting equity and social solidarity' (DETR, 1999a, p. 47).

Urban renaissance thus involves a vision for the future of towns and cities that sees them as better places in which to live and work. An aspect of this vision is more housing development in existing urban areas and less in the countryside, but the economic, social and environmental benefits of this pattern and form of residential development are difficult to evaluate. The degree and complexity of the change and the associated costs and benefits go beyond the boundaries of conventional economic analysis. More evidence to support specific aspects of the urban renaissance agenda would enable a more reasoned judgement to be made about its impact. These specifics relate, for example, to the costs and benefits of alternative patterns of residential development and alternative types of residential production.

The Urban Task Force report puts much emphasis on improved design to achieve urban renaissance objectives, but an overemphasis on design solutions and a lack of appreciation of the economic dimensions of urban form have been viewed as weaknesses of the report. Evans (2003), for example, has argued that the report's authors should have shown a better understanding of the impact of fuel prices on urban densities and not accepted that higher densities will inevitably reduce carbon fuel use: 'Whilst attributing causality is difficult, the economic relationship is more probably that across countries, high petrol prices lead to less use of fuel, shorter journeys and hence more dense cities' (ibid., p. 527). Although it does not advocate increased fuel prices as the key to obtaining more environmentally sustainable patterns of development, the Urban Task Force report does see roles for both new economic policy instruments and new land use planning mechanisms in promoting change. These aspects, rather than design solutions, are the focus of our attention in this chapter.

What is new urbanism?

New urbanism in the USA has much in common with urban renaissance in Britain. It is a reaction to the problems of conventional suburban development or sprawl, and is essentially a campaign for integrated neighbourhood developments oriented towards public transport and based on a belief that suburban sprawl has resulted in environmentally and socially destructive development patterns:

> A growing movement of architects, planners and developers, the New Urbanism is based on the belief that a return to traditional neighbourhood patterns is essential to restoring functional, sustainable communities. Still in its infancy, the trend is beginning to have an impact. More than 300 new homes, villages and neighbourhoods are planned or under construction in the US, using principles of the New Urbanism. Additionally, more than 100 small-scale new urbanist 'infill' projects are restoring the urban fabric of cities and towns by re-establishing walkable streets and blocks ... The heart of the New Urbanism is in the design of neighbourhoods. (Steuteville, 2000)

Like urban renaissance, new urbanism emphasizes, and arguably overemphasizes, the importance of design and compact development in producing sustainable communities. Unlike urban renaissance there is considerable weight attached to applying new design principles to new settlements; the priority in urban renaissance is making existing urban areas better places to live. It has been suggested that the claims of new urbanism, however, should not be exaggerated:

> Although it is often advertised as a panacea, the New Urbanism is only one alternative to suburban sprawl. It will probably function most successfully in a broader planning context that may include significant investments in transit incentives to reinvest in the inner city, and disincentives to build at the metropolitan fringe. (Fulton, 1996)

New urbanism in the USA is strongly allied to the smart growth movement:

> In contrast to prevalent development practices, smart growth refocuses a larger share of regional growth within central cities, urbanized areas, inner suburbs, and areas that are already served by infrastructure. Smart growth reduces the share of growth that occurs in newly urbanizing land, existing farmlands, and in environmentally sensitive areas. In areas with intense growth pressure, development in newly urbanizing areas should be planned and developed according to smart growth principles . . . Many organizations and individuals are now promoting smart growth. Over 60 public interest groups across the U.S. have joined together to form *Smart Growth America*, a coalition advocating better growth policies and practices . . . Many communities embrace specific aspects of smart growth, such as urban service boundaries, pedestrian- and transit-oriented development, controls on sprawl, compact mixed uses, and the protection of agricultural and environmental resources. (APA, 2003)

Smart growth is thus in line with the objectives of sustainable development as set out in Chapter 5. It argues for re-using brownfield sites before open land, and for reducing the use of the car.

New urbanism and smart growth emphasize the role of local communities in achieving sustainable development through better use of planning mechanisms. However, as with urban renaissance in Britain, the role of central government in providing appropriate policy instruments is essential. This is particularly so in relation to fiscal incentives which have been used on both sides of the Atlantic to promote brownfield development.

Promoting brownfield residential development

In America both tax reliefs and grants have been used to promote brownfield development. The Brownfields Tax incentive which was introduced in 1997 and broadened in 2000 provides an estimated $300 million in annual tax reliefs, and levers in $3.4 billion in private investment. The incentive reduces the costs of decontaminating and preparing sites for development. The Brownfield Revitalization Act of 2002 authorizes up to $250 million in funds annually for brownfield grants. These are used to support the development assessments, the clean-up costs and the development of brownfield sites (more information can be found on the web site of the US Environmental Protection Agency: www.epa.gov).

In Britain, reforms to the planning system were viewed by the Urban Task Force as essential to promoting more urban housebuilding: 'The necessary shift from greenfield to brownfield development can be accelerated by streamlining planning permissions for recycled land. Simpler development plans, supported by neighbourhood "masterplans" and design guidance, will enable faster decision making' (DETR, 1999b, p. 12). However, the Urban Task Force also acknowledged the potential for economic policy instruments to support the planning system and commissioned a report on fiscal incentives to promote brownfield development (DETR, 1999c). The report evaluated a range of tax changes for owner-occupiers, tenants, developers and investors that might influence urban residential development. The Task Force report suggested changing value added tax (VAT) to harmonize the development costs of brownfield and greenfield housing (rather than the 17.5 per cent VAT applied to refurbishment or conversion of existing residential properties and the zero per cent applied to new development); it also suggested that consideration be given to the introduction of a system of environmental impact fees through the planning system. The latter was seen as a possible means of reflecting the full environmental costs of new development in the costs borne by developers (DETR, 1999a, pp. 221–3 and p. 255).

In the Urban White Paper (DETR, 2000a), the British government announced its intention to use a series of fiscal measures to encourage the development of brownfield sites and bring empty property back into use. It began to introduce these measures in the 2001 Budget, including:

1   Accelerated tax relief for cleaning up contaminated land. The intention is to effectively reduce the cost of preparing sites for development.

2   A 100 per cent capital allowance for creating flats over shops and commercial premises. This is intended to encourage the residential use of vacant and under-utilized space.

3   VAT reforms. These include cutting VAT to 5 per cent for residential conversions and zero VAT on the sale of renovated properties that have been vacant for ten years or more. The aim is to encourage more conversion of properties for residential use.

4   Exemption from stamp duty (which is effectively a tax on purchasing properties) for all property transactions in selected 'disadvantaged wards'. This is intended to encourage the refurbishment and return to use of existing properties as well as new development.

In examining the potential impact of these measures, it will be useful to refer to the analyses in the report by KPMG for the Urban Task Force on *Fiscal Incentives for Urban Housing* (DETR, 1999c), and a Joseph Rowntree Foundation-funded report on *The Contribution of Economic Instruments to Planning Objectives* (Evans and Bate, 2000).

As the KPMG report acknowledges, 'Market forces are the principal drivers of housing location. Where demand is strong, brownfield opportunities will continue to be attractive to developers, provided abnormal development costs can be overcome, with or without public sector support' (DETR, 1999c, p. 5). If demand is not strong, fiscal incentives may have a role in strengthening demand for dwellings in urban areas. This may be at the expense of weakened demand for dwellings in other locations. Demand-side measures that affect owner-occupiers or tenants may be distinguished from supply-side measures that are designed to influence landowners, investors and developers, principally by changing the relative costs and rates of return from housing production and investment on brownfield and greenfield sites. Changes in taxes which make it less expensive to develop brownfield sites and more advantageous to invest in urban housing have the potential, in principle, to raise levels of brownfield construction.

The use of fiscal instruments for urban renaissance objectives assumes that it is possible to change the behaviour of the demanders and suppliers of new housing in ways that influence both the location and the type of housing produced. To be effective, the financial incentive will have to impact on items that households and developers consider when making their decisions.

Switching demand effectively in favour of inner-city locations through fiscal measures may be very expensive if the incentives have to overcome real or perceived disadvantages of such locations. For households who are concerned about high crime rates, poor schooling and noise in inner cities, the tax incentives required will be more than for households who perceive such locations to have good access to work, entertainment and shops, and who value these attributes highly. Low transaction costs associated with house purchase (through, for example, stamp-duty exemption) may have very little effect on the locational decisions of families who have decided against inner-city living because they believe that life will be better in suburbia or the countryside. Single people or couples without children buying for the first time might on the other hand be persuaded by such incentives. KPMG suggested that tax reliefs on house-insurance premiums might provide a viable incentive. However, if such insurance costs are not factors that enter into the decision-making frameworks of owner-occupiers or tenants they will not have an impact.

Switching demand in favour of inner urban areas involves shifting demand in favour of specific house types as well as specific locations. KPMG produced data to show 'that urban developers produce more terraced houses, generally at higher densities, whereas mixed and greenfield developers produce more detached housing, inevitably at lower densities' (DETR, 1999c, p. 20). They show that greenfield development has produced 75 per cent detached and semi-detached housing compared with 26 per cent in urban areas. Flats have comprized 3 per cent of greenfield development and 14 per cent of urban development.

Fiscal incentives will need to attract households towards high-density living as well as urban locations if they are to be successful in promoting brownfield targets. Fiscal measures that reduce property transaction costs are likely in the long run to have only a small impact on demand. In fact, stamp-duty exemptions are likely to increase house prices, and the tax reduction may thus benefit sellers. If all of the benefit is capitalized into house prices the benefits will be wholly with existing owners.

A reduction in VAT on residential conversions is likely, in principle, to increase the rate of conversions. With a 5 per cent rate for conversions and zero per cent for new building, there is still no 'level playing field' between the two forms of production as the Urban Task Force suggested. Evans and Bate discuss the option of a more radical change to VAT that imposes a 17.5 per cent rate on new building. If this was levied only on new building on greenfield sites it could both act as a disincentive to such development and provide a source of revenue to promote brownfield development. It is argued that such a tax would have little effect on house prices and be borne mainly by landowners. It would be applied only to the first sale of dwellings, be easy to collect and provide a considerable volume of revenue (Evans and Bate, 2000, pp. 8–9). If the disincentive effect was, however, sufficient to reduce the total volume of housing development, as opposed to shifting the balance of production in favour of brownfield sites, the overall consequences for housing supply would be undesirable.

If fiscal measures are to target brownfield development, a major issue is defining 'brownfield' in a way that is sufficiently clear for tax laws to be applied effectively, and for policy objectives to be promoted efficiently. It has been argued that brownfield development opportunities fall into three categories:

1   Disused sites with low levels of land remediation costs.
2   Contaminated sites with high levels of remediation costs.
3   Disused buildings with refurbishment potential (DETR, 1999c, p. 11).

Each of these categories presents a different set of problems and different policy instruments are required to overcome the distinctive issues that each case presents. The costs and the risks vary between the categories. If sites are in good market locations, high development costs might be covered by revenue and fiscal incentives may be unnecessary.

A wide-ranging review of the problems of defining 'brownfield' proposes that 'a brownfield site is any land or premises which has previously been used or developed and is not currently fully in use, although it may be partially occupied or utilized. It may also be vacant, derelict or contaminated' (Alker *et al.*, 2000, p. 49). It is shown that according to this definition brownfield land exists in rural and urban locations. Given the complexity of the definitional problem, it is not surprising that the fiscal measures in use do not try to tackle brownfield sites as a generic entity. Rather, it is specific subsets of issues and types of property that have been targeted. Thus the current measures in England focus on 'contaminated land', 'space over shops and commercial premises', 'vacant property', and 'disadvantaged wards'.

The problem of definition might be easier if attention was switched to some form of greenfield tax, but devising a greenfield tax which does not reduce the total volume of housing development but does encourage brownfield development is likely to be difficult. The Urban Task Force considered the option and was unable to recommend a form of greenfield tax that would meet the core objective of shifting the balance of development (DETR, 1999a, p. 221). Evans and Bate view a greenfield tax as both a deterrent to greenfield development and a source of revenue to support brownfield development. Their proposed 17.5 per cent VAT on new building on greenfield sites would amount to a greenfield land tax if, as they argue, it was effectively paid mainly by the landowner rather than the developer who would pass on the added cost in the form of reduced bids for land.

In formulating a package of economic incentives for brownfield production, it is important to be quite clear on the policy objectives. An increased proportion of new housing from brownfield sites is compatible with either a lower or a higher total volume of housebuilding on greenfield sites. An increased proportion of new housing from brownfield sites is also compatible with either a smaller or a larger total volume of housebuilding. If we want more houses built in total, but we want a larger proportion to be on brownfield sites, we may be content for the total volume of housing on greenfield sites to increase. If this is the case, the Urban Task Force approach of more incentives for brownfield development rather than disincentives for greenfield development might be the correct approach.

Evaluations of economic policy instruments suggest that they can provide an important stimulus to development but only if combined with other measures. KPMG conclude that 'Fiscal measures will, in isolation, have only a limited impact on behaviour. A measure to stimulate brownfield housing demand may have limited impact if the supply of suitable development opportunities is constrained by planning or ownership difficulties' (DETR, 1999c, p. 83). Evans and Bate suggest that economic instruments 'must be seen as supporting the planning system. It is the planning system which decides what development can take place and where' (2000, p. 25). An alternative view is that the market and the planning system determine the pattern of development and fiscal incentives can have an important influence on both the demand and the supply sides of the residential housing market.

Urban capacity studies

In response to the government's aim of increasing the proportion of housing development that results from conversions and construction on brownfield sites, urban capacity studies – which attempt to estimate the volume of such development that might occur in given locations – are proliferating. English local planning authorities are required to undertake urban-housing capacity studies, and regional planning bodies are to coordinate capacity studies to maintain a consistency of approach.

The conclusions of a Round Table report on urban capacity (UK Round Table on Sustainable Development, 1997) stated that in order to present an unfettered assessment of urban capacity, studies should:

(a)   be based on original site survey work;
(b)   include a significant physical design component; and
(c)   reject limitations imposed by existing policies and standards.

A number of concerns were expressed about the methods used in practice. Local authorities did not always consider alternatives to existing restrictive policies such as those involving design standards, densities and parking provision. The report also identified a tendency to underestimate the housing capacity of both windfall and very small sites, in particular sites with a capacity of 10 houses or less, and in consequence a large portion of capacity was overlooked. Local planning authorities generally accepted the specified land allocations, and, as such, land designated for employment use might not be included in an assessment of physical capacity. This was so even if there was no apparent demand for its development. Sites have also been rejected because of assumptions about market demand, contamination, ownership and access.

Capacity assessments have relied heavily on extrapolation. An overreliance on the projection of past trends carries the risk of an assumption that there will be a constant land supply, building stock and steady market conditions: in short, an assumption of stability. The implications of these conclusions are that there has been an underestimation of urban housing capacity that has led to the proposition that more greenfield sites are required for development than is necessary. Urban capacity studies have, in many cases, engaged in debatable grossing-up exercises, where results from small-scale studies of sites (which may not in any useful sense be representative of a wider area) are used to estimate overall capacity. Several studies have involved detailed design briefs which have been costly, time consuming, and highly subjective.

All studies involve assumptions, and a major problem is the validity of the assumptions made. Different assumptions lead to different conclusions. The capacity of towns to accommodate more houses is a matter of their potential to change the use of land and buildings. This potential is a function of a number of constraints and any quantification of capacity is dependent on what assumptions one makes about these constraints and the possibility of the constraints being removed. At one extreme, all future housing development could take place in existing built-up areas and, at another, there could be no more urban housing development. Where between these two extremes reality lies depends on a range of economic, social and political factors and a range of decisions made by governments, local authorities, developers, financial institutions and many other corporate decision-makers and individuals.

In *Tapping the Potential: Assessing Urban Housing Capacity: Towards Better Practice* (DETR, 2000b), a review of published housing capacity studies concluded that studies of physical availability produce an 'unconstrained' capacity figure and that to predict how much of the unconstrained capacity will be developed some 'discounting' is required. This discounting includes a consideration of the market viability of the housing. It is evident from the studies reviewed that current economic evaluations are sometimes completely absent or are afterthoughts to a physical capacity study driven by design considerations. The economic evaluation is then somewhat cursory in nature. Market demand has been, for example, measured only by ranking sites according to developer preferences or by simply formulating 'optimistic' and 'pessimistic' scenarios about market conditions.

The housing development potential of urban areas is a function of economic as well as land-use and physical planning variables. Estimates of urban housing capacity should thus routinely consider the potential costs and returns from housing development, with such financial viability estimates becoming an integral part of, and not an occasional add-on to, urban capacity studies. A viability analysis should attempt to answer three questions:

1   How much of the physical capacity is, and will be, commercially viable for private-sector developers to develop (a) as 100 per cent market housing for sale, and (b) as a mixture of housing for sale and social-rented housing?
2   What are the probable levels of profit to be achieved on developments?
3   What residual values arise from specific developments identified in the capacity study?

The theory driving the evaluation might be based on the assumption that private sector residential developers try to maximize their profits, which are primarily a function of the revenue from house sales and the costs of development. It can be further assumed that land values are determined residually. In other words, they depend on the profits the developer expects from the revenue from house sales minus all non-land costs. The principles underlying economic viability that were developed in relation to affordable housing development in Chapter 8 apply in general terms to all types of residential development. For development to occur, the maximum that the developer will be prepared to pay for land (R) must be positive and it must be greater than what the landowner is prepared to accept, (L) When the maximum that the developer will be prepared to pay for land (R) is greater than what the landowner is prepared to accept (L), there is a potential for a surplus (technically economic rent) from the land transaction. This surplus may be termed S. Therefore, $S = R - L$.

A capacity study should ascertain whether or not there is potentially a positive residual before any payments are made for land. This residual with 100 per cent market sales should be estimated, and the impact on this residual of providing varying proportions of affordable housing can also be estimated.

Estimating what the landowner is prepared to accept involves making assumptions about the landowner's behaviour. It may be reasonable to assume that the landowner wants to sell for the largest sum possible. This will depend on the existing and alternative uses that are viable and, in planning terms, possible on a given site. If the housing developer is willing to pay an amount that the landowner is willing to accept for a particular site, we may conclude that the site meets the viability requirement. The site may then be included as part of the housing capacity of the urban area in which it is located.

Government guidance on urban housing capacity studies (DETR, 2000b) contains detailed advice on how local authorities should identify the physical sources of supply. There is much information on identifying potential land and buildings and estimating how many dwellings might occupy the available space. This leads to an estimate of the 'unconstrained' capacity figure: 'The unconstrained housing capacity of an area is the theoretical total number of dwellings that it could accommodate if all of the potential capacity was developed optimally' (DETR, 2000b, p. 29). The guidance offers no definition of 'optimally', but does, however, suggest that 'discounting' will be necessary to determine how much of the unconstrained capacity might actually get developed. Viability is deemed to be one item that might be relevant to discounting but no advice on how to estimate viability is offered.

To complement and extend the government's *Tapping the*

Potential guidance on capacity studies (DETR, 2000b), the House Builders Federation published its own guide *Realising Capacity* (HBF, 2001). It states that 'Whilst "Tapping the Potential" identifies the need to test the availability, deliverability and marketability of capacity, it provides little guidance on how they should be taken on board' (ibid., p. 1). Furthermore, market appraisals are often absent from capacity studies or are a weak element of such work:

> Many local authorities fail to identify or develop the market appraisal element of a study and many omit it all together . . . It is essential that understanding is gained by utilizing the knowledge of the industry and local agents . . . Many areas may well be unmarketable as housing sites. It is imperative to ensure that capacity studies acknowledge and explore local housing market variations and reflect them appropriately within their assumptions. (Ibid., p. 18)

An approach to viability and capacity that explores what the developer is prepared to offer for land and what the owner is willing to accept would meet the House Builders Federation's requirements and provide a clearer approach to effective policy implementation. Research funded by the Economic and Social Reseach Council (ESRC) at the Centre for Residential Development at Nottingham Trent University has shown that whilst many urban capacity studies either completely ignore, or treat in a derisory fashion, considerations of economic viability, an appropriate evaluation can be incorporated in a cost-effective fashion using secondary data. Published information on house prices and building costs can give a broad indication of the viability of housebuilding at varying locations, which can be supplemented as necessary by site-specific appraisals (Weston *et al.*, 2003).

Low housing demand

Lack of effective demand for housing in urban locations works against urban renaissance and smart-growth objectives. Low and falling demand for housing in some inner cities, particularly in the north of England, became a recognized phenomenon in the late 1990s in Britain, resulting in the most extreme cases in falling house prices, empty properties and social housing which is deemed to be 'difficult to let'. In such locations, urban renaissance presents particularly significant challenges. Bramley and Pawson (2002) suggest that the causes of low demand and the unpopularity of particular neighbourhoods may be grouped into three categories:

1   Broader regional and sub-regional effects of demographic trends, particularly migration, which are often seen as linked to economic restructuring and employment changes.
2   Changes in preferences and behaviour, generally associated with a declining popularity of social housing and greater turnover and instability in the tenant population.
3   'Micro-social processes at the neighbourhood level which lead to particular areas being stigmatized by reputations for poverty, crime and other problems, leading into processes of cumulative deterioration of conditions which may ultimately culminate in abandonment' (ibid., p. 369).

They also suggest that localities can be divided into three broad groups which have:

1   Generic low demand across all tenures, generally of serious magnitude and impact.
2   Low demand and/or oversupply of social-sector housing accompanied by adequate or buoyant private-market conditions.
3   Isolated patches of unpopular social housing in generally high-demand areas (typically in London and the South, and typically involving particular types of housing such as high-rise or bedsit flats) (ibid., p. 403).

On the basis of their research evidence, Bramley and Pawson suggest that generic low demand is usually a consequence of economic decline and job losses with associated outmigration. Where low demand is felt mainly in the social rented sector it is suggested that it,

> may reflect the relative strength rather than the weakness of the local economy, as affordable home-ownership is brought within reach of former tenants gaining a foothold in a growing labour market. Such a scenario is particularly likely in housing markets where social housing is relatively oversupplied. (Ibid., p. 419)

The appropriate policy response depends on the causes of low demand and the economic circumstances of the city. It is suggested that where economic performance is weak it may not be possible to maintain current population levels and some 'thinning out' of the housing stock, focused on less-popular types of housing in poor condition, is required. This applies mainly to non-central inner areas of cities. Where there is a historically large public-sector housing stock, a vigorous local economy, and demand for social housing has been undercut by economic success, some restructuring of the housing stock may be in order. This might involve transfer of social housing stock to the private sector and possibly some demolition and replacement to achieve a similar effect. Where the local economy is strong and there is no tenure imbalance, pockets of unpopular social rented housing can be tackled by management and investment measures. Bramley and Pawson suggest that the policies propounded by the Urban Task Force are broadly related to the third of these scenarios (ibid., p. 420).

Based mainly on a study of Manchester and Newcastle, Power and Mumford (1999) suggest that pockets of low demand are a consequence of severe poverty and joblessness. In neighbourhoods with the most extreme problems they found:

> Streets with a majority of houses empty; Demolition sites scattered throughout the area; Empty property across the neighbourhood; Falling property values; and Intense demand problems in all property types, all tenures and all parts of the neighbourhood. This means too few people wanting to live in those properties. (Joseph Rowntree Foundation, 1999)

Low demand, it is argued, has generated falling school rolls, loss of confidence in locations, a vacuum in social control, anti-social behaviour and intense fear of crime. The research suggests that concentrated poverty is the single biggest explanatory factor in neighbourhood decline.

Conclusions

Environmental and social arguments have combined in many advanced economies to make a case for more compact urban forms. More compact cities are argued to reduce energy consumption, consume less rural land and produce ecological benefits. More investment in existing urban areas, it is proposed, will also bring improvements in the quality of life to present and future residents. These claims have underpinned urban renaissance in Britain and new urbanism in America.

Urban renaissance in Britain has been promoted through a

government target for 60 per cent of all future housebuilding to be on 'brownfield' sites, thereby reusing land and buildings that have low values in their existing use. Planning and fiscal policy instruments have combined to limit the probability of planning permission for new greenfield residential developments where brownfield options are available and to provide financial incentives for urban housebuilding. Significant changes in patterns of residential development are, however, unlikely without more extensive policy processes that take account of the links between housing location and the wider economy. In particular, the relationships between urban form and the costs and availability of transport options should be approached more holistically.

Urban capacity studies have improved knowledge about the availability, and to a limited extent the economic viability, of sites for new residential development. Successful urban renaissance will, however, have to put even more emphasis on an improvement in the quality of living in towns and cities if demand is to match the supply of new urban development opportunities.

The issue of low housing demand related to low incomes and low levels of employment illustrates the weakness of both conventional land-use planning policies and newer economic policy instruments in tackling the problems of urban renaissance. None of the instruments on offer can create demand. Demand may be focused and steered towards certain locations, but if there is a fundamental lack of underlying demand little of significance will change. Capacity studies that show that space is available for housing are of little value if there is no demand for housing to fill the space. Better-designed cities may shift demand in favour of urban locations but better design does not provide resources for households that lack the ability to demand good-quality housing. Where poverty and unemployment are the underlying problems, these need to be tackled directly; they cannot be planned away or designed away.

Chapter 10

Policy Instruments in a Comparative Context

In this chapter the merits of examining housing and planning policies in different countries will be set out, with ideas from a cross fertilization of experiences in Europe and the USA to the fore. The limitations of obtaining lessons from other countries in the light of differences in institutional arrangements and varying perceptions of problems will be acknowledged. There will be a consideration of policy instruments which address the supply of housing through subsidy and land-use mechanisms, and issues of land assembly and the supply of land for social housing in Europe will be explored. The use of 'inclusionary zoning' arrangements to support the supply of affordable housing through the planning system in the USA will be examined.

The purpose is not to provide detailed descriptions or a fully comparative analysis of policy approaches in several countries, it is rather to point to selected examples of varying approaches in order to demonstrate the varieties of policy instruments and contexts. The analysis will show that the operation of markets in housing and land and the nature of public policy are influenced significantly by political and institutional contexts, and that ideas for new policy solutions should take account of these complexities. It will also be shown that the way that problems are formulated and solutions proposed can be usefully challenged by looking across international boundaries.

The merits of a comparative context

It has rightly been argued that 'Policies are the cultural products of history, time and place: they are rarely exportable' (Cullingworth, 1993, p. 177). However, with appropriate sensitivity to the problems of 'transferability', knowledge of policy instruments and outcomes in one country can inform analysis of similar issues in another country.

189

The generation of new policy ideas as the result of a stimulus from information about how problems are tackled elsewhere is very different from trying to duplicate instruments used elsewhere (Oxley, 2001). Ideas for new initiatives in the form of new tax allowances or personal subsidies, for example, might reflect current or past practice in other countries, whose experience may then provide evidence to inform debate about applicability in the country under consideration.

Exposure to approaches in a variety of countries can help to challenge insular beliefs about the causes of problems and the effects of policy instruments. A varying perception of barriers to the delivery of housing and planning in one country can inform notions of ways to tackle similar goals (but different perceptions of barriers) in another country. Some attitudes, like those towards land ownership and private property rights, contrast markedly between countries. They are often tied up with long traditions and are unlikely to change easily. Institutional arrangements may also be deeply imbedded in culture and history. However, some institutional arrangements can change, and if for example land-assembly mechanisms or the nature of the bodies that own and manage subsidized housing appear to have advantages in one country, these might also – despite differences – have some applicability in another country.

However, the deeper value of comparisons lies not so much in the exportability or otherwise of policies as in enhanced understanding of the process of which policies are part. Understanding differences and similarities between societies can help us to better understand the process at work within societies (for a discussion of types and uses of comparative analysis see Oxley, 1991, 2001, and Pickvance, 2001).

Perceptions of housing problems

The policies that governments use to tackle housing problems should logically be linked to some analysis of the nature of the problems that are being addressed. For example it is possible to view housing problems as essentially a lack of demand for decent housing; thus some households have a 'need' but not a 'demand' for decent housing. These terms were discussed in Chapter 2. Demands are a function of income and economic power, whilst needs are socially determined and linked to acceptable standards of decent housing. Governments can tackle the problem mainly from the demand side by trying to boost the effective demands of those with significant needs but inadequate financial resources to exercise effective demand. Governments can alternatively tackle the supply problem by trying to increase the supply of housing of an acceptable quality (see the discussion in Chapter 2 and especially Figure 2.5). They can also, of course, combine both approaches. For a detailed analysis of the range of responses which governments might have to the problem of a lack of demand for effective housing see Oxley (2000, pp. 70–124).

From the demand side, governments might try to increase incomes using some sort of income supplement. With the extra income, individuals may choose to purchase more housing but they may choose not to do so. The extent to which extra income results in extra housing demand depends on the income elasticity of demand for housing. That is, it is a matter of individual choice and preferences for housing compared to other items. The extent to which the extra demand is effective in increasing the supply of decent housing depends on the price elasticity of supply of such housing. Whether or not supply is very responsive, that is elastic, and a large volume of additional decent housing results, is dependent on the conditions in the housing market and the institutional arrangements for organizing supply (again see the discussion in Chapter 2).

A second response involves increasing the demand for decent housing by subsidizing its consumption, which means tying additional income to the consumption of housing. There are several variants of how this can be done in practice. It could be done by using housing vouchers which can be used to obtain certain types of housing which was the essence of the Section 8 Housing Allowance Programme in the USA, although this approach has not found favour in Europe (Howenstine, 1986, and Oxley, 1998). Here the common variant is the use of some form of housing allowance, like housing benefit in the UK, to meet part of the cost of housing consumption. Some of the benefits of subsidy will, as with the first approach, end up with housing suppliers: how much depends on supply elasticity.

Given that the majority of house purchase decisions rely on borrowed money, the demand for housing can also be raised by making this credit cheaper and/or more easily available. Here there are a variety of methods which may be used. Borrowing costs from private-sector institutions may be subsidized. Borrowing from such institutions could be guaranteed and thus risk and interest rates reduced, or borrowing could be made available at sub-market rates from public-sector providers of finance. If the objective is to only selectively enhance effective demand, the benefits of cheaper finance should be targeted at households with inadequate demand and the arrangements for credit subsidization and supply orientated to this goal.

It is usual for economists to assume that lack of income is the cause of insufficient demand. In addition, the significance of interest rates is frequently acknowledged and so credit is sometimes made cheaper as discussed above. It is rare in economic analysis for additional personal factors to be recognized as constraints on demand, for their recognition tends to violate the assumption of rational decision-makers. However, in practice, individuals may be unable to demand decent housing not because they lack the financial capacity, but because they are constrained by other personal attributes including mental and physical incapacity.

Furthermore, many households fail through ignorance or the complexity of provision to claim financial benefits to which they are entitled. This is a case of not being able to cope with the way a system works. For those who cannot cope with the complexities of housing markets, simply providing them with cash to enhance their effective demand may be inappropriate or insufficient. They may need other help if they are to exercise effective demand.

From the supply side, governments might subsidize supply without price and allocation conditions. Thus, housing suppliers might receive incentives to increase supply and to reduce the price of decent housing, so enabling more households to afford the commodity and to exercise effective demand. A variety of subsidies which reduce housebuilders' and landlords' costs are possible in principle, but the consequences of this approach are dependent on the effectiveness of the subsidy in reducing the price of decent housing and the reaction of consumers to the lower price. The price elasticity of demand is therefore influential in determining how much more housing will be supplied and the price at which it will be made available to consumers.

Another approach subsidizes suppliers, be they housing developers or landlords, and encourages them to reduce prices and increase supply. However, rather than leaving the degree of price reduction and the degree of supply-increase only to the consequences of market demand and supply, the subsidy is conditional on specified rent levels and production levels. The subsidy can also depend on the personal circumstances, including incomes, of those who occupy the housing. Through subsidizing supply conditionally governments may influence the allocation of the housing and suspend market-determined allocation. This is the approach that many European governments have used through their support for housing associations and other social-sector landlords.

Another supply-side approach involves the use of tax reductions to the suppliers of housing, particularly suppliers of housing intended for people on low incomes. Such fiscal incentives typically reduce the costs of developing new housing and increase the rates of return to investors or developers. In the form of Low-Income Housing Tax Credits (LIHTC) this type of subsidy is an important means of stimulating investment in 'affordable housing' in the USA.

Supply-side approaches can also involve the land-use planning system in stimulating the supply of housing generally, or in particular for lower-income households. This might mean using mechanisms which assist in the assembly of land for such development or establishing a requirement for local governments to ensure an adequate supply of land to social housing developers. There are many examples of such mechanisms and requirements in Europe. More radically, the granting of planning permission for private-sector housing development can be conditional on the developer providing a required volume of 'affordable housing' as part of the scheme, or sometimes on another site. This is the essence of 'affordable housing though planning' in the UK (as discussed in Chapter 8) and 'inclusionary zoning' in the USA.

Each of the approaches above involves working with market processes and maintaining individual consumption decisions. There is individual choice in housing consumption but the constraints on choices are moderated. There are also choices for housing suppliers; they can take the subsidies or fiscal incentives on offer or respond to the land-use planning incentives or requirements, but they do not have to. An alternative stance rejects reliance on the market and replaces market supply by state supply. This means that the state or an agent of the state becomes directly involved in the supply of housing. In principle this could be state supply of an amount sufficient only to bridge the gap between what households can effectively demand and what they are deemed to need, or it could be all of the supply of housing. The state-supplied housing will have to be allocated in some way. In principle it could be assigned prices and allocated according to ability to pay. This would, in effect, mean a state supply and a market allocation process. Ability to pay should be enhanced if the net effect of the extra production is lower prices. If effective demand is appropriately expanded through lower prices, housing need will be met.

Governments could decide to supply housing directly or to use some sort of agent of the state (a local housing authority for example) to supply housing and it could seek to determine the allocation of this housing according to some sort of needs criteria so that ability to pay is not a barrier to access to decent housing. The volume of housing which the state supplies, directly or indirectly, could be either an amount to bridge the gap between market demand and social need, or it could be total housing supply if the government determines that it wishes to eliminate private-sector production.

A more cynical government approach involves trying to change the volume of housing needed. This volume is a function of acceptable standards of housing, and what is acceptable and what constitutes decent housing is a matter of public policy determination. Governments may simply try to reduce total need by lowering the standard, and may seek to make need correspond more closely or ultimately to coincide with market demand and supply.

Rather than taking any one of the approaches set out above, governments could combine elements of two or more of these approaches to produce some sort of mix of approaches. This is, in reality, what European governments, and indeed most governments throughout the world, have done. Governments in practice do not stand to one side and leave housing entirely to the individual decision-making of markets.

Western European approaches to housing policy

In the aftermath of the Second World War, Western European housing policies were geared to reducing housing shortages, and housing production was clearly an aim of policy in most countries in the 1950s and 1960s. Social housing systems developed in response to shortages. It has been argued that:

> The social housing systems that were developed in the 1950s and 1960s have some common features. First, social housing was seen primarily as a construction rather than a management responsibility. Secondly, policy was mainly concerned with the number of units built; quality and variety were minor issues. Thirdly, the development perspective focussed on housing estates. Little attention was devoted to the residential environment or any linkages with the local economy, the local community or existing amenities. Last but not least, the market did not come into the picture. Social housing was predominantly a matter of bureaucratic planning and allocation processes ... [and] ... there was a general tendency to finance and subsidize property rather than give direct support to individual households who need help in paying their housing bills. (Priemus and Dieleman, 1999, pp. 624–6)

Subsequent developments put increasing emphasis on improving the quality of the stock and on improving the distribution of subsidies so that they were 'better targeted'. In the 1990s most governments tried to reduce public expenditure on housing in the light of improving housing conditions and budgetary pressures related to the control of inflation and compliance with European Monetary System convergence criteria. There is growing evidence of increased concern with allocation processes and the need to make these more responsive to consumer preferences.

There are wide differences between countries in institutional arrangements and housing subsidy systems, but the governments of all European Union countries have adopted and continue to exercise, even in times of strict public expenditure constraints, much influence over the provision of housing. In no country has a free-market approach with much reliance on individual determination in the demand and supply of housing been allowed to prevail. Nowhere do we find governments relying on a general increase in household incomes as the means for raising effective housing demand. There are, however, many examples of governments, especially from the 1970s onwards, giving considerable emphasis to housing allowances to relieve household budgetary pressure and to support housing demand. There was a decisive switch in favour of housing allowances in a period in which supply subsidies were being reduced and more emphasis was based on market forces. It is important to recognize that the systems in several countries were trying to ameliorate the consequences of rising rents and inconsistent pricing where rents varied widely without any clear association with housing quality (Oxley, 1987).

Support for housing consumption costs has typically taken the form of tax allowances for interest payments. The once very generous mortgage interest tax relief in the UK has now been phased out, but variants of this form of subsidy remain in many European countries. Such measures have been heavily criticized as a means of supporting housing demand, on both efficiency and equity grounds. Large benefits, without appropriately designed systems, can go to those on high incomes, and as a means of promoting home ownership, tax exemptions usually fail to target marginal purchasers.

Supply subsidies have most usually been given with conditions attached, and such 'conditional object subsidies' have been a principal means by which social housing has been promoted in Western Europe. A significant distinctive feature of the UK is that such subsidies have gone in large measure to support local authority housing and thus large municipal landlords have been the main suppliers of social housing. The emphasis in the last two decades on housing associations as the key social-housing developers has to some extent depleted the predominance of local councils as owners of the social rented stock, but they remain the largest landlords in many cities.

In Germany, in contrast, social-housing subsidies have been available to a variety of private and public-sector landlords who have been prepared to meet rent and allocation criteria. In several countries, including Greece and Spain, social-housing subsidies have supported owner-occupation, not social renting. An article entitled 'General trends in financing social housing in Spain' (Pareja Eastaway and San Martin, 1999) is entirely about specific forms of subsidized home ownership. It is shown that, 'One of the characteristics of social housing programmes in Spain is that they have historically encouraged the buying of a house as a means to get access to housing' (ibid., p. 710).

Supply subsidies have generally declined in importance relative to demand subsidies, largely as a reaction to changing perceptions of the housing problem that is being addressed. The more housing has been seen as a problem of distribution and low incomes (rather than as a problem of production), the more the emphasis has been on housing allowances and the less the emphasis has been on object subsidies. It has been shown that in Western Europe, 'There has been rapid growth in targeted assistance in the form of housing allowances and housing benefits since about 1980. That development entails a dramatic shift away from property subsidies towards income linked subsidies' (Priemus and Dieleman, 1999, p. 627). However, this has been seen to have serious drawbacks: 'First and foremost, housing allowances have much less impact on the supply side of the residential construction market and the housing market. If the main goal is to mobilize the supply, property subsidies would be more effective than housing allowances' (ibid.). In the light of this, support for housing supply is still important in several counties and is likely to remain so as long as there is a lack of confidence in the ability of consumer subsidies to fully deliver affordable housing of an acceptable quality. Governments have thus in practice tended to rely on a variety of approaches which redistribute resources through subsidizing both housing producers and consumers.

The European Union has no direct responsibility for housing provision. There cannot, according to the principle of 'subsidiarity', be a European housing policy, and responsibility for housing issues rests with the member states. There is thus supposed to be no European housing expenditure and the only budgets for housing should be national, regional or local (Oxley, 1999). However, where housing investment which improves the quality and quantity of the housing stock also promotes economic growth, urban regeneration and increased prosperity, there is no reason why such support should not, in selective cases, come from EU funds. This would not amount to abandoning the principle of subsidiarity, but it would amount to a pragmatic recognition of the very significant links between housing investment and wider aspects of well-being. This would require a change in the rules regarding EU finances (Stephens, 1999), and the probability is that there will continue to be no explicitly European housing budget, and national governments will continue to bear the responsibility for housing issues. The actions which national governments take and the freedom of choice they give to individuals in housing matters will continue to be significant policy issues.

Support for housing demand relative to housing supply has increased in recent decades and the emphasis has been on the financial rather than the non-financial impediments to effective demand. Supply-side subsidies, which have been used as the principal means of supporting the development of social housing, have had more explicit price and allocation conditions attached in countries such as Germany, France and the Netherlands than has been the case in the UK. A greater reliance on direct state provision in the form of local authority housing has also been a distinguishing feature of the UK's institutional arrangements. It is the allocation mechanisms for social housing which are now receiving fresh attention in several countries, including the UK. It is on this issue that the role of individual decision-making has particular significance and where further changes can be expected.

Land assembly and residential development

Land-use planning throughout Europe has a variety of objectives including promoting social and environmental objectives, and aspects of planning are used in a variety of ways to promote the provision of land for housing. There are important contrasts in basic approaches. The role of local development plans in the UK is, for example, much less prescriptive than in the Netherlands, Germany and France. Indicative and flexible plans in the UK contrast with more detailed plans in these countries that are not only land use plans but also infrastructure provision plans. It has been argued that:

> Binding detailed land use plans 'fix' land values within a narrow range with the potential consequence that local authorities may

end up paying more for land than they otherwise would have had to do, had they left land unzoned, or provided plans that were only 'indicative'. This is the dilemma facing Dutch, German and French authorities wishing to acquire land through compulsory purchase, pre-emption rights or other land assembly techniques. (Golland, 2001 p. 15)

Land speculation and large land-development profits for the private sector have not been significant features of the Dutch land-supply system. This is, however, changing. The traditional model worked on the basis of municipal acquisition and disposal of development land, where the municipality would acquire land at existing use value, take responsibility for site preparation, infrastructure and layout and pass the land on to developers. Any profit from the development process would go to the local authority.

In the 1990s the Dutch government identified specific housing expansion areas and declared that subsidies would be available to support the required development outcomes. A consequence has been to highlight development locations and the opportunities to invest and speculate in land. Although there is no guaranteed certainty that the largest locations will be built on, because every site requires an appropriate local plan, 'buying land directly from farmers is not such a risky activity because the locations are identified in a (non-binding) national plan' (ibid., p. 20). Under the emerging 'building-rights' model, which represents a departure from customary procedure, developers are taking the initiative in purchasing land from the original owners. A 'building right' is granted by the municipality to a developer to build a number of houses in a given area and developers are given some influence over the emerging local spatial development plan. Developers can trade land in one part of a municipality for building rights in another. Land passes temporarily to the local authority, which provides the infrastructure and then sells the land in a 'building-ready state' to developers including those with whom it has concluded 'building-rights' contracts. A key benefit for the developer is the certainty of building permission.

An increase in speculation by parties who have purchased strategic areas of land (with the specific objective of a realizing a maximum gain once the land is assembled in accordance with a local plan) has been met with some concern from both developers and municipalities with such speculators being regarded as 'pariahs' (Needham, 1997, p. 295). Municipalities can use their rights of preemption as a tool of antispeculation policy; preemption gives the authority the right of first refusal when potential development land comes on the market under specific circumstances:

> Once a right of pre-emption has been established for a particular plot of land, it becomes illegal to transfer the land to a third party other than the local authority who have the right to purchase it. Thus those who have acquired land on a speculative basis and who would usually have several potential (development company) buyers, then, as the result of a pre-emption order, find themselves with one (municipal) buyer. (Golland, 2001, p. 24)

The municipalities also play a significant part in the land-assembly process in Germany where they have a legal duty to ensure a sufficient land supply. It has been suggested that only around 8 per cent of all land for housing is assembled by developers in Germany compared with 80 per cent in Britain (ibid., p. 26; B.M.Bau, 1993, p. 143). Germany has a distinctive solution to the problem of multiple ownership of complex sites: 'A key obstacle to land assembly is land ownership. This is particularly the case where a larger site has to be assembled from many small land plots. The process of "Umlegung" in Germany (literally, the "turning over" of land) offers a tried and tested solution to this problem scenario' (Golland, 2001, p. 29). Umlegung involves land 'pooling'. Several owners agree to securitize their bundle of rights and obligations so that a larger more developable site can be realized. The benefit for owners lies in realizing the 'marriage value' that will be created by planning, infrastructure provision and the pooling of land resources. Prior to the Umlegung process, legally binding plans typically set out the areas required for infrastructure, roads and open space. The municipality can acquire public space without any direct compensation to land owners, but the increase in overall land value created by the granting of planning permission will usually be sufficient for land owners to accept this position. The Umlegung process can be voluntary or it can have statutory authority. It is normally used for greenfield sites although it can also be used in urban areas to promote regeneration (Barlow *et al.*, 2002). Furthermore, municipalities can use preemption rights in the absence of agreement if acquisition can be shown to be in support of well-defined planning objectives.

Although local authorities play a strong role in the French supply process through infrastructure provision and monitoring, a peculiarity of land assembly in France is the role of the 'lotisseur'. The lotisseur is a specialist private-sector operator, and the process of lotissement involves infrastructure provision and the subdivision of land into lots that can be sold for housing. The model is most significant for housing at the urban fringe where lotisseurs have been able to deliver land in a cost-effective way. In France, permission to subdivide land for development is seen as a separate and distinctive step in the planning process which requires specific permission. The right of preemption by local authorities enables a municipality to assist in land assembly by exercizing a right of first refusal. In the absence of agreement between the land owner and the authority, the price is settled by a court. It has been suggested that 'local authorities and other public sector players in France, Germany and the Netherlands possess an extensive range of instruments with which to manage the land assembly process. In the UK, by contrast, local authorities have few policy instruments, apart from compulsory purchase, by which to directly assemble land' (Golland, 2001, p. 53). It is not surprising, therefore, that difficult land-assembly problems, including multiple ownerships which can impede inner-urban development (Adams and Watkins, 2002, pp. 230–5) have been addressed by agencies outside of local government. In the past, urban development corporations promoted urban renewal in selected areas through 'extraordinary powers of land acquisition' (Cullingworth and Nadin, 2002, p. 298). Currently, English Partnerships – a public body separate from, but working with, local authorities – has an important role in urban regeneration through positive land-market activity working with private and public-sector partners (ibid., pp. 301–2).

Land for social housing

A study of the supply of land for housing in 18 European countries (Needham and de Kam, 2000) reveals a variety of means by which the public sector supports the providers of social housing including reserving land for social housing in land-use plans, using powers of preemption to secure land, and subsidizing the costs of acquisition.

There are also typically, within countries, a variety of means by which social housing developers acquire land, with open-market acquisition often sitting alongside low-cost provision from the public sector. In many countries (including Denmark, England, France, Germany, Portugal and Spain) municipalities supply land directly to providers at sub-market prices. In the Netherlands municipalities acquire land at market prices, and when selling it for social housing prevent losses by increasing the density in land-use plans and by cross-subsidizing from the sales of land for market housing. Land acquired from developers of market housing in return for 'building rights' is supplied more cheaply for social housing than for market housing.

In the Netherlands,

> There are no legal instruments especially for acquiring land for social housing. However, because many municipalities actively support social housing and also are active in the land market, they can help housing associations to acquire necessary land. In doing so, they may apply their legal powers of preferential acquisition (pre-emption) or compulsory purchase. These instruments do not reduce prices, but are occasionally used to enforce development of sites according to the municipal standards including a certain proportion of social housing. (Needham and de Kam, 2000, p. 31)

In Germany and the Netherlands, unlike in Britain, land can be specifically designated as social-housing land in land-use plans. This can have the effect of restricting competition and lowering the value of the land compared with the land for market-housing development. Of course, if the alternative is, say, agricultural use or social-housing development (but there is no market-housing possibility) it might be argued that designation can increase the value of the land.

In France,

> The municipalities (communes) have the task of realizing a certain number of social dwellings. They also have the task of land-use planning, and as part of that they can designate land for housing. It is not, however, permitted to reserve some of the designated land especially for social housing. One method of discouraging the building of market housing (and thus increasing the chances that social housing be built) is to restrict the number of parking spaces . . . Some local governments acquire land so as to be able to offer it to the providers of social housing. Then they sometimes accept a price for the land below the market price . . . Another way in which social housing is sometimes aided is when a local government pays some of the costs of land servicing. (Ibid., p. 18)

German municipalities are legally obliged to ensure a sufficient supply of cheap land for housing, especially for low-income groups. Some municipalities have engaged in long-term land banking and others in short-term intermediate ownership:

> The Bund, the Länder, and the municipalities are required to sell land from their stock at a reduced price: this land is especially

important for the low-rent housing programme . . . The municipality can designate land in a land-use plan for housing, and in a
building plan for social housing. However, this does not have
much effect, as the owner is not obliged to offer land for sale, and
will not do so if the designation reduces the value too much.
Municipalities have pre-emption rights in some circumstances:
compulsory purchase is in principle possible but in practice hardly
ever used. Also, municipalities can exercise influence through their
rights to provide local infrastructure . . . Sometimes social housing
is provided as part of a mixed development: then the developers
can subsidize the land for social housing by using the profits on
the land sales from high paying uses. (Ibid., p. 20)

The use of cross-subsidies working with the planning system is an
increasingly important way of supporting social housing not just in
Europe, but also, as will be shown, in the USA.

Housing supply subsidies in the USA

To put American policy instruments in context, it is worth pointing
out that the largest housing subsidy in the USA supports neither
housing supply nor any of the housing demand and need-oriented
objectives outlined earlier in this chapter, instead it supports the
consumer costs of owner-occupation. Mortgage interest and local
property taxes are deductible against taxable income for the
purposes of federal income tax. The annual cost in revenue foregone
by the US Treasury is about three and a half times the annual budget
of the Department of Housing and Urban Development which,
among other things, is tasked with supporting low-income housing.
This home-ownership tax expenditure subsidy is concentrated
within the top 25 per cent of the income distribution.
    The largest capital subsidy programme in the USA is the low-
income housing tax credit (LIHTC). This has been seen as one of the
most powerful tools for the development of affordable housing
because it provides incentives for private industry to work with the
state and local governments (Bast, 2002). The programme, which
was established by the Tax Reform Act of 1986, provides for federal
tax incentives for the construction or rehabilitation of rental housing
units occupied by low-income households. Each state receives an
annual allocation of LIHTC based on the state's population. States
allocate the credits to developers according to various public policy
objectives including affordability and geographic distribution. The

amount of credit available for a project is proportional to the value of the developer's investment in the affordable housing component of the project. The LIHTC is a dollar for dollar credit or offset for income taxes otherwise payable, and is taken annually over a 10-year period. While available to owner/developers as an enhancement to the ordinary investment returns of the property, most developers elect to convert the future stream of tax credit benefits to a single lump sum which is used to partially finance the development of the property. This factoring mechanism typically involves a limited partnership structure in which the developer sells an ownership interest in the property and its associated tax benefit stream to an investor in exchange for a lump-sum capital contribution (Black-Plumeau, 1998). LIHTC and additional privately supplied debt capital results in about $7 billion each year in affordable housing capital investment and produces around 70,000 apartments annually in the USA.

In addition to the production of affordable housing, LIHTC produces other benefits of potential interest to policy-makers. First, LIHTC is a 'pay for performance' regime in that the tax benefit does not begin to flow to investors unless the affordable property is developed and placed in service. Further, the benefit may not continue to be claimed (or be subject to claw back by the taxing authorities) if the property does not continue to operate as an affordable property. This web of incentives substantially privatizes the delivery and continued compliance risks otherwise borne by government. A second benefit to policy-makers is embedded in the LIHTC's primary reliance on private debt and equity capital. The experience has been that affordable housing properties capitalized in this fashion have tended to be better maintained and more professionally managed relative to other forms of affordable housing. Most American observers attribute this outcome to the risk oversight concerns of private capital suppliers.

The affordable apartments cannot be rented to anyone earning more than 60 per cent of the median family income for the area in which they live, and the apartments should be available on such a condition for at least 30 years. The maximum rent charged to low-income tenants is 30 per cent of the maximum income for a qualified low income household. At least 20 per cent of the units in a tax-credit project should be occupied by households earning 50 per cent or less of the area median, or at least 40 per cent must be occupied by tenants earning 60 per cent or less of the area median income adjusted for household size. These specific occupancy rules must be met for at least 15 years. In practice, the restricted occupancy requirements often substantially exceed this statutory minimum.

Impressed by the success of LIHTC, the 'Millennial Housing Commission', appointed by Congress to review and advise on housing policies in America included among its many suggestions a proposal to model a new state-administered home-ownership tax credit on LIHTC (MHC, 2002). States would use this credit to stimulate new home-ownership developments and rehabilitation where costs exceeded market values, or to support lenders who provide low-cost mortgages to qualified buyers. The proposal is intended to extend the benefits of home-ownership to more low-income households.

Community Development Block Grant (CDBG) is allocated by the federal government to more populous cities and counties. It may be applied to support housing development costs and non-housing community development processes. The HOME Investment Partnerships programme features a block grant used by state and local governments to address affordable housing needs. Recipient jurisdictions can develop their own programmes and activities to meet affordable rental or home-ownership needs.

Whilst in Britain council housing has provided and continues to provide (despite the 'right to buy' and transfers to housing associations in recent years) housing for a significant proportion of the population, 'Public Housing' in the USA houses only 1.3 million households. Run by local 'Public Housing Authorities' (PHAs) with the aid of federal operating subsidies, American public housing targets very low-income households (on less than 50 per cent of area median income). No significant additions to this stock have occurred since the early 1970s, and public housing has a poor public image. It has been suggested that 'despite the ongoing problems facing the public housing program, this stock represents a critical national housing resource. Although it has been much neglected, it provides decent-quality affordable housing for millions of low-income people for whom other options are lacking' (Bratt, 1998, p. 446). The Millennial Housing Commission (MHC, 2002) proposed changes in the regulatory framework and new powers for PHAs to borrow on the private capital market as part of a package of measures to transform the public housing programme.

A quantitively more significant form of federally assisted housing is the Federal Housing Choice Voucher Program (formerly known as 'section 8 vouchers'). Unlike public housing, which is owned by the public sector, the housing supported under this scheme is provided by private landlords who rent to low-income households at affordable rents. Because the vouchers are associated with particular households rather than particular properties, households holding vouchers have a degree of choice over which approved units they occupy, and subsidies cover the difference between the rent charged and an acceptable proportion of the household's income. The maximum reimbursement-setting formulas associated with the vouchers are more modest and some measure of rental dwelling vacancy is present. In high rental-rate/low-vacancy areas, it is common for a portion of the available vouchers to be returned unused due to the lack of landlord interest in cooperating with the programme.

In addition to the Housing Choice Voucher Program, there exists a companion programme known as 'project-based section 8'. The key difference between this programme and its voucher sibling is that, under project-based section 8, the subsidy mechanism is attached to a specific property rather than to a specific household. About 3.5 million households live in privately- owned units that are supported either through direct federal support or through the voucher programme.

In addition to federal housing initiatives there is a vast array of measures operating at state, country and city level that support housing for low-income households. The nature of the support varies with the laws and political priorities of the localities but often involves some kind of tax incentive for the production of affordable housing. For example, some 35 states operate a system of Tax Increment Finance (TIF) whereby increases in property tax revenues can be dedicated to specific public purposes including affordable housing. In some states affordable housing is exempt from local taxation. States rarely commit their own resources to housing but a $2.4 billion bond issue for affordable housing in California in 2002 is a notable exception.

Whilst it is clear that affordability of housing by low-income households is perceived as a significant issue in America, and that through the voucher programme there is demand-side assistance, an important part of federal and local support is targeted at increasing the supply of housing for low-income households. The pros and cons of demand versus supply-side assistance have been debated at least as much in America as in Europe (see for example the evidence cited in Sirmans and Macpherson, 2003). As in Europe, much of the government support for housing takes the form of fiscal incentives rather than direct expenditure and much goes to homeowners, including those on high incomes. In 2001 tax incentives totalling $121.2 billion made up the majority of federal housing support, and it is estimated that $64.5 billion of this comprized mortgage-interest deductions. Direct spending on housing assistance, by comparison, was only $34.9 million, almost all of which was targeted at low-income renters (MHC, 2002, pp. 30–1).

Planning and inclusionary zoning in the USA

Differences in attitudes to land ownership and to the rights of government to 'interfere' with individual property rights underlie important contrasts in the role of planning in Britain and America. Whereas British planning is designed to serve public policy objectives and the 'public interest', in the USA planning is frequently concerned with resolving conflicts between private interests in land (Cullingworth, 1993). In Britain, development rights have been nationalized since 1947; the state owns the right to develop, and almost all development requires permission from the local authority. Permissions are considered within the context of a development plan but this is not legally binding. An appeal against the local authority's decision is to central government, in the form of the appropriate secretary of state; the courts have very little part in the process. In America there is much greater concern for private property rights. The discretion given to planning agencies in the USA is small, as discretion can be deemed to imply differential treatment of similar cases and thereby be contrary to the equal protection clause of the Constitution and the guarantee given in the Bill of Rights that individuals are free from arbitrary government decisions. Ensuring that planning decisions are in conformity with the law means that 'A striking characteristic of American land use planning is its domination by lawyers and the law' (Cullingworth, 1993, p. 219).

Zoning can be seen as a means of minimizing discretion and determining the land uses to which individuals have a right. It has been argued that

> Much if not most of the land use planning in the US is not planning but zoning and subdivision control. The former implies comprehensive policies for the use, development, and conservation of land. Zoning is the division of an area into districts with differing regulations; subdivision is the legal division of land for sale and development. (Cullingworth, 1997, p. 55)

A zoning ordinance details the restrictions and conditions which apply in each zone in a way that makes zoning essentially an extension of the law of nuisance to land uses. It has been claimed that 'some states require zoning to be consistent with a comprehensive plan, though consistency is rarely defined; even when it is, the machinery for enforcing it is generally weak ... There are many local governments who use zoning as a means of precluding comprehensive planning' (ibid., pp. 65–8). As such, zoning can be a way of excluding unwanted neighbours. Indeed, it has been stated that zoning is used to 'protect real estate values . . . and to exclude most low income households from suburban communities' and, indirectly, exclude most minority groups, and that, 'The need to protect the security of real estate investments took equal precedence with the need to provide the public with more air and light and less unhealthy congestion in housing' (Krumholz, 1998, pp. 641).

As explained in Chapter 9, there is an emerging interest on the part of some policy-makers/advocacy groups regarding a constellation of issues sometimes collectively referred to as 'smart growth'. Its relevance to this discussion is that one of the key lines of thinking amongst smart-growth advocates is that the dominant postwar American pattern of single-use zoning (known as 'Euclidian zoning') is a major contributing factor to sprawl and excessive reliance on private-car usage. The solution, according to some smart-growth advocates, lies in changes to zoning which permit the mixing of land uses including various types of residential tenure and the mixing of residential and selected supporting commercial uses.

A counter to the exclusionary nature of zoning is the use of 'inclusionary zoning' to address affordable housing needs. With inclusionary zoning,

> developers are typically asked or required to contribute to the community's affordable housing stock in exchange for development rights or zoning variances. Some programs are mandatory, where others provide incentives. Some involve cash contributions to an affordable housing fund, while others involve the construction of affordable units within the development. (Schnare, 2000)

Inclusionary zoning ordinances typically detail that a minimum percentage of units to be provided in a specific residential development are affordable to households in a particular income group. Controls may seek to ensure that the units remain affordable for minimum periods of 20 years or more. In many ordinances, some form of incentive in the form, for example, of high-density development (a 'density bonus'), a relaxation of development restrictions relating to height, or open space, wavers of permit fees or fewer developer-required amenities are provided. Generally an inclusionary programme is designed to save rather than spend public funds.

Advocates of inclusionary zoning claim that it helps to create economically diverse communities, increases the supply of affordable housing and helps to limit sprawl by concentrating more development in a single location. Critics argue that it reduces the saleable value of new units and constitutes an unwarranted tax on developers who should not bear the costs of affordable housing provision. It has also been claimed that inclusionary zoning shifts upwardly-mobile poor citizens from central to suburban locations so threatening the revival of inner-city areas and placing undue pressure on the expanding locations (Burchell and Galley, 2000).

A further argument against zoning is that it is a 'taking' and is contrary to the Constitution of the United States. This means that government may not take private property rights for public use without paying just compensation, and selected persons should not be forced to bear public burdens that should be borne by society as a whole. There have been many cases of landowners challenging land use and environment regulations as takings. It has, however, been argued that: 'Inclusionary zoning ordinances are legally vulnerable only if they make it impossible for a developer to earn a reasonable return on the project as a whole' (Kayden, 2002, p. 12). The provision of compensation, for example in the form of a density bonus, can compensate a developer and ensure a reasonable rate of return. This is a technique that is frequently used in those localities where inclusionary zoning is practised.

Whilst it is claimed by advocates that inclusionary zoning can make significant contributions to affordable housing provision, it is only a minority of American cities and states that use this technique. Montgomery County, Maryland, is claimed to provide 'the leading national example of the use of this technique at the county level', where around 10,000 affordable housing units were produced through inclusionary zoning between 1993 and 1999 (Burchell and Galley, 2000, p. 4).

Conclusions

A perception of housing policy problems as problems of access to decent quality housing by low-income groups is common to Europe and America. Viewed as an affordability problem the issue has encouraged governments on both continents to support demand by low-income households through a variety of direct and indirect subsidies. European housing allowance systems that are designed to ease the affordability problem differ markedly from American housing voucher programmes in that the latter are strongly linked to consumer choice and private-sector supply of rented housing. There are two important elements to this distinction: the linkage of the demand-side support to supply-side provision, and the reliance on the private sector to provide the accommodation. The strength of the dual distinction is strongest between the USA and Britain where, for example, housing benefit has been more a 'conditional subject subsidy' supporting households, than a 'conditional object subsidy' supporting landlords who provide accommodation to low-income households at specified 'affordable rents'. In the USA the 'voucher system' and 'section 8 assistance' have directly helped private landlords and low-income tenants. The reliance on the public sector for 'affordable' supply is much stronger in Britain than other European countries where, in many cases (especially in Germany) private- sector suppliers have a stronger role. Housing associations in many European countries, whatever the nature of their ownership, have become, in recent years, much more subject to market pressures and reliance on private finance.

The role of governments in specifically supporting an expansion of home ownership presents a mixed picture. In both the USA and several European countries (the Netherlands for example), large fiscal advantages, mainly in the form of tax relief on mortgage interest, go to homeowners. In Britain such subsidies have been significantly reduced and mortgage-interest tax relief abolished. The expansion of home-ownership has, however, been supported in Britain by 'right to buy' transfer from the public sector.

The use of tax incentives to promote housing supply has been an important feature of policies in some European countries and also in the USA. However, the use of LIHTC in the USA to promote private investment in the supply of affordable housing is very different from the tax advantages available to housing associations and other social-housing providers in Europe. LIHTC is usually factored to specialized investors and the proceeds are applied to the development of the associated properties. A similar mechanism would be particularly innovative in a British context; as a form of fiscal incentive to private developers and as a form of conditional supply-side subsidy it would be very different from other supply-side incentives concentrated on housing associations.

Fundamentally different attitudes to private property rights, land ownership and the legitimate role of government in the USA and Europe underpin different approaches to land-use planning and the supply of land for housing. The protection of private property rights, to the fore in the USA, contrasts with public policy objectives of planning that dominate in Europe. The role of public authorities in Europe in using their powers of acquisition and ownership to enhance the supply of land for housing, and particularly to promote the provision of land for social housing, would seem unthinkable in an American setting.

The use of inclusionary zoning in the USA and affordable housing through the planning system in Britain provide both significant similarities and an important difference in approaches. In both cases the land-use planning system is being used to cream-off development profits to cross-subsidize the provision of housing for those who cannot afford market housing. In both countries the arguments about the appropriateness of such cross-subsidization and the possible detrimental affects on private sector development are similar. However, the idea that such a provision might amount to an unconstitutional 'taking' is peculiarly American. The way this has been countered in America, by the use of planning-system incentives to developers, might nevertheless provide ideas about how an increased volume of low-cost housing development might be prised out of private developers in Britain.

It is supply-side initiatives in Europe and America which directly influence the volume and affordability of housing that are of particular interest to the British situation. Financial measures that increase private-sector involvement and initiatives which make connections between the planning system and the fiscal system potentially provide new policy ideas. Whilst one must be aware of cultural, institutional and geographical differences, including such basic factors as population density and volumes of urban and rural land, the mix of instruments in use in other countries can provide a stimulus to at least a consideration of the feasibility of policy transfer.

Chapter 11

The Economic Consequences of Planning

Land-use planning systems have a variety of objectives such as protecting the countryside, improving the quality of the physical environment, locating new housing where it is needed and producing patterns of land use that minimize incompatible uses and maximize compatible uses. These might be termed 'intended' consequences; but there will also be many 'unintended' consequences. These might be higher house prices, lower rates of increase in housebuilding and higher costs of development. The empirical evidence on the overall impact of planning is thin and typically open to variable interpretations, and much of the academic commentary on the consequences of planning is therefore based on conjecture. This relates to alternative views of the interactions between planning, development, the behaviour of individuals and firms and the overall economy. Exploring this area is thus more about exploring ideas and modelling relationships than it is about identifying 'facts'.

In principle the consequences of planning can be examined by investigating four sorts of outcomes:

1   *Microeconomic impacts.* Here, a consideration of how planning changes the behaviour of households and firms, leading them to modify their consumption, production and location decisions is involved. The microeconomic decisions of all the players in development and planning processes might be considered and thus the actions of housebuilders and landowners in particular will come under the spotlight, and the perspective might be widened to view the behaviour of planners and politicians.
2   *Macroeconomic impacts.* This requires an examination of the ways that planning influences the national economy. Are there consequences for inflation, unemployment and economic growth and if so what is the magnitude of these effects? Are there causal connections between planning and the stability of

the macroeconomy? Does planning have any effects on the cyclical nature of some macroeconomic aggregates?

3   *Welfare impacts.* This implies an overall evaluation of the costs and the benefits for society of a planning system. The wide external costs and benefits as well as private costs and benefits would need to be measured. The scope of the inquiry would include the distributional impacts of planning controls and thus the losses and gains to different groups in society.

4   *Market-specific impacts.* The consequences for prices and outputs in specific markets becomes the focus of intention with this approach. In particular, the land markets and housing markets have been major sources of concern. The key questions relate to the effect of planning on the supply of land for housebuilding, the volume of housebuilding and the resulting impacts on land prices and house prices.

Microeconomic impacts

An understanding of the impact of planning on developer and landowner behaviour can be aided by recognizing whether or not planning leads to a more certain environment in which developers and landowners operate. It might be argued that by defining where residential development will occur and linking new housing supply to the provision of infrastructure and services, planning reduces the risk and the uncertainty of development. Housebuilders can be assured that with supply focused on specific locations demand must inevitably be focused on those locations, and thus the probability of sales and profits is enhanced. However, a lack of clarity in the planning system, a large degree of discretionary power by the planning authorities and much room for negotiation may be seen to increase uncertainty and impose additional costs on developments. The view that is taken on uncertainty is crucial to the conclusions about the impact of planning. Leisham *et al.* (2000) state:

> It can be agreed that the effect of planning regulations is to exacerbate the uncertainty which exists in the land market in relation to the permissibility and intensity of uses to which land may be put. Even British land use planning, which does not apply strict land use zoning but is characterized by flexibility, is likely to exacerbate uncertainty. The existence of uncertainty in the land market makes it possible for speculative gains to be made through land trading. (2000, p. 148)

However, Leisham *et al.* argue that 'the inherent risks in speculative development suggest that housebuilders will be risk averse and exercise caution in their valuation of land. Our essential hypothesis is that uncertainty deflates housing land values because of a collective caution by the building industry' (ibid., p. 154).

A contrasting perspective is provided by Gillen and Fisher (2002) who suggest that British planning and market conditions combine to create circumstances in which 'Residential development companies optimistic about future trends in the market are prone to bidding up land prices, accelerating prices whilst the market remains sluggish and house prices stable' (2002, p. 41). Land prices, they suggest, are driven by overoptimism on the part of developers and landowners: 'The latter withhold land from the market in anticipation of a quick return to the upswing phase of the housing market and the former incite price rises by overzealous bidding and procurement behaviour' (ibid., pp. 55–6).

The degree of consistency with which planning is applied over and between localities can impact on the degree of certainty within which developers make decisions. High degrees of consistency will increase certainty. Strong degrees of prescription in planning may also simplify the demands to which developers respond. In a loosely planned environment consumer preferences with respect to items such as density and location will be of more importance than in a strongly planned environment where decisions on such items are determined by planning. Developers may find that responding to planners' demands is simpler than responding to consumer demand.

Pressure to develop more housing in central urban locations and to build at higher densities may lead firms to respond by adapting the nature of the products they supply. High-density urban flats are very different products from low-density rural houses. Also, some firms may adapt to changing planning preferences better than others. Over time, changes in planning may lead to changes in the type, number and size of housebuilding firms. Healey (1998), reviewing changes in planning and the development industry over several decades, suggests that 'the industry has been shaped by public policy towards land and development' (1998, p. 212).

Planning will bring about changes in behaviour of both producers and consumers of housing. Its purpose is to bring about behavioural changes, but whether or not the actual changes that occur are the desired changes that promote planning objectives is a topic on which there is much disagreement. Protagonists of public choice theory (for example Pennington, 2002b) believe that planning has been 'captured' by special-interest groups and planning bureaucracies and thus the actual changes are very different from the intended changes. This view was examined in Chapter 6.

Macroeconomic impacts

There is general agreement that there are significant links between planning, housing and the macroeconomy (see for example Evans, 1988; Muellbauer, 1990; Muellbauer and Murphy, 1997a; Maclennan, 1994; Meen, 1996, 2003). The nature and the quantitative significance of the links is, however, far from clear and the application of both theory and empirical evidence is inconclusive. In principle it is highly probable that planning has had significant impacts on national economic growth and inflation. These impacts are arguably transmitted through the effects of the planning system on the production and pricing of housing. The conclusions reached on these issues are thus closely connected to the arguments about the effects of planning on housebuilding and house prices which are discussed later in this chapter. An important point is that the magnitude of any effect of planning on housing supply and prices is likely to be tempered by the quantitative significance of supply from the existing stock.

If planning acts as a constraint on the total volume of housebuilding (a proposition which in itself is highly debatable), then the output of a significant industry is reduced. However, it does not necessarily follow that the total output and the growth of the economy as a whole is impeded. This would follow only if resources that would have been employed in housebuilding are otherwise idle. If they are not idle but employed in alternative industries, the effect on output depends on whether productivity is higher or lower in the other industries. A more complex analysis of growth effects acknowledges that a planning system itself consumes resources in both the public sector and the private sector that is subject to the system. Less planning would free resources that could be employed elsewhere. Again the net effect on output depends on whether or not resources are redeployed to more productive activities.

If planning redistributes housebuilding activity (as it undoubtedly does), it may have important implications for labour markets. The availability and price of labour will be related to the availability and price of housing. A restriction of housing relative to employment-generating activity is likely to reduce the availability and increase the price of labour. A shortage of so-called key workers (such as teachers, nurses and policemen) in London is, for example, sometimes blamed on a lack of 'affordable' housing for such employees (LGA, 2002). Specifying precise housebuilding and labour-market relationships will, however, be extremely difficult given the multitude of factors that influence housebuilding (apart from planning) and all those factors that influence labour markets (apart from the supply of new housing).

Monk *et al.* (1996) suggest that because planning constraints reduce the elasticity of housing supply, the land-use planning system in the UK exacerbates cycles in house and land prices. If such cycles impact on the stability of macroeconomic aggregates, planning may be argued to have an effect on economic stability. A major problem with such reasoning is that it is only a relatively small proportion of housing supply that can be influenced by planning if supply is dominated by sales from the stock.

However, if we concentrate on the effects of changes in housing production, rather than total housing supply, changes in production may have important effects on the economy. These changes may be significant because of their short-run consequences for volatility if not their long-run effects on output. Reviewing research evidence on the long-run macroeconomic effects of changes in housing construction, Meen (2003) suggests that the evidence is inconclusive but, 'Even if additional housing construction has limited long-run effects on the national economy, housing is one of the most volatile sectors of the economy and, clearly, volatility causes problems for the design of macroeconomic policy' (2003, p. 97). The role of planning in producing the short-run fluctuations in housing construction remains, however, an open question.

Welfare impacts

If a planning system is intended to compensate for market failures which impede economic welfare, it seems logical that the consequences of planning should be examined with reference to the changes in economic welfare that it engenders. Corkindale (1999) suggests that the British land-use planning system costs over £1 billion per annum in public expenditure and imposes further costs on business and private individuals and 'unless there is some evidence that these costs are outweighed by the benefits, it is hard to justify the system'. However, 'it has not been subject to the kind of sustained evaluation advocated by economists and other social scientists' (1999, p. 2053). Three reasons for this are proposed by Corkindale:

- First it is suggested that, 'The planners' concept of evaluation equates success with the achievement of a planning policy objective regardless of cost. The economists' concept of evaluation, on the other hand, compares the costs and benefits of a policy in order to judge whether it yields net benefits for society at large.
- Second, 'The public policy objectives of land use planning are often not very precisely specified and this tends to make policy evaluation rather difficult. Thus, there has been little explicit attempt to relate the physically defined policy objectives – such as urban containment or the protection of rural land – to fundamental objectives related to the value systems of people'.
- Third, it is argued that little evaluation has been done because of 'the difficulty of measuring the benefits of land use planning, many of which are essentially environmental in character' (1999, p. 2054).

Despite the difficulties, there have been some attempts at evaluation using a welfare framework. Cheshire and Sheppard (1997), for example, examine development control as a policy measure that restricts the supply of certain land uses and generates benefits in the form of unpriced local public goods. There are implicit taxes and implicit benefits which are reflected in changes in land values. Cheshire and Sheppard estimate that households experience net costs from the provision of public open space in urban areas. There are, however, considerable distributional effects with middle-income households benefiting at the expense of both richer and poorer households.

Rather than try to evaluate the welfare benefits to society as a whole, cost–benefit analysis has been used to consider specific projects such as a new road or airport. In an American context, McDonald and McMillan (2003) examine the application of cost–benefit analysis to local land-use decisions at 'individual parcel or block level'. They consider the benefits to the local jurisdiction associated with land-use decisions, and they suggest that the annual benefits of a particular choice of land-use fall into three categories: land rents, employment effects, and the net costs of additional public services. They conclude, not unsurprisingly, that benefits to the local jurisdiction are not necessarily maximized if the land is allocated to the use with the highest land rent. Whatever the costs and benefits to 'the local jurisdiction' these will, of course, be potentially very different to the benefits to the wider society.

Walker (1980) argued that an assessment of the effect of urban planning on social welfare depends on which welfare criteria and in particular which distributional judgements one chooses. These choices have implications for what is deemed to constitute an increase in social welfare and 'must be chosen by reference to values outside of welfare theory itself' (1980, p. 224).

Planning involves costs in the form of resources used in operating the system. These are both public and private-sector costs and benefits in the form of externalities and public goods. The costs are borne by taxpayers, householders and firms; the benefits accrue to households and firms. Some costs and benefits, however, cannot easily be assigned to specific households and firms. Environmental benefits such as the preservation of rural land or less traffic congestion have effects across a variety of individuals, and identifying these individuals is necessary before any distributional judgements can be made.

A welfare approach to the impacts of planning thus provides a theoretical framework which suggests that all the costs and all the benefits to society as such be evaluated. Identifying and measuring these impacts does, however, provide a considerable range of challenges.

Market-specific impacts

It is the fourth set of outcomes identified at the beginning of this chapter (market-specific impacts) that has become a significant source of debate and controversy in the UK. The argument ranges from an assertion that planning has no significant effects on land and house prices to a belief that planning has been an important source of land and house price inflation. A series of questions underlie the debate. These include: How are house prices determined? How are land prices determined? and, What effect does planning have on the supply of housing? The debate has been conducted in the UK in relation to the market for owner-occupied housing.

Production effects

The price of owner-occupied housing is not subject to any direct controls and thus, in an elementary sense, price is a function of the level of demand and the level of supply. Demand depends mainly on demographic and financial factors, the key demographic variable being the total number of households. The key financial variables are incomes and the cost and availability of mortgage finance. In the short run the level of demand is also likely to be influenced by expectations about future levels of house-price inflation with demand increasing when there are high expectations of further increases. How the aggregate level of demand is distributed spatially and by type of house depends on where jobs are located, the cost and ease of travelling from home to work, the spatial distribution and the physical configurations of the existing housing stock, the existing pattern of house prices and household preferences for locations and dwelling types. These preferences are likely to be related to the detailed composition of the stock of households, and the size and the age composition of households will be important.

The supply of housing has two components: the supply from the existing stock and the supply from new building. Together these components provide the total flow of dwellings supplied to the market. The supply from the existing stock is the volume of 'old' housing that is coming onto the market over a given time period. It is thus a function of the turnover in the existing stock. Understanding this source of supply thus requires an answer to the question: 'Why do people put their houses on the market?' There are, of course, many reasons. Households may wish to move because their personal circumstances change, for example in the sense of the household becoming larger or smaller, or because of a change of jobs or a wish to invest more or less in housing.

The supply of owner-occupied housing that comes from new building depends on all those factors that influence the production decisions of the housebuilding industry. The firms that make up the industry may have a variety of motives including maximizing profit and expanding market share. The profitability of housebuilding depends on the revenues from house sales and the costs of production, and firms may be prevented from reaching their profit-maximizing or market-share-optimizing level of output by constraints. These might be constraints that are internal to the industry such as shortages of skilled labour, or constraints that are external to the industry such as a lack of building land because of planning restrictions.

Planning acts as a restraint on housebuilding if the total volume of land that is available with planning permission over any time period is less than the volume of land that the industry demands. It is not of course inevitable that a planning system restricts land supply and acts as a production constraint. Whether or not it does is an empirical issue. It depends on what level of production would be achieved with more or less land available with planning permission. Within a country there may be some areas where planning acts as a restraint on production and others where it does not, or areas where it is more of a constraint and areas where it is less of a constraint. In principle it is possible that a planning regime, by exercising variable levels of constraint from area to area, will redistribute production without having any effect on the aggregate level of production. Again, whether this happens is a matter for empirical investigation. One should also recognize that in principle, by influencing densities, planning could encourage an increase in production levels at some locations and reductions at others. Planning may sometimes encourage higher-density developments than developers would opt for in an unrestricted regime and thus raise outputs on specific sites.

In 2003 the British government began a review of the causes of volatility in housebuilding and the historically low level of housing construction. The review was driven by concerns about the low price elasticity of supply from housebuilding and the inflexibility in the housing market as a barrier to adopting the euro (with the consequent dimished national control of interest rates). The government was also concerned about the constraints on the housebuilding industry and the causes of housing shortages. (The review was termed the 'Barker Review' – after the person appointed to lead the review – and more information is available at www.barkerreview.org.uk.) Evidence to the review from the Royal Institution of Chartered Surveyors suggested that planning was not the principal cause of low levels of housebuilding:

> The rapid decline in housebuilding levels is primarily due to the collapse of the social and affordable housing programme . . . we see no convincing evidence that planning has played a significant role in the decline of housebuilding. (RICS, 2003, pp. 1, 10)

However, the House Builders Federation clearly believed that its members could build more houses if planning constraints were loosened and more land on which housebuilding is viable was made available:

> The shortage of new housing of all tenures is primarily due to the pressure put on government by the nimby [not in my backyard] lobby which has resulted in planning policies demanding an increase in housebuilding on brownfield land without sufficient corresponding public investment to make these sites viable for development. (HBF, 2003)

House price effects

If planning acts as a constraint on the supply of new housing one might expect this to have consequences for land prices and house prices. If the supply of housebuilding land is less than it would be without constraints then, other things being equal, one would expect land prices to be higher as a result of planning constraints. Similarly, if the supply of housing is reduced as a result of planning one would expect house prices to be higher. However, the occurrence and the magnitude of such price effects depends on the processes of price formation in the land and housing markets.

In the housing market any restriction on new housebuilding is an influence on one source of housing supply. The other source of supply, determined by the turnover in the existing stock, is unaffected. A significant empirical question is 'What are the relative magnitudes of these two sources of supply?' If 'new supply' is very small relative to 'supply from the stock', large changes in new supply may have small impacts on the total housing supply. In practice, the significance of 'new supply' varies from country to country and region to region, and there may also be important temporal variations.

According to the Land Registry, in the two years from January 2000 to December 2001 around 11 per cent of the 180,000 dwellings sold in the English East Midlands were 'new'. The remainder were 'old' properties and thus supplied from the stock. Over the same period around 6 per cent of the dwellings sold in Greater London were 'new'. Thus in the mixed urban and rural East Midlands 89 per cent of dwellings sold were a result of turnover in the existing stock. In urban London 94 per cent of dwellings sold were a result of turnover in the existing stock. Very large changes in levels of new housebuilding will have only small impacts on these proportions. If twice as many new dwellings had been built and sold in the East Midlands without any change in the number of 'old' houses traded from the existing stock, 80 per cent of supply would still have consisted of sales from the existing stock. A doubling of housebuilding in London would on a similar assumption have resulted in 89 per cent of dwellings sold being 'old' properties. Of course a doubling of output is highly improbable even with a doubling of planning permissions because the capacity of the industry would be limited; internal constraints would restrict output even if external constraints were removed. There would, furthermore, be some increase in trading within the existing stock to accompany the increase in sales of new properties. A significant proportion of households buying a 'new' property would have to sell an 'old' property. This would limit the significance of 'new' sales as a proportion of total sales.

The supply of dwellings for sale is thus likely to be dominated by sales from the existing stock. This dominance exists in highly urbanized and less urbanized areas of England, and will continue under any plausible assumptions about an increase in the supply of new housing. With only 6 per cent of all houses sold in London being newly built, the idea that the price of houses generally in London would fall if there was an increase, even a massive increase, in housebuilding is highly implausible. It is also improbable that a large increase in the 11 per cent of houses supplied from new construction in the East Midlands could result in reductions in house prices in, for example, Leicester, Derby and Nottingham.

The market in new houses is not a separate market from the market in 'old' houses traded from the stock. Within limits, 'new' houses and 'old' houses are substitutes for each other. Housebuilders cannot simply increase the price of their dwellings by whatever percentage they choose and have buyers coming forward to make purchases. Prospective purchasers will in these circumstances demand relatively 'old' houses. Of course new houses will be able to command some sort of 'newness premium', but given an adequate supply from the stock, buyers will turn elsewhere if this premium is too high. What would happen if the cost of building houses fell? Would housebuilders reduce the prices at which they sell houses? They may not. If the prices of 'old' houses have not fallen they will have no need to reduce their prices in order to attract buyers.

The essence of the arguments above is that in large measure housebuilding firms are 'price-takers' rather than 'price-makers'. The central proposition is that the price of houses is determined principally by the interaction of the demand and supply of houses traded within the existing stock, and housebuilders have to accept price levels determined by this interaction. They do not have the power to charge what they like for their dwellings nor the incentive to reduce their prices when prices generally remain high.

The degree to which housebuilders are price-takers is subject to limits and caveats. A limit is determined by the degree of substitutability between old and new dwellings and the caveats relate to understanding this substitutability in specific market circumstances. A new three-bedroomed detached house may attract more demand and a higher price than an old three-bedroomed detached house in a similar location because it has new applicancies included, is better insulated and has prospectively lower maintenance costs. However, it is sometimes the 'old' property that demands the higher price because is has architectural features that are highly valued and it is in an established neighbourhood with desirable characteristics.

Housebuilders might engage in marketing techniques that concentrate on 'product differentiation'. That is, they might emphasize the positive differences between their new dwellings and old dwellings, reinforcing this with glossy new fittings and 'trade-in deals' that give sellers of old dwellings buying new dwellings a guaranteed immediate sale of their property. The more successful the positive product differentiation, the higher the demand and the higher the price that can be achieved for new dwellings.

Housebuilding may create new products and establish new housing markets in which there are few competing substitutes from the existing stock. For example, conversions of factories and warehouses in inner-city locations to luxury apartments can respond to a demand for high-quality inner urban dwellings that is not being met by supply from the existing stock. In these circumstances housebuilders may be able to demand high prices for a specific sort of dwelling that is in limited supply. If there is sufficient new housing production in a given location, whether it be in the centre of a city or in a rural haven, the new building can transform an area, create new neighbourhoods and establish new products for which there are new demands. However, there will still be limits on the demand for these new products because ultimately there will be housing elsewhere that can be a substitute. If the new inner-city apartment or the new five-bedroom, two-bathroom rural detached property is too expensive, buyers will opt, for example, for old suburban alternatives. The degree of substitutability between types of dwellings and locations is crucial to the power that housebuilders have over house prices and consequently the relationships between 'old' and 'new' house prices.

With this notion of substitutability in mind, it can be argued that it is not just the volume of new housebuilding but the physical and locational characteristics of new building that has to be considered to ascertain the likely effects on house prices. New houses that do not have good substitutes in the existing stock but meet specific demands may sell at prices that reflect their scarcity. Large volumes of such building will not have significant downward effects on prices. New houses that are good substitutes for existing housing and compete with that housing will have different effects. The extra supply of such housing might if it is on a sufficient scale have, without any increase in demand, a dampening effect on prices. The scale of the extra supply would, however, have to be very large for the price effects to be significant.

Land price effects

An increase in the supply of housebuilding land may be expected to have some downward effect on land prices. However, an examination of the demand for housebuilding land is essential to an understanding of the possible land price effects. Housebuilders' willingness to pay for land depends on how much they can afford to pay for land and still expect to make profits from housebuilding. If we think of the willingness to pay as a residual, it is a function of revenue from house sales minus non-land costs. (This approach was set out in general terms in Chapters 2 and 7, and in relation to affordable housing and planning in Chapter 8.) In this approach, land is treated as a factor of production and its demand is derived from the demand for the final goods, in this case houses that the land helps to produce. If housebuilders expect more revenue from house sales, without any increase in production costs, they will be willing to bid more for land. If they expect less revenue from house sales, without any reduction in housebuilding costs, they will be willing to bid less for land. If house prices fall or housebuilders expect house prices to fall, other things being equal, they will be willing to pay less for land. If an increase or an expected increase in housebuilding, as a result of an increase in the supply of housebuilding land, does reduce house prices it may have a downward effect on housebuilders' willingness to pay for land and consequently a reduction in land prices.

The direction of cause and effect in the argument above is from house prices to land prices. Changes in house prices may have consequences for land prices, but it does not follow that changes in land prices will necessarily have consequences for house prices. If land prices fall, how will housebuilders react? Will they lower the prices of the houses they sell? If they can continue to sell at the previous prices the answer may be 'no'. They will instead increase their profit levels. We can think of the residual referred to above as a sum to be shared between the landowner and the housebuilder; the relative shares will depend on the relative bargaining strengths and skills of each party. An increase in land supply will tend to reduce the relative bargaining power of the land-owner and from this point of view some reduction in land values may follow. This is more likely to be accompanied by increases in housebuilders' profits than a reduction in house prices unless there are other factors at work that are depressing the demand for new houses. If the housing market is dominated by sales from the existing stock, large increases in the supply of housebuilding land are unlikely to have significant downward effects on either house prices or land prices.

The argument presented above is close to the position presented by Grigson (1986) who argued that the operation of the planning system cannot increase land or house prices because house prices are demand-determined and housing land prices are determined as a residual. The analysis is also in line with the view of Barlow, Cocks and Parker (1994, p. 11) that, 'the price of new housing is essentially determined by the market in second-hand housing, with the land price representing a residual after the developer has carried out a financial appraisal of the scheme'. Monk (1999) characterizes the Grigson position as 'extreme' and posits the 'Evans–Grigson' debate, citing Evans (1983, 1988, 1989, 1996) as the key proponent of the opposing view that the planning system operates to push up land and house prices and reduce the quantity of housing built. Evans' argument that planning increases the price of land with permission for housebuilding significantly above alternative agricultural values is supported by clear empirical evidence. What is less clear is that the high land prices are the cause of high house prices.

Significant contributions to the empirical evidence on the relationships between planning, land prices and house prices have been provided by the work of Bramley (1993a and 1993b). Cross-sectional analysis using data for English local planning authorities suggests fairly modest price and quality effects from planning controls. With land allocation doubled, the long-run reduction in house prices is estimated at less than 10 per cent. In an extension of the research to Scotland, Leishman and Bramley (2001) suggest that a 50 per cent reduction in land supply would lead to private-sector completions falling by 13 per cent after two years and 27 per cent after three years, with house prices rising by 2 per cent after two years and 4 per cent after three years. If land supply was doubled, a 15 per cent increase in completions with 2 per cent reduction in house prices is predicted after two years, with a 36 per cent increase in completions and 4 per cent fall in prices after three years.

Evans (1996) argues that the approach used by Bramley (1993a, 1993b) understates the likely changes in house prices and housing output as a result of the land made available for possible development through the planning system. The underestimation is (1) because Bramley uses a cross-sectional approach to predict changes that will occur over time, and (2) because of the use of 'structure plan provision for housing' as a predictor of output. There is, Evans argues, an extremely weak relationship in practice between structure plan provision and housing production. In responding to the first of these criticisms, Bramley (1996) argues about the nature of the equilibrium or disequilibrium that Evans assumes exists in a cross-sectional situation and distinguishes between stock and flow equilibrium. On the second criticism Bramley acknowledges the historical weakness of the plan provision/housing output relationship but argues that the strength of the connection has grown as changes in the planning system have increased the probability of land allocated in plans getting developed. Further discussion of empirical studies of the effects of planning constraints on housing markets can be found in Adams and Watkins (2002, pp. 247-61) and Bramley (2003).

'New' and 'old' housing transactions

Earlier in this chapter it was argued that if the supply of new housing is small relative to the supply of housing from the stock, the impact on house prices of any change in the supply of new housing is likely to be small. Thus, even if planning brings about very large changes in the supply of new houses, the change in the total supply of housing may be small if much of this total results from turnover in the existing stock. Where turnover in the existing stock is high, house prices determined by the interaction of the demand and supply of 'old' houses are likely to influence new house prices and housebuilders are likely to be 'price-takers' rather than 'makers'.

Table 11.1 shows that turnover in the existing stock is particularly high in the UK with nearly 6 per cent changing hands in a given year. Comparable data for other European countries is difficult to obtain. However, estimates for Belgium and Germany show lower rates of turnover in the stock in those countries. 'Old' dwellings sold as a result of turnover in the stock represent a higher proportion of total private housing transactions in the UK than in either of those countries. With only 11 per cent of housing transactions being sales of new dwellings in the UK, compared to 72 per cent of transactions in Germany, the UK housing market is significantly different. In Germany, with a large proportion of housing on the market coming from new production, new housing output will have a much bigger impact on total supply and on house prices than is the case in the UK. In Germany, the argument that changes in the volume of new housebuilding will have significant consequences for house prices is much easier to sustain than it is in the UK.

Table 11.1   *'Old' and 'new' transactions in housing, 2000*

Transactions	Belgium	Germany	UK
New private dwellings sold (000s)	36.1	393.39	153.28
Old private dwellings sold (000s)	72.01	156.61	1277.72
Total private housing transactions (000s)	108.19	550.00	1431.00
Total private housing transactions as percentage of housing stock (%)	4.3	1.4	5.8
Old dwellings sold as percentage of total transactions (%)	66	28	89

Source: Estimates based on data from United Nations Housing and Building Statistics for Europe, Eurostat Housing Statistics in the European Union, and the European Mortgage Federation.

Conclusions

It has been argued that the economic consequences of planning can be considered by evaluating the microeconomic impacts, the macroeconomic impacts, the welfare impacts and the market-specific impacts. In principle the most comprehensive approach is to evaluate the welfare impacts. This involves a consideration of all the costs and benefits, viewing planning as an aspect of public policy that promotes a series of social costs and social benefits which may or may not bring about a net social benefit. Identifying and measuring these costs and benefits does, however, involve complex challenges, and practical attempts at such evaluations are sparse.

Whilst there are claims about the impact of planning on individual behaviour, specific markets and the macroeconomy, such claims are difficult to evaluate because of the lack of clear evidence. Planning is but one part of a complicated economic system and isolating its particular contribution requires more sophisticated modelling than has yet been developed.

Many of the effects of planning are assumed to impact upon housing and land markets, with planning influencing levels of housebuilding and house prices. Because of the significance of these claims, much attention has been given in this chapter to the relationships between planning and housing markets, and it has been argued that planning affects mainly the supply side of the market. The volume of housing supply that comes from new building as opposed to turnover in the existing stock varies significantly between countries. In Britain, where new building constitutes only a very small proportion of supply, changes in planning that bring about changes in housebuilding will have only a very small effect on total supply and thus only a small effect on house and land prices.

Chapter 12

Conclusions

We have considered several sets of relationships: the relationships between economics and planning, economics and housing, and planning and housing. As these relationships have been explored, a fourth set of relationships – those between markets and government – have been a recurring theme influencing the analysis of how each of the other sets of relationships might work and does work in practice. We have considered these relationships in the context of institutional arrangements in Europe and America, with some of the more detailed evaluation concentrating on Britain. Throughout the exploration the emphasis has been on the use of economics to analyse problems and to propose solutions to those problems. The purpose of land-use planning, the instruments of planning and the consequences of planning have been considered. In European countries, the purpose of planning is couched in a variety of terms including regulating development in the public interest, coordinating decisions about land use, avoiding incompatible land uses, and ensuring a supply of socially desirable land uses. Public policy objectives for planning in Europe have been contrasted with objectives tied to preventing conflicts between private interests in land in the USA.

In Europe, planning has been seen as a means to improve living conditions contributing to solving a diversity of housing, transport and employment problems. A strong redistributive theme has been occasionally prominent, with planning seeking to redistribute resources to the less well-off and, more specifically, contributing to the 'betterment' issue which is concerned with disproportionate gains in income and wealth to some land-owners as they have prospered through the progress of society. A redistributive objective has been more significant in countries such as Britain and the Netherlands than in the USA. In Britain and the Netherlands the right of individual landowners to prosper from ownership has been weaker than in the USA where individual property rights have assumed a far stronger position.

In America and in Europe, planning has been called on in recent decades to achieve environmental objectives, and such objectives have been linked to the concepts of sustainable development, urban renaissance and the new urbanism. In its broadest manifestation the environmental agenda calls on planning to take a role in controlling land use for the benefit of future as well as existing populations. All these diverse objectives for planning have one thing in common: they require planning to achieve goals that markets cannot or have not achieved. The role of planning as a reaction to market failure has been a recurrent theme throughout this book. If planning is to do things that markets cannot do, it is important to understand why markets cannot do these things. Only then can one hope to find ways of using planning to effectively address market failure. It is through this process that one may discover both the pros and cons of existing methods of planning and the need for innovations in planning. It is also through this process that one may discover that land-use planning is unable to address specific market failures or that there are more appropriate policy instruments that come out of some other conceptual toolbox.

If planning is to respond to market failures, planners must understand market success as well as market failure. Housing and land markets can distribute resources on the basis of consumer and supplier choices; they can reflect the values that individuals place on alternative resource-allocation options, and they can, under certain conditions, produce efficient allocations of resources. In many circumstances market forces cannot guarantee efficiency and they can never be relied on to make judgements about equity or fairness.

Planning can be informed by an understanding of implicit as well as explicit markets. In the latter, prices can be observed for items for which monetary exchanges actually occur, whilst implicit markets involve indirect trading. The price of houses and land near to desirable amenities may be higher than properties further away because buyers are putting an implicit value on the amenities which is reflected in the exchange value of the house or land. Disentangling the bundle of attributes purchased in complex property markets can enable one to understand values placed on such diverse phenomenona as schools, shops, transport and open space.

It is, furthermore, extremely valuable to view trading in dwellings and land as trading in property rights rather than in physical items. These rights are defined in law, by planning regulations, building controls and a range of governmental and social controls. Property rights govern what one can do with land and buildings, and they are typically underwritten by the state. Property rights endow privileges of use and occupation and the ability to engage in exchange, usually for money; they thus help to determine values and prices.

An important argument in this book has been that markets work on the basis of property rights endorsed by the state, and thus the division often posed between markets and the state is a false dichotomy and the notion of government interference in markets is misleading. Without the state's role in property-rights protection, underwriting and enforcement, market exchanges would cease to have significance. The state, through a range of laws and regulations, changes property rights and changes market values, and it is instructive to see land-use planning as part of the process of moderating property rights. The moderation can take many forms including nationalizing development rights, creating zoning ordinances, implementing density controls, imposing taxes on increases in value, and requiring a proportion of dwellings on a site to be designated as affordable housing.

In applying market analysis to housing and land the fundamental characteristics of demand and supply have been emphasized, and the demand for housing has been clearly distinguished from the need for housing. The former as an expression of a willingness and ability to pay can be expressed in the marketplace; the latter, being defined by a socially acceptable requirement for housing unmatched by ability to pay, cannot be expressed in the marketplace and may thus be a driver for some policy action, including some planning. The concept of a derived demand for land has been used to emphasize the point that land is demanded for the contribution it makes to the production of goods and services. The relationship of the demand for housing to the demand for land for residential development has been viewed as one in which the latter as a factor of production is dependent on the former.

The supply of housing has been distinguished from the stock of housing and the production of new housing. The supply is the amount coming on to the market in a given time period and it has two basic sources: turnover in the existing stock, and the development through conversions and new construction of additional dwellings. The stock of housing is the amount of housing existing in a given geographical area at a given moment in time. Demolition reduces the stock and new development adds to the stock. Changes in the supply of housing can occur without any new production; but positive changes in the stock require new production. It has also been shown that the volume of housing supply that comes from new building as opposed to turnover in the existing stock varies significantly between countries. In Britain where new building constitutes only a very small proportion of supply, changes in planning that increase the supply of land for housebuilding will have only a small effect on total housing supply and thus a small effect on house prices and land prices.

The stock of land within any geographical area is fixed. The supply of land, and more specifically the supply of land for residential development, is not fixed. It varies with the price offered for alternative land uses and it varies as a result of planning. Planning can thus influence the distribution of land values. It has been shown that part of the rewards to landowners may be necessary to ensure supply and some may be a surplus or economic rent over and above this minimum. Planning can influence the volume of economic rent. Whilst there are sound arguments for taxing economic rent there are no sound arguments for taxing all of the returns to landowners. The practical difficulty, as we have discussed, is distinguishing the necessary payment from the economic rent.

The failure of housing and land markets to cope with the problems of externalities, the provision of quasi-public goods and the problems of disequilibrium have been seen as central to the case for some form of land-use planning and specifically for the planning of residential development. A concern with externalities implies a consideration of the external costs and external benefits of developments at all geographical levels from the very local to the international. External costs may be as narrow as the implications of new building for neighbours' peace and quiet, or as broad as the consequences of dispersed patterns of development for traffic generation and energy depletion. The positive externalities of well-planned development may reach as far as the consequences for health improvements, educational attainment and crime reductions.

Roads, drainage, sewerage and the other infrastructure associated with development are typically quasi-public goods whose provision may require public expenditure and public planning. Land-use planning mechanisms sometimes encourage a shift of such costs on to developers. Effective planning can also influence the efficient resourcing, provision and the use of quasi-public goods.

Many of the problems of land and property markets can be viewed as disequilibrium in the marketplace. Run-down neighbourhoods, derelict buildings, vacant sites and poor-quality housing can be seen as symptoms of the time that it takes for markets to adjust to a new equilibrium. Eventually market forces may deal with these problems, and low values may in due course encourage redevelopment. However, waiting for markets to promote urban regeneration may mean waiting a very long time, and in the meantime resources are idle and individuals suffer. With an understanding of the causes of disequilibrium, planning can speed up processes of adjustment.

In its broadest form, externalities embrace fundamental environmental issues. It has been argued that these can be seen as specific forms of external costs that markets ignore, and from this perspective environmental economics, with an emphasis on externality issues, can be viewed as a distinctive branch of welfare economics. The inability of markets to value environmental items in an optimal fashion is a specific form of market failure. We have seen that land-use planning can provide but one set of policy instruments as part of environmental strategies. The use of financial incentives, permits and standards together with national and international redefinitions of property rights can form part of the broader approach.

Whilst externalities, quasi-public goods and disequilibrium issues are examples of barriers to the ability of markets to achieve efficiency outcomes, it is the fairness, the social acceptability and the political reaction to distributions of resources that pose even more significant challenges to market processes. The fairness and distribution problems are questions of equity, and are thus questions of opinion. Normative positions on social exclusion, poverty and excess profits are at the centre of arguments for planning to react to the failure of markets to achieve equitable outcomes.

To use planning as a redistributive mechanism addressing questions of equity it is necessary to both understand the reasons for the existing distribution and to predict the redistributional consequences of planning. The analysis underpinning this approach is complex and empirical verification imperfect. However, it is important to apply a conceptual framework that highlights such issues, even if it does not resolve them.

Distributional questions arise at local, national and international levels, and also arise importantly between generations. A decision to give planning permission on plot A rather than plot B distributes resources in favour of those who have property rights in plot A. Many housing policy objectives concern redistributing national resources between households so that those on lower incomes can enjoy improved standards of accommodation. When environmental objectives are couched in sustainable development terms their achievement can involve international and intergenerational redistribution. However, distributional effects are frequently obscured. We have shown, for example, that affordable housing through planning policies brings about redistributions from landowners and developers in favour of the beneficiaries of affordable housing. But the nature and the size of these redistributions are rarely explicit, and the acceptability of the redistributions are rarely discussed. Analysis which reveals, measures, questions and appraises such redistributions is essential to informed policy debate.

The application of land-use planning instruments should occur in the context of analysis of the causes of problems and the full range of planning and other options available to address the problems. The provision of low-cost housing may be enhanced by planning instruments, but an analysis which sees the lack of provision in terms of the weak effective demand of low-income households suggests a wide range of options including the use of housing allowances, grants to housing suppliers, tax breaks for developers and fiscal incentives for investors in social housing.

In practice there is a lack of strategic analysis that links these options. Decisions on housing allowances are made in a different mindset, by a different set of decision-makers, to decisions on land allocations for affordable housing. The lack of residential development land in urban areas can be seen as a planning and residential land-use allocation problem but it can also be seen as a transport problem and a distribution of employment problem. Changes in transport and employment can in principle negate the need for additional housing development land. Again, strategic analysis and long-term solutions require broad thinking and critical appraisals of well-defined options.

If the roots of housing problems lie in unemployment, low incomes and social exclusion, land-use planning policies may have very little effect on housing provision. If the roots of energy consumption choices lie with fuel prices, technological change and technical innovation, land-use planning policies may have very little effect on sustainable patterns of development. The limitations of planning need to be understood. It cannot solve deep-rooted social, environmental and political problems. Too much should not be expected of planning, but neither should planning be blamed for too much. Planning is sometimes blamed for low levels of housebuilding and high levels of house prices, but, as we have shown, both are determined by a complexity of factors of which planning may be but one fairly insignificant example.

We have argued that markets and planning systems need to be viewed in the appropriate institutional contexts, which vary temporally and geographically. The context influences the choice and the effectiveness of policy instruments. In Britain, a context which favours a better integration of land-use policy instruments with fiscal policy instruments is developing. Government has acknowledged the case for more imaginative use of fiscal policy options, and lessons in the use of such instruments are, as we have shown, available from other countries. An improved use of fiscal policy instruments linked to land-use planning can counter some of the anti-planning arguments of the public choice school of thought.

The liberal interventionist perspective which supports a market-failure approach to planning has been challenged by public choice analysis. A strong critique of the ability of land-use planning systems to respond efficiently to market failure and achieve public policy objectives is provided by public choice theorists who argue that public-sector planners have neither the information nor the motivation to act in the public interest. They argue that the costs of planning do not necessarily outweigh the benefits, particularly when public-sector failure is set against market failure. Whilst a liberal interventionist viewpoint argues that planning can, and does, as part of a wider system of government activity, make people better-off by compensating for the inefficiencies and inequities of a market-determined system of land use, the public choice perspective is that planning cannot and does not achieve this objective. Planning, in practice, so the public choice school suggests, will benefit special interest groups including developers and planners.

In this book it has been argued that rather than accept the public choice theorists' critique as a demonstration of the inevitable outcomes of planning, it is better to view them as a warning of what might happen under a planning system that is not subject to appropriate governance and is not sufficiently responsive to consumer choice. An appropriate lesson from the public choice critique is that better use can be made of markets and market information. House price and land price data, in particular, can inform the planning process. It must, however, be remembered that although prices are an indicator of preferences, they are fundamentally an indicator of ability to pay. If planning is to respond to demand, price information is valuable. If planning is to have social objectives, price information combined with indicators of need and environmental effects is essential.

Planning can work with and moderate markets through careful integration with financial policy instruments such as taxes and subsidies, and we have noted the use of such instruments in promoting urban renaissance and brownfield development. In the use of economic policy instruments to promote environmental objectives there are examples that Europe could borrow from the USA. Similarly, stimulation to residential development and particularly the development of affordable housing can be usefully supported by fiscal incentives. We have noted the merits and the weaknesses of a system of tariffs to promote affordable housing through planning in

Britain; this is an idea that government has mooted but as yet not implemented.

An extension of the logic of bringing economic policy instruments to bear on planning issues is that all land uses involve opportunity costs and ultimately a price may be assigned to the values associated with alternative uses. In a system under which development rights rest with the state, one can imagine the scope for these rights to be traded by the state. Alongside a potential land-use map could be placed a planning-permission price map. There might be several possible uses for given land plots, and different uses could have different prices at which planning permission might be given. Socially desirable uses, for example, would be cheaper than uses with high social costs. There might be minimum threshold prices at which the auctioning of planning permission would begin. For some options the base price would be infinity, ruling out any question of developing Hyde Park for 10-bedroomed mansions with gardens, or St Paul's Cathedral for conversion to social-housing apartments. For brownfield sites with high pollution-irradication and infrastructure costs the planning permission price for residential development might be negative if such use was to be promoted.

A major problem with this approach, as the public choice theorists would remind us, is that public administrators lack the knowledge to determine the socially optimal prices at which permissions might be sold or at which the bidding might start. However, affordable housing through planning, as we have shown, implies finding an implicit negotiated price at which permission for a particular use is given. A system of tariffs would make such pricing more explicit. The socially optimum rate of taxation on cigarettes and petrol is not known precisely, but that does not prevent acceptance of such taxes in the knowledge that they not only raise revenue but they also limit consumption. Without going all the way to the wholesale selling of planning permission, undesirable land uses can be limited by taxation and desirable uses promoted by fiscal concessions.

In planning regimes where property rights rest more firmly with individuals, and the state plays more of a moderating than a land-use-determining role, pricing has a place in the evaluation of compensation payments for those adversely affected by development. However, whatever the initial configuration of property rights, financial compensation for significant external costs (such as those associated with environmental pollution and resource depletion, falling on dispersed communities in many jurisdictions and on future generations) is not practically feasible. This does not mean that financial persuasion may not have a place in limiting undesirable uses. It does mean that land use cannot be universally determined by the level of compensation payments that are acceptable for adverse uses.

The application of economic principles to housing and planning encourages an evidence-based approach to the analysis of policy problems and the formation of appropriate strategies to solve the problems. Land-use planning informed by such analysis, assisted by fiscal policy instruments and placed within a broad social policy setting, can achieve social objectives that markets will inevitably fail to promote.

References

Adams, D. and Watkins, C. (2002) *Greenfields, Brownfields and Housing Development* (Oxford: Blackwell).

Alker, S., Joy, V., Roberts, P. and Smith, N. (2000) 'The definition of brownfield', *Journal of Environmental Planning and Management*, 43(1), pp. 49–69.

Alonso, W. (1964) *Location and Land Use* (Cambridge, Mass.: Harvard University Press).

APA (1997) *Policy Guide on Impact Fees*, American Planning Association (www.planning.org).

APA (2000) *Policy Guide on Planning for Sustainability*, American Planning Association (www.planning.org).

APA (2003) *Policy Guide on Smart Growth*, American Planning Association (www.planning.org).

Ball, M. (1998) 'Institutions in British property research: a review', *Urban Studies*, 35(9), pp. 1501–17.

Ball, M. (1999) 'Chasing a snail: innovation and house-building firms' strategies', *Housing Studies*, 14(1), pp. 9–22.

Ball, M. (2003) 'Markets and the structure of the housebuilding industry: an international perspective', *Urban Studies*, 40(5–6), pp. 879–916.

Barlow, J., Bartlett, K., Hooper, A. and Whitehead, C. (2002) *Land for Housing: Current practive and future options* (York: Joseph Rowntree Foundation and York Publishing Services).

Barlow, J., Cocks, R. and Parker, M. (1994) *Planning for Affordable Housing*, Department of the Environment Planning Research Programme, (London: HMSO).

Barlow, J. (2000) *'Private Ssector House-Building: Structure and Strategies into the 21st Century'* (London: Council of Mortgage Lenders).

Barr, N. (1998) *The Economics of the Welfare State*, 3rd edn (Oxford: Oxford University Press).

Bast, C. (2002) 'Low-income housing tax credits', *Real Estate Finance Journal*, 17(3), pp. 82–5.

Becker, L. C. (1977) *Property Rights* (London: Routledge & Kegan Paul).

Begg, D., Fischer, S. and Dornbusch, R. (2003) *Economics*, 7th edn (London: McGraw-Hill).

Bhatti, M. (2001) 'Housing/futures? The challenge from environmentalism', *Housing Studies*, 16(1), pp. 39–51.

Bishop, D. (2001) *Delivering Affordable Housing Through the Planning System* (London: RICS and The Housing Corporation).

Black-Plumeau, L. (1998) 'Low-income housing tax credits', in W. van Vliet (ed.), *Encyclopedia of Housing* (Thousand Oaks, Col.: Sage), pp. 344–5.

Blaug, M. (1997) *Economic Theory in Retrospect*, 5th edn (Cambridge: Cambridge University Press).

237

Blaug, M. (1990) *Economic Theories, True or False?* (Aldershot: Edward Elgar).

Blowers, A. (1993) *Planning for a Sustainable Environment* (London: Earthscan).

B.M. Bau, (1993) *Functionsweise Städtische Bodenmärkte in Mitgliedstaaten der Eurospäischen Gemeinschaft* (Bad Godesburg: Bundesministerium für Raumordnung, Bauwesen und Städtebau).

Boyne, G.A. and Walker, R. (1999) 'Social housing reforms in England and Wales: a public choice evaluation', *Urban Studies*, 36(13), pp. 2237–62.

Bramley, G. (1993a) 'The impact of land-use planning and tax subsidies on the supply and price of housing in Britain', *Urban Studies*, 30(1), pp. 5–30.

Bramley, G. (1993b) 'Land-use planning and the housing market in Britain: the impact on house-building and house prices', *Environment and Planning A*, 1021–51.

Bramley, G. (1996) 'Impact of land-use planning on the supply and price of housing in Britain: reply to comment by Alan W. Evans', *Urban Studies*, 33(9), pp. 1733–7.

Bramley, G. (2003) 'Planning regulation and housing supply in a market system', in T. O' Sullivan and K. Gibb (eds), *Housing Economics and Public Policy* (Oxford: Blackwell), pp. 193–217.

Bramley, G., Barlett, W. and Lambert, C. (1995) *Planning, the Market and Private Housebuilding* (London: University College London Press).

Bramley, G. and Pawson, H. (2002) 'Low demand for housing: incidence, causes and UK national policy implications', *Urban Studies*, 39(3), pp. 393–422.

Bratt, R.G. (1998) 'Public Housing' in W. van Vliet (ed.). *Encyclopedia of Housing* (Thousand Oaks, Cal.: Sage), pp. 442–466.

Breheny, M. and Congdon, P. (eds) (1989) *Growth and Change in a Core Region* (London: Pion).

Brown, T. (ed.) (1999) *Stakeholder Housing: A Third Way* (London: Pluto).

Brown, T., Dearing, A., Hunt, R., Richardson, J. and Yeates, N. (2003) *'Allocate or Let? Your choice: Lessons from Harborough Home Search'* (Coventry: Chartered Institute of Housing).

Buchanan, J.M. (1968) *The Demand and Supply of Public Goods* (Chicago: Rand McNally).

Burchell, R.W. and Galley, C.C. (2000) 'Inclusionary Zoning: Pros and Cons', pp. 3–12 in 'Inclusionary zoning: a viable solution to the affordable housing crisis?' *New Century Housing*, vol. 1, issue 2, October 2000 (Washington, DC: The Center for Housing Policy).

Burrows, P. (1979) *The Economic Theory of Pollution Control* (Oxford: Martin Robertson).

Chamberlin, E.H. (1993) *The Theory of Monopolistic Competition*, reprinted 1974 (Harvard: Harvard University Press).

Cheshire, P. and Sheppard, S. (1997) *The Welfare Aspects of Land Use Regulation*, LSE Research Papers in Environmental and Spatial Analysis (London: London School of Economics).

Coase, R. (1937) 'The nature of the firm', *Economica*, 4, pp. 386–45.

Coase, R.H. (1960) 'The problem of social cost', *Journal of Law and Economics*, 3, October, pp. 1–44.

Coase, R. (1973) 'The problem of social cost', in R. Staaf and F. Tannian (eds), *Externalities: Theoretical Dimensions of Political Economy* (New York: Dunellen), pp. 119–62.

Coleman, A. (1985) *Utopia on Trial: Vision and Reality in Planned Housing* (London: Hilary Shipman).

Conway, J. (1999) 'Health and housing', in T. Brown (ed.), *Stakeholder Housing: A Third Way* (London: Pluto), pp. 54–66.

Coppin, L. (2000) 'Housebuilders rail against Livingstone's homes plan', *Estates Gazette*, 28th October, p. 51.

Corkindale, J. (1999) 'Land development in the United Kingdom: private property rights and public policy issues', *Environment and Planning A*, 31, pp. 2053–70.

Cullingworth, J. (1993) *'The Political Culture of Planning: American Land Use Planning in Comparative Perspective'* (London: Routledge).

Cullingworth, B. (1997) *Planning in the USA: Policies, Issues and Progress* (London: Routledge).

Cullingworth, B. and Nadin, V. (2002) *Town and Country Planning in the UK*, 13th edn (London: Routledge).

Cullis, J. and Jones, P. (1998) *Public Finance and Public Choice*, 2nd edn, (Oxford: Oxford University Press).

Demsetz, H. (1969) 'Information and efficiency: another viewpoint', *Journal of Law and Economics*, 12, pp. 1–22.

DETR (1997) Circular 1/97, *Planning Obligations* (London: Department of Environment, Transport and the Regions).

DETR (1998) *Modernising Planning* (London: Stationery Office).

DETR (1999a) *Towards an Urban Renaissance: Report of the Urban Task Force* (London: Spon).

DETR (1999b) *Towards an Urban Renaissance: Urban Task Force Report Executive Summary* (London: Department of Environment, Transport and the Regions).

DETR (1999c) *Fiscal Incentives for Urban Housing: Exploring the Options*, produced for the Urban Task Force by KPMG (London: Department of Environment, Transpot and the Regions).

DETR (1999d) Planning Policy and Guidance Note 3, *Planning and Affordable Housing* (London: Stationery Office).

DETR (2000a) *Our Towns and Cities: The Future: Delivering an Urban Renaissance* (London: Stationery Office).

DETR (2000b) *Tapping the Potential: Assessing Urban Housing Capacity: Towards Better Practice* (London: Department of Environment, Transport and the Regions).

DoE (1991) Circular 7/91, *Planning and Affordable Housing* (London: HMSO).

DoE (1996) Circular 13/96, *Planning and Affordable Housing* (London: Stationery Office).

Downs, A. (1957) *An Economic Theory of Democracy* (New York: Harper & Row).

DTLR (2001) *Planning Obligations: Delivering a Fundamental Change* (London: DTLR).

Evans, A. (1973) *The Economics of Residential Location* (London: Macmillan).

Evans, A. (1983) 'The determination of the price of land', *Urban Studies*, 20, pp. 119–29.

Evans, A. (1985) *Urban Economics* (Oxford: Blackwell).

Evans, A. (1988) *House Prices, Regional Policy and Labour Supply in a Conceptual Framework*, report to DTI South East (Reading: SE Associates).

Evans, A. (1989) 'South East England in the eighties: explanations for a house price explosion', in M. Breheny and P. Congdon (eds), *Growth and Change in a Core Region* (London: Pion), pp. 130–49)

Evans, A. (1991) 'Rabbit hutches on postage stamps; planning, development and political economy', *Urban Studies*, 28(6), pp. 853–70.

Evans, A. (1995) 'The property market: ninety per cent efficient?' *Urban Studies*, 3 (1), pp. 5–29.

Evans, A. (1996) 'The impact of land use planning and tax subsidies on the supply and price of housing in Britain: a comment', *Urban Studies*, 33(3), pp. 581–5.

Evans, A. (2003) 'The development of urban economics in the twentieth century', *Regional Studies*, 37(5), July, pp. 521–9.

Evans, B. and Bate, B. (2000) *A Taxing Question: The Contribution of Economic Instruments to Planning Objectives* (London: Town and Country Planning Association).

Field, B.C. (1994) *Environmental Economics* (New York: McGraw-Hill).

Fleming, M.C. and Nellis, J.G. (1984) *The Halifax House Price Index: Technical Details* (Halifax: Halifax plc).

Fletcher, J., Adamowicz, W. and Graham-Tomasi, T. (1990) 'The travel cost method of recreation demand', *Leisure Sciences*, 12, pp. 119–47.

Fulton, W. (1996) 'The new urbanism challenges conventional planning', *Land Lines*, 8(5), September (www.lincolninst.edu).

Gallent, N. (2000) 'Planning and affordable housing: from old values to new labour?' *Town Planning Review*, 71, pp. 123–47.

Gans, H.J. (1991) *People, Plans and Policies: Essays on Poverty, Racism and Other National Urban Problems* (New York: Columbia University Press).

George, H. (1879) *Progress and Poverty* (New York: Appleton; London: Kegan Paul, Trench).

Gillen, M. and Fisher, P. (2002) 'Residential developer behaviour in land price determination', *Journal of Property Research*, 19(1), pp. 39–59.

Gilpin, A. (2000) *Environmental Economics: A Critical Overview* (Chichester: John Wiley & Sons).

GLA (2000) *Homes for a World City: Report of the Mayor's Housing Commission* (London: Greater London Authority).

Golland, A. (2001) *Models for Land Assembly in the UK: A Comparative Analysis of other European Approaches* (London: Royal Institution of Chartered Surveyors).

Grigson, W.S. (1986) *House Prices in Perspective: A Review of South East Evidence* (London: SERPLAN).

Hanley, N., Shogren, J.F. and White, B. (1997) *Environmental Economics in Theory and Practice* (London: Macmillan).

Hanley, N., Shogren, J.F. and White, B. (2001) *Introduction to Environmental Economics* (Oxford: Oxford University Press).

Harrison, A. (1977) *Economics and Land Use Planning* (London: Croom Helm).

Harvey, J. (1998) *Modern Economics*, 7th edn (Basingstoke: Macmillan).

Hayek, F.A. (1948) *Individualism and Economic Order* (Chicago: Chicago University Press).

Hayek, F. (1967) *Studies in Philosophy, Politics and Economics* (London: Routledge).

Hayek, F. (1978) *New Studies in Philosophy, Politics, Economics and the History of Ideas* (London: Routledge).

HBF (2001) *Realising Capacity: Urban Potential Good Practice Guidance* (London: House Builders Federation).

HBF (2003) 'Social housebuilding drops', Press Release, 29 April (London: House Builders Federation (www.hbf.co.uk)).

Healey, P. (1992) 'An institutional model of the development process', *Journal of Property Research*, 9, pp. 3334.

Healey, P. (1998) 'Regulating property development and the capacity of the development industry', *Journal of Property Research*, 15(3), pp. 211–27.

Healey, P., Purdue, M. and Ennis, F. (1993) *Gains from Planning? Dealing with the Impacts of Development* (York: Joseph Rowntree Foundation).

Howenstine, E. (1986) *Housing Vouchers: A Comparative International Analysis* (New Brunswick, NJ: Centre for Urban Policy Research).

Hughes, W.T. and Sirmans, C.F. (1992) 'Traffic externalities and single family house prices', *Journal of Regional Science*, 32, pp. 487–500.

Jacobs, M. (1991) *The Green Economy: Environment, Sustainable Development and the Politics of the Future* (London and Boulder, Col: Pluto Press).

Jaffe, A.J. (1996) 'On the role of transaction costs and property rights in housing markets', *Housing Studies*, 11(3), pp. 425–34.

Jevons, S. (1871) *Theory of Polictical Economy*, reprinted as Penguin Paperback, 1970 (Harmondsworth: Penguin).

Jones, C. (2002) 'The definition of housing market areas and strategic planning', *Urban Studies*, 39(3), pp. 549–64.

Joseph Rowntree Foundation (1994) *Inquiry into Planning for Housing* (York: Joseph Rowntree Foundation).

Joseph Rowntree Foundation (1999) 'The problem of low housing demand in inner city areas', *JRF Findings* 519, May (York: Joseph Rowntree Foundation).

Joseph Rowntree Foundation (2001) 'The effectiveness of planning policies for affordable housing', *JRF Findings*, November (York: Joseph Rowntree Foundation).

Kayden, J.S. (2002) 'Inclusionary Zoning and the Constitution', pp. 10–13 in 'Inclusionary Zoning: Lessons Learned in Massachusetts', *NHC Affordable Housing Policy Review*, vol. 2, issue 1, January (Washington, DC: The National Housing Conference).

Keogh, G. and D'Arcy, E. (1999) 'Property market efficiency: an institutional economics perspective', *Urban Studies*, 36(13), pp. 2401–14.

King, P. and Oxley, M. (2000) *Housing: Who Decides?* (London: Macmillan – now Palgrave Macmillan).

Krumholz, N. (1998) 'Zoning', in W. van Vliet (ed.), *Encyclopedia of Housing* (Thousand Oaks, Cal.: Sage), pp. 641–4.

Lafferty, W.M. and Meadowcroft, J. (2000) *Implementing Sustainable Development* (Oxford: Oxford University Press).

Lane, R. (1998) 'Transfer of development rights for balanced development', *Land Lines*, 10(2), March, Lincoln Institute of Land Policy (www.lincolninst.edu).

Leicestershire Health Authority (1999) *Annual Report of the Director of Public Health* (Leicester: Leicestershire Health Authority).

Leisham, C., Jones, C. and Fraser, W. (2000) 'The influence of uncertainty on house builder behaviour and residential land values', *Journal of Property Research*, 17(2), pp. 147–68.

Leisham, C. and Bramley, G. (2001) *A Local Housing Market Model with Spatial Interactions and Land-use Controls*, Discussion Paper, Heriot-Watt University, Edinburgh.

LGA (2002) *Key Workers and Affordable Housing* (London: Local Government Association).

Lipsey, R.G. and Chrystal, A. (1995) *An Introduction to Positive Economics* (Oxford: Oxford University Press).

Litchfield, N. and Connellan, O. (1997) 'Land value taxation in Britain for the benefit of the community: history, achievements and prospects', Lincoln Institute of Land Policy Working Paper (www.lincolninst.edu).

Maclennan, D. (1994) *A Competitive UK Economy: The Challenges for Housing Policy* (York: Joseph Rowntree Foundation).

Malpezzi, S. (1996) 'Housing prices, externalities and regulation in US metropolitan areas', *Journal of Housing Research*, (2), pp. 209–41.

Marx, K. (1881) 'On Henry George' [a letter written to Friedrich Sorge, a prominent figure in the US working-class movement, from London, 30 June 1881] (www.cooperativeindividualism.org).

McDonald, J.F. and McMillen, D.P. (2003) 'Costs and benefits of land use regulations: a theoretical survey', *Journal of Real Estate Literature*, 11(2), pp. 157–75.

Meen, G. (1996) 'Ten propositions in UK housing macro-economics: an overview of the eighties and early nineties', *Urban Studies*, 33(3), pp. 425–44.

Meen, G. (2003) 'Housing, random walks, complexity and the macroeconomy', in T. O'Sullivan and K. Gibb (eds), *Housing Economics and Public Policy* (Oxford: Blackwell), pp. 91–109.

Menger, C. (1871) *Principles of Economics*, re-printed by Atlantic Books, 1994 (London: Atlantic Books).

MHC (2002) *Millennial Housing Commission Report to Congress* (www.mhc.gov/home.html).

Mill, J.S. (1909) *Principles of Political Economy* (London: Ashley).

Minton, A. (2000) 'Ken turns developers red', *Estates Gazette*, 28th October, pp. 89–90.

Minton, A. (2001) 'Housing targets in the firing line', *Estates Gazette*, 20 October, pp. 61–3.

Monk, S. (1999) *The Use of Price in Planning for Housing: A Literature Review*, Discussion Paper 105, Department of Land Economy (Cambridge: University of Cambridge).

Monk, S., Pearce, B. and Whitehead C. (1996) 'Land use planning, land supply and house prices', *Environment and Planning A*, 28, pp. 495–511.

Monk, S. and Whitehead, C. (2000) *The Use of Housing and Land Prices as a Planning Tool: A Summary Document*, (Cambridge: Cambridge Housing and Planning Research, University of Cambridge).

Muellbauer, J. (1990) 'The great British housing disaster', *ROOF*, May/June, pp. 16–20.

Muellbauer, J. and Murphy, A. (1997a) 'Booms and busts in the UK housing market', *Economic Journal*, 107, November, pp. 1701–27.

Muellbauer, J. and Murphy, A. (1997b) *Booms and Busts in the UK Housing Market*, Research Discussion Paper Series no. 1615 (London: Centre for Economic Policy).

Mueller, D.C. (1989) *Public Choice II* (Cambridge: Cambridge University Press).

Mulhearn, C. and Vane, H. (1999) *Economics* (London: Macmillan).

Needham, B. (1997) 'Land policy in the Netherlands', *Tijdschrift Voor Economishe en Sociale Geographie*, 88(3), pp. 291–6.

Needham, B. and de Kam, G. (2000) *Land for Social Housing* (Nijmegan, Hilversum: CECODHAS [Comité Européen de Coordination de l'Habitat Social]).

Newman, O. (1973) *Defensible Space* (London: Architectural Press).

Ng, K.W. (1992) *Welfare Economics: Introduction and Development of Basic Concepts* (London: Macmillan).

O'Byrne, P., Nelson, J. and Seneca, J. (1985) 'Housing values, census estimates, disequilibrium and the environmental cost of airport noise', *Journal of Environmental Economics and Management*, 12, pp. 169–78.

ODPM (2003a) 'Consultation paper on a proposed change to Planning Policy Guidance Note 3, Housing: supporting the delivery of new housing' (London: Office of the Deputy Prime Minister).

ODPM (2003b) 'Consultation paper on a proposed change to Planning Policy Guidance Note 3, Housing: influencing the size, type and affordability of housing' (London: Office of the Deputy Prime Minister).

O'Sullivan, T. and Gibb, K. (eds) (2003) *Housing Economics and Public Policy* (Oxford: Blackwell).

Oxley, M. (1975) 'Economic theory and urban planning', *Environment and Planning A*, 7(5), pp. 497–508.

Oxley, M. (1987) 'Housing allowances in Western Europe', in W. van Vliet (ed.), *Encyclopedia of Housing* (Thousand Oaks, Cal.: Sage), pp. 165–78.

Oxley, M. (1991) 'The aims and methods of comparative housing research', *Scandinavian Housing and Planning Research*, 8, pp. 67–77.

Oxley, M. (1995) 'Private and social rented housing in Europe: distinctions, comparisons and resource allocation', *Scandinavian Housing and Planning Research*, 12, pp. 59–72.

Oxley, M. (1998) 'Demand-side subsidies', in W. Van Vliet (ed.), *Encyclopedia of Housing* (Thousand Oaks, Cal.: Sage), pp. 107–8.

Oxley, M. (1999) 'Housing in Europe', in T. Brown (ed.), *Stakeholder Housing: A Third Way* (London: Pluto), pp. 94–5.

Oxley, M. (2000) 'Governments and Social Welfare', in P. King and M. Oxley, *Housing: Who Decides?* (London: Macmillan – now Palgrave Macmillan).

Oxley, M. (2001) 'Meaning, science, context and confusion in comparative housing research', *Journal of Housing and the Built Environment*, 16, pp. 9–106.

Oxley, M., Cousins, L., Dunmore, K. and Golland, A. (2001) *Affordable Housing in London: Spatial Development Strategy Technical Report One*, July (London: Greater London Authority (www.london.gov.uk).

Page, D. (1993) *Building for Communities* (York: Joseph Rowntree Foundation).

Page, D. (1994) *Developing Communities* (York: Joseph Rowntree Foundation).

Paraja Eastway, M. and San Martin, I. (1999) 'General trends in financing social housing in Spain', *Urban Studies*, 36(4), pp. 699–714.

Pearce, D.W. and Turner, R.K. (1990) *Economics of Natural Resources and the Environment* (Hemel Hempstead: Harvester Wheatsheaf).

Pennington, M (2002a) *Liberating the Land: The Case for Private Land-use Planning* (London: Institute of Economic Affairs).

Pennington, M. (2002b) *Planning and the Political Market: Public Choice and the Politics of Government Failure* (London: Athlone Press).

Pickvance, C.G. (2001) 'Four varieties of comparative analysis', *Journal of Housing and the Built Environment*, 16, pp. 7–28.

Poulton (1991a) 'The case for a positive theory of planning. Part 1: what is wrong with planning theory?' *Environment and Planning B*, 18, pp. 225–32.

Poulton, M.C. (1991b) 'The case for a positive theory of planning. Part 2: a positive theory of planning', *Environment and Planning B*, pp. 18, 263–75.

Power, A. and Mumford, K. (1999) *The Slow Death of Great Cities? Urban Abandonment or Urban Renaissance* (York: Joseph Rowntree Foundation and York Publishing Services).

Power, A. and Tunstall, R. (1997) *Dangerous Disorder: Riots and Violent Disturbances in 13 Areas in Britain in 1991–92* (York: Joseph Rowntree Foundation).

Power S. and Whitty, G. (1995) *No Place to Learn* (London: Shelter).

Prest, A.R. (1981) *The Taxation of Urban Land* (Manchester: Manchester University Press).

Priemus, H. and Dieleman, F. (1999) 'Social housing finance in the European Union: developments and prospects', *Urban Studies*, 36(4), pp. 623–31.

Ratcliffe, J. (1976) *Land Policy* (London: Hutchinson).

Ricardo, D. (1951) 'The works and correspondence of David Ricardo', in P. Sraffa (ed.), vol 1, *On the Principles of Political Economy and Taxation* (Cambridge: Cambridge University Press).

RICS (1998) *Planning Permissions – RICS Policy Position* (London: Royal Institution of Chartered Surveyors).

RICS (2003) *Submission to the Barker Review of Housing Supply* (London: Royal Institution of Chartered Surveyors) (www.rics.org).

Robinson, J. (1933) *The Economics of Imperfect Competition*, reprinted 1969 (London: Macmillan).

Robinson, R. (1979) *Housing Economics and Public Policy* (London: Macmillan).

Rosen, S. (1974) 'Hedonic prices and implicit markets', *Journal of Political Economy*, 82, pp. 35–55.

Rosenthal, L. (1984) 'Income and price elasticities of demand for owner-occupied housing in the UK: evidence from pooled cross sectional and time series data', *Applied Economics*, 2(6), pp. 761–75.

Rothstein, B. (1998) *Just Institutions Matter: The Moral and Political Logic of the Universal Welfare State* (Cambridge: Cambridge University Press).

Rudlin, D. (1998) *Tomorrow: A Peaceful Path to Urban Reform* (London: Friends of the Earth).

Rydin, Y. (2003) *Urban and Environmental Planning in the UK*, 2nd edn (Basingstoke: Palgrave Macmillan).

Samuelson, P. (1954) 'The pure theory of public expenditure', *Review of Economics and Statistics*, 36, pp. 387–9.

Samuelson, P.A. and Nordhaus, D. (2001) *Economics*, 17th edn (Boston, Mass.: McGraw-Hill).

Schnare, A. (2000) Introduction, pp. 1–3 in 'Inclusionary zoning: a viable solution to the affordable housing crisis?', *New Century Housing*, vol. 1, issue 2, October 2000 (Washington, DC: The Center for Housing Policy).

Scottish Office (1996) 'Structure plans: housing land requirements', *Planning Advice Note 38* (Edinburgh: Scottish Office).

Sirmans, G.S. and Macpherson, D.A. (2003) 'The state of affordable housing', *Journal of Real Estate Literature*, 11(2), pp. 133–55.

Smith, A. (1976) *The Wealth of Nations*, eds R.H. Cambell and A.S. Skinner (Oxford: Oxford University Press).

Smith, V.K. and Huang, J. (1993) 'Hedonic models and air quality; 25 years and counting', *Environmental and Natural Resource Economics*, 3(4), pp. 381–94.

Smolka, M.O. and Amborski, D. (2000) *Value Capture for Urban Development: An Inter-American Comparison* (Cambridge, Mass.: Lincoln Institute of Land Policy) (www.lincolnist.edu).

Staaf, R. and Tannian, F. (eds) (1973) *Externalities: Theoretical Dimensions of Political Economy* (New York: Dunellen), pp. 119–62.

Stephens, M. (1999) 'The fiscal role of the European Union: the case of housing and the European structural funds', *Urban Studies*, 36(4), pp. 715–35.

Steuteville, R. (2000) 'The new urbanism: and alternative to modern, auto-mobile-orientated planning and development', *The New Urban News*, 28 June (www.newurbannews.com).

Stewart, J. (2001) 'Monopoly Rules', *Housebuilder*, November, pp. 8–9.

Stewart, J. (2002) *Building a Crisis: Housing Under-Supply in England* (London: The House Builders Federation).

Summers, L.H. (1993) *The Economist Year Book 1993*, pp. 255–6.

Thorsnes, P. and Simons, G.P.W. (1999) 'Letting the market preserve land: the case for a market-driven transfer of development rights program', *Contemporary Economic Policy*, 1 (2), April, pp. 256–67.

UK Round Table on Sustainable Development (1997) *Housing and Urban Capacity* (London: HMSO).

Uthwattt Report (1942) *Report of the Expert Committee on Compensation and Betterment*, Cmd 6386 (London: HMSO).

van Vliet, W. (ed.) (1998) *Encyclopedia of Housing* (Thousand Oaks, Cal.: Sage).

Walker, B. (1980) 'Urban planning and social welfare', *Environment and Planning A*, 12, pp. 217–25.

WCED (World Commission on Environment and Development) (1987) *Our Common Future* (Oxford: Oxford University Press).

Webster, C.J. (1998) 'Public choice, Pigouvian and Coasian planning theory', *Urban Studies*, 35(1), pp. 53–75.

Webster, C. and Wu, F. (2001) 'Coarse, spatial pricing and self-organising cities', *Urban Studies*, 3 (11), pp. 2037–54.

Weston, R., Oxley, M. and Golland, A. (2003) *A Methodology for Assessing the Economic Viability of Urban Housing Development*, Centre for Residential Development (Nottingham: Nottingham Trent University).

Willis, K. and Garrod, G. (1991) 'An individual travel cost method for evaluating forest recreation', *Journal of Agricultural Economics*, 42, pp. 33–42.

Winch, D. (1971) *Analytical Welfare Economics* (Harmondsworth: Penguin).

Wolf, C. Jr (1987) 'Market and non-market failures: comparison and assessment', *Journal of Public Policy*, 7, pp. 43–70.

Index